EVIDENCE-BASED HEALTHCARE DESIGN

ROSALYN CAMA, FASID, EDAC

Foreword by Craig Zimring, PhD

WILEY

John Wiley & Sons, Inc.

Library of Congress Cataloging-in-Publication Data:

Cama, Rosalyn.
  Evidence-based healthcare design / by Rosalyn Cama.
      p. ; cm.
  Includes index.
  ISBN 978-0-470-14942-3 (cloth : alk. paper)
  1. Health facilities—Design and construction. 2. Evidence-based medicine. I. Title.
  [DNLM: 1. Facility Design and Construction—methods. 2. Hospital Design and Construction—methods. 3. Evidence-Based Medicine—methods. 4. Outcome Assessment (Health Care) WX 140 C172e 2009]
  RA967.C256 2009
  725'.51068—dc22

                                        2008026777

Printed in the United States of America

10 9 8 7 6 5 4 3 2 1

DEDICATION

"He who has health has hope, and
he who has hope has everything."
—Arabian Proverb

For John

None of us are immune from health challenges but some deal their whole life with the management of chronic illness. It is for them that I write this book and in particular for my brother John, who since his early twenties has learned to live with Cancer and the consequences of its treatment. He has done so with grace and courage while maintaining a zest for life. It is his internal struggle that inspires me to be part of a community that is building a body of knowledge about the best environments in which to deliver care. This base of knowledge, if possessed by all who design healthcare facilities, should make the journey for John and others like him less stressful, much healthier, and incredibly hopeful.

Button bush.
Picture by Henry Domke,
www.henrydomke.com.

CONTENTS

Lowbush blueberry.
Picture by Henry Domke,
www.henrydomke.com.

Chapter 5: Step 4: Measure and Share Outcomes   155

Part III: Nexus

Chapter 6: Evidence-Based Design in Practice   201

Chapter 7: Growth Opportunities for the Design Professional   229

The Practical Use of Evidence in Design

Craig M. Zimring, PhD
Environmental Psychologist
Professor of Architecture
Georgia Institute of Technology, Atlanta, Georgia

We are now starting a building boom that will shape healthcare for another generation. As Roz Cama writes in this important book, demographic, technical, economic, and competitive forces have converged to create the need for hundreds of billions of dollars of healthcare construction. This is occurring just as a quality revolution is changing healthcare. Reports such as the Institute of Medicine's *Quality Chasm* series have helped alert healthcare and the public to the need to significantly improve healthcare quality; groups such as the *Institute for Healthcare Improvement* have made significant strides in helping to improve healthcare processes. At the same time, the public, payers and others are calling for significant and visible improvement in healthcare quality and safety, while making healthcare much more centered on the needs of patients and their families.

Moon scallops.
Picture by Henry Domke,
www.henrydomke.com.

I am an environmental psychologist and have devoted my career to exploring how the built environment affects individuals and organizations. So I was particularly interested when the Robert Wood Johnson and the Center for Health Design asked me to partner with Roger Ulrich and an extraordinary group of colleagues from Texas A&M and Georgia Tech—Young-Seon Choi, Jennifer DuBose, Anjali Joseph, Xiaobo Quan, Hyun-Bo Seo, Xeumei Zhu—in 2004 and again in 2008 (R. S. Ulrich, Zimring, Joseph, Quan, & Choudhary, 2004; R.S. Ulrich et al., 2008) to explore whether there is convincing scientific evidence that the built environment affects healthcare quality and particularly outcomes for patients, family, staff and organizations. This question is of particular urgency. A variety of demographic, technical, competitive and financial pressures have converged to create one of the largest healthcare building booms in US history. Over the next decade we will create hundreds of billions of dollars of new healthcare construction that will shape US healthcare for a generation.

When we reviewed this literature we found that there were many more strong scientific studies than we had anticipated. They were scattered among hundreds of scientific journals and scores of disciplines such as medicine, nursing, epidemiology, architecture, environmental psychology and others. Almost all were in peer-reviewed journals. Although most changes in the built environment are multi-factorial, involving changes in care process, culture technology, along with physical changes, a number of these studies were actually randomized field experiments or cohort studies where clever researchers were able to take advantage of natural experiments to explore whether differences in qualities such as light or noise influenced pain, stress or sleep. There is much more to be studied, but the overall conclusion of our reviews was that there is convincing evidence that design can significantly impact outcomes. Some of these impacts are direct—there is good reason to believe that natural light and view can reduce stress and reduce the need for analgesic drugs—and much more has to do how the built environment can support improved ways of providing care. For example single rooms have multiple advantages: they help reduce infections, improve sleep, reduce the necessity of moving patients due to roommate incompatibility and help reduce falls.

This evidence has helped visionary healthcare leaders and designers to create a new generation of healthcare facilities that serve as tools for healthcare improvement. The Center for Health Design is working with more than 50 Pebble partners committed to using evidence-based design in their healthcare building projects and to study the resulting outcomes. The Military Health System, serving some 9.4 million people in 70 hospitals and 814 medical clinics worldwide is committed to using evidence-based design. The Global Health and Safety Initiative, representing some 100,000 hospital beds is using evidence- based design to increase patient, staff and environmental safety.

The emerging results are very encouraging. The new evidence-based designed Ohio-Health Dublin Methodist Hospital, in which Roz Cama played a significant role, has been open for nine months as of the writing of this foreword and has yet to experience a single healthcare acquired infection. Their Press-Ganey patient satisfaction scores are above the 98th percentile. Many other evidence-based facilities are opening and showing very promising results.

So Roz Cama's book comes just at the right time. While there is growing evidence about the importance of the built environment for healthcare improvement, design practitioners have relatively little experience creating, judging, assembling and using rigorous evidence. Academic disciplines such as environment and behavior studies and environmental psychology have been around since the 1960s but it is only recently that even the largest design firms have hired directors of research and have committed themselves to learning about, creating, using and sharing research. In general, unlike engineering or medicine, the design professions have tended to focus on products rather than process. Design processes often are invented by individual firms or designers or even re-invented for individual projects.

My colleagues Fried Augenbroe, Eileen Malone, Blair Sadler and I have recently had the opportunity to interview some 23 senior healthcare executives about how they were able to deliver innovative healthcare projects (Zimring, Augenbroe, Malone, & Sadler, 2008). We found that evidence played a key role. Understanding the evidence helped the project leaders establish innovative but realistic principles and goals and to choose cost-effective design strategies for achieving them. An evidence-based approach helped create accountability, where the teams set quantitative goals for improved quality and safety outcomes.

At its best, the use of evidence can reduce risk for the owner because it helps guide the design team toward solutions that will achieve the owner's goals and discard solutions that will not. Like the use of evidence in medicine, the use of evidence in design can help eliminate strategies that are not cost-effective or that are even harmful. At its worst, evidence-based design is simply a new buzzword with little substance, a rhetorical device for attempting to convince the client to do what the designer would have done anyway.

But even for the most thoughtful and experienced practitioners, the use of evidence in design is complex. A design project builds on previous experience but must also respond to the unique requirements of a specific context, and this is even more so during times of rapid change. What I like most about Roz Cama's book is that it is both inspirational and practical. Recognizing the real change will only occur if we understand how designs can help fuel changes in care process and culture, it avoids the magical thinking that we so easily fall into in design. It helps designers create a realistic process where evidence can play a range of roles in helping the client become excited about more ambitious goals, helping align the team to create creative solutions to achieve the goals and helping everyone become more accountable. This book also can have a more global impact. The design professions are seldom involved in the most important strategic discussions because they lack the knowledge base needed to provide them a role in helping clients achieve that which is most important for them: patients healing, families being treated respectfully as partners, staff being productive and effective. This book is a significant contribution in helping to solve this problem.

Ulrich, R. S., Zimring, C., Joseph, A., Quan, X., & Choudhary, R. (2004). *The role of the physical environment in the hospital of the 21st century: A once-in-a-lifetime opportunity.* Concord, CA: The Center for Health Design.

Ulrich, R. S., Zimring, C. M., Zhu, X., DuBose, J., Seo, H., Choi, Y., et al. (2008). A review of the research literature on evidence-based healthcare design. *Health Environments Research & Design, 1*(3), 61-125.

Zimring, C. M., Augenbroe, G., Malone, E. B., & Sadler, B. (2008). Implementing healthcare excellence: The vital role of the CEO in evidence-based design. *Health Environments Research & Design, 1*(3).

ACKNOWLEDGMENTS

"Different people are not that separate, they are all enfolded into the whole, and they are all a manifestation of the whole. It is only through an abstraction that they look separate. Everything is included in everything else."
—Joseph Jaworski, Synchronicity,
The Inner Path of Leadership

Several years ago I had the pleasure of meeting Ray Anderson, CEO of Interface Carpets, a legend at so many levels. We met at an ASID leadership retreat in Sedona, a magical setting that inspired our thinking about the future of our profession. Ray encouraged me to read Joe Jaworski's book *Synchronicity*. The lessons learned in that reading confirmed many things for me about my life but more importantly taught me to be open to possibilities. The opportunity to write this book has certainly been one of those possibilities. An

Indian woodoats.
Picture by Henry Domke,
www.henrydomke.com.

endeavor like this does not come easily, nor does it come from being alone; it comes from being part of a whole. I'd like to acknowledge the synchronistic moments in my life that have led me to this place and to those with whom I have bonded and are enfolded in all that I do.

At the age of 11 I described my desire for how I'd like to spend the rest of my life to my maternal grandfather, Poppet, and he defined it as interior design. At Dad's insistence I headed to college to earn a Bachelors Degree. It was at the University of Connecticut where I stumbled upon a note in the college catalogue for interior design majors and the transfer from Fine Arts was almost immediate. Upon graduation Warren Platner rescinded a job offer because of a failing economy which sent me looking for a temporary position as I prepared for graduate school. My mother found an ad for a draftsperson at Yale-New Haven Hospital where Harold Mindell convinced me that a six-year stint on a $73 million building project with Russo + Sonder/Davis Brody would be better than a Masters in Architecture. Upon project completion, Sam Brody encouraged me to start my own firm. Dr. David Parke drew my attention to a new building program at Meriden-Wallingford Hospital and my first contract for professional services was signed. Rhoda Russota taught me enduring business principles. Lloyd Acton taught me to listen with my heart, and our collaboration with Marna Borgstrom taught us the power of value-driven leadership. The ten years following took me on a leadership tract with the American Society of Interior Designers including an immersion with the Center for Creative Leadership. Lou Williams exposed me to a research-based approach toward design, which opened the door for an invitation to sit on the board of The Center for Health Design. Under the leadership of Derek Parker at The Center, I became part of an amazing think tank that continues to transform the way healthcare facilities are designed using an evidence-based design methodology for improving outcomes. It is in the camaraderie I share with Debra Levin and the faith I have gotten from Bob Levine that has forced me to own and develop a strong voice in evidence-based design. It is in my passion for this design methodology that I caught the attention of John Czarnecki of Wiley, who invited me to write this book.

I must acknowledge the support and love I have from those closest to me, as I have been on an overloaded, unsympathetic schedule this past year and a half. To my husband, Ron Mazzacane, and two nieces Elizabeth and Sarah Guidone, who are holding me to all of my promises upon completion of this endeavor. To my business partner, Ed Bottomley, for his stunning editing and our incredible staff at CAMA, Inc., for allowing me sabbaticals at critical project moments. They are all brilliant, talented, and doing great work creating interiors that improve outcomes. For the dedication given by my assistant Angela Vallejera and designers Elizabeth O'Brien and Javier Ferro, as well as Sadie Abuhoff and others at Wiley on the assembly of this manuscript, without whose talents I would not have made it to the finish line. For Kim Plavcan, whose brilliant design solutions are the foundation upon which we all stand, and whose own lost battle with Cancer makes us ever so committed to the cause.

This book is the representation of so many that have been on a similar journey either with me or parallel to me. It is their contributions that make this manuscript as rich as it is. Cheryl Herbert and Greg Mare and the Karlsberger/Big Red Rooster team on the Dublin Methodist Hospital for being truly evidence-based. Roger Ulrich, Ian Morrison, Mary Malone, Craig Zimring, Len Berry, Derek Parker, Kirk Hamilton, Ann Hendrich, Blair Sadler, Robin Guenther, Debra Levin from The Center for Health Design Board for the sharing of their wisdom. Anjali Joseph, Sara Marberry, Natalie Zensius, Carolyn Quist, Amy Keller for their support and quick answers. Bill Rostenberg and Rachael Ginsberg from Anshen + Allen for a story well told. Richard Thomas and Louis Meilink from the Weill, Cornell team; IDEO and Bob Porter from the SSM Healthcare team; Brad Seamons and Nicola Majchrzack from the Massachusetts General Hospital team; Linda Haggerty, Amy Starling, Wilson Mertens, MD from the Baystate Health team; Lyn Geboy at Kahler Slater; Teri Zborowsky at Ellerbe Becket; Debajyoti Pati at HKS; Maggie Calkins on the long-term care perspective; Denise Guerin from the University of Minnesota; and Frank Becker from Cornell University; Patrick McKenna and the American Cancer Society team; and Michael Berens from ASID; Mark Strauss and Wing Leung at *Interior Design Magazine* and its top 40 healthcare firms that responded to our questionnaire—thank you for all of your knowledge sharing and inspirational evidence-based pioneering work.

I acknowledge the collaborative members of all of the interdisciplinary teams too many to mention especially the following firms who shared project work and photography: The American Cancer Society, Anshen + Allen, Ballinger, Big Red Rooster, Bruce Komiske, BSA Lifestructures/Maregatti, CAMA, Cannon Design, The Center for Health Design, Farrow Partnership, FKP, Graphics Press/Edward Tufte, Gresham, Smith, Guenther 5, HDR, Heery, HOK, IDEO, Interior Design Magazine, Kahler Slater, Kasien, Karlsberger, KMD, Leonard Berry, MSI, NBBJ, Perkins + Will, Salvatore Associates, Steffian Bradley, and to Gilles Thibault and Henry Domke for exceptional healing photography.

Lastly I'd like to acknowledge the people who lead the interdisciplinary teams with whom I share current evidence-based collaborations and thought-provoking journeys: Jim Valenti at El Paso Children's Hospital with Jim Diaz at KMD, Barry Rabner at The University Medical Center at Princeton with Ken Drucker at HOK, Pat Sodomka and Rick Tobias at The Medical College of Georgia with Jim Kukla at Heery and Dan King at 2KM, Dr. Brian Smith at Yale-New Haven Hospital with Vassilios Nicolaouilios at Karlsberger, Bobbe Young and Mike Moran at Baystate Health with Kurt Rockstroh at SBA, and Norm Roth, Pat Luddy, and Brad Beavers at Yale-New Haven Hospital with Alberto Salvatore at Salvatore Associates. May we take evidence-based design to a new level of exploration.

Godspeed to all.

INTRODUCTION

"New strategy always implies change, and the potential of a new strategy is often threatening to the existing success formula."
—Peter Schwartz, The Art of the Long View

The Long View

A new strategy has emerged for the design of our buildings and in particular the design of our healthcare facilities; it is called evidence-based design. The strategy is a shift, not a radical change, but a shift nonetheless that all who are involved in the design of a healthcare facility must become aware of and ultimately own within their practice model. If you have not begun to modify your practice methodology or the filters within your "request for design qualifications" then you are falling drastically behind because the shift has begun and its tipping point is near.

Some have healthy skepticism about the lack of rigor within the research phase of this methodology, others fear the loss of the creative process, while others think it will cost more to provide this service. This book will dispel all of those fears. In fact, it will guide you through a process that will take you gradually into an evidence-based mindset and give you choices in levels of practice. There are four levels and four components to this new methodology—some of which is already familiar and some will require further investigation and training for the non-evidence-based designer. It does not require that the standard design phases be discarded, but rather suggests some upfront reorganization of team format, a more rigorous level of investigation in gathering intelligence, and the formulation of more scientific questions or hypotheses before the design begins. It will suggest a more critical process for arriving at a design solution that will foster innovation within a framework that intelligently supports the risk associated with change. In the end it will encourage an interdisciplinary team to be fully accountable by measuring, sharing and building a body of knowledge the skeptics fear is weak.

This book is intended for all design professionals, owner representatives, healthcare administrators, clinicians and educators, providing a methodology and examples for each of the four evidence-based components. It offers a way to understand the process but does not offer a prescriptive approach. With an understanding of the process, each team will find its own way to one of the four levels, the level in which they choose to participate. It takes into consideration the interdisciplinary nature of the design team that assembles to assess, analyze, and develop new environments in which to deliver the best possible care in a most complex building type.

The format presented in this book is a four-step process explained and supported by examples, expert testimony, and checklists for easy future reference. The examples in this book are collected from actual projects, gathered in qualitative interviews with practitioners and owners about how they are transforming their practices. There are a number of firms today that are beginning to provide this service, but the author is not convinced that every studio in these firms has climbed on board.

This book's differential is in its use as a tool at the start of a healthcare project, for the developing proposals, defining scope of services, creating an interdisciplinary team, and creating project schedule of tasks and deliverables. At a more ambitious level it can inform a new generation of practitioner if adopted by educators for use in the classroom. Although it uses evidence gathered to illustrate its points, it primarily focuses on the methodology of practice. It is timely, therefore, for a book that defines an outcome-based practice and outlines a methodology for deliverable services.

The long view.
© courtesy of Gilles Thibault.

It is the author's hope that this book will challenge and inspire new concepts in practice, for what is outlined here is truly the launch of a shift in the thinking of how the built environment impacts human behavior. Please read on and be inspired to challenge your design practice methodology. The author aims to inform, instruct, and inspire a transformation in design practice.

The author hopes to immerse you into the topic, to allay your fears, and to encourage you to work toward accepting and building this necessary body of knowledge hereby enhancing the process of improving healthcare delivery as quickly as possible.

Part I
Medical Specialty
Area, Riley Hospital for
Children.
Michael O'Callahan
Photography,
KMD/CAMA/
Roll•Barresi

PART I

DRIVERS FOR CHANGE

"There is nothing wrong with change,
if it is in the right direction."
—Winston Churchill

Chapter 1
Understanding the Shift toward Evidence-Based Design in Healthcare

"Grant me the serenity to accept the things I
cannot change, the courage to change the things
I can and the wisdom to know the difference."
—Reinhold Niebuhr

It is difficult to discuss a practice methodology without giving it context within the field in which it is to be practiced. This chapter opens the discussion by defining what evidence-based design is. It continues by identifying drivers for change in healthcare as well as in the design professions and offering a brief synopsis of all four components of this process. It graphically aligns traditional phases of the design process with the shift necessary to be evidence-based. Like every chapter in this book, it offers expert testimony from supporters of evidence-based design who have experienced a positive change as a result of this practice methodology.

The practice of design is constantly evolving. Why? It evolves according to the demands being made on the design professions and transforms according to the practice's ability to respond to that demand. These shifts in evolution are never as obvious as the one that is occurring right now toward an outcome-driven approach to the design of the built environment. Firms are struggling to embrace this shift because, after all, design is an art not a science. Or is it?

A well-designed building is generally aesthetically pleasing, functionally effortless, and extraordinarily experiential, yet measurement of its success is often subjective. The abstract solution of how to divide space and capture light is often studied, but rarely is its impact on behavioral outcomes. If science is the study of the physical world and its manifestations, especially by using systematic observation and experiment[1], then the design of the built environment has a natural place in the world of science. A design with a measurable outcome is so akin to evidence-based medicine that it is only natural that this methodology has caught on with healthcare clients. The growing popularity of this design methodology is being fueled by

Figure 1.1
Nautilus shell.
Picture by Henry Domke,
www.henrydomke.com.

medicine's familiar logic. It is here in the healthcare specialty where the practice of evidence-based design has emerged most prominently. How to embrace this shift in design methodology is the premise behind this book.

An evidence-based approach to design is not new. In fact, it is quite commonplace when it is linked to academia, though rarely does it fall within the basic services of a professional design practice. One problem is that the design of the built environment has not been considered a factor in health and organizational outcomes. (See Essay 2-1.) For example the essential act of hand-washing is conducted in every specialty of design. It is critical to food service and healthcare delivery. How many times have you gone to a new restaurant and sent a dining companion to the restroom to see an amazing bathroom design feature? The design detailing catches your fancy and adds to the overall experience, but does it increase the chance of getting staff to wash their hands? Does making it attractive elicit the action or will smart placement increase the behavior? In healthcare, where the failure to wash hands between examining patients increases the spread of infection, little effort is made to understand how to improve that experience or, more importantly, increase compliance. We need to understand how to improve this outcome. In two separate hospital-user meetings in the last year, Emergency Department physicians asked to reorient the hand-washing sink so they could begin the task of hand-washing while immediately engaging in conversation with the patient

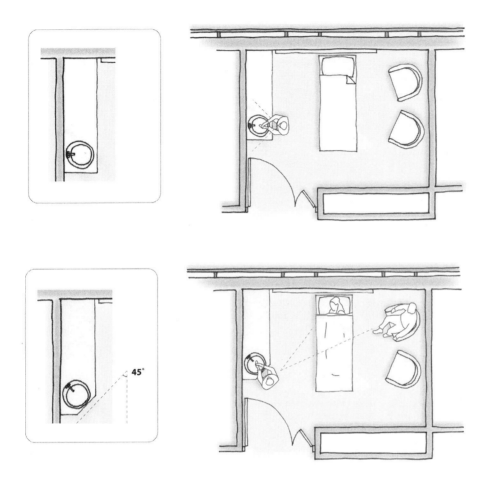

Figure 1.2
Typical emergency exam room layout where caregivers must turn backs to the patient and family while washing their hands at the sink on a parallel wall.

Figure 1.3
At Yale-New Haven Hospital's pediatric emergency room, placing the sink on an angle allows caregivers to maintain eye contact with the patient and family while washing their hands. The design hypothesis is to improve hand-washing compliance and improve staff-to-patient and staff-to-family communications. Studies not yet complete.
Salvatore Associates Architect of Record/ CAMA, Inc.

or family. (See Figures 1.2 and 1.3.) The jury is out as to whether this change in a design feature will improve compliance, but follow-up measurement will show if in fact a simple design adjustment can improve a chronic flaw in healthcare outcomes. Chapter 2 will look at why important knowledge like this is lacking and what can be done to build a base of knowledge about design features that improve performance statistics such as hand-washing compliance. In evidence-based healthcare design a body of knowledge is being captured, however, like the missing knowledge on how design can improve hand-washing compliance, it has many voids. The importance of adopting an evidence-based approach to build this base of knowledge is that it will contribute to an industry struggling with ways to improve safety and quality services—outcomes we should never take for granted in our healthcare system.

Figure 1.4
Japanese Method of
Inquiry asks why five
times to get to the root
of an answer changing
a user's perspective of
the status quo.

▶ *WHY are U.S. Railroad tracks spaced 4'8" apart?*
Because the U.S. adopted the British standard.

WHY are British tracks spaced that way?
↓ **The dimensions were adopted from trams that preceded railroads.**

WHY were British tramways spaced that way?
↓ **The jigs used for trams were the same as the jigs for horse drawn wagons.**

WHY did the jigs for wagons set wheels 4'8" apart?
↓ **That was the distance between wheel ruts on ancient British roads, built by Imperial Rome for chariots.**

…and WHY were the wheels of Roman chariots spaced 4'8" apart?
↳ **That's the optimum width to accommodate two horses in harness, side to side.**

why ?

that's
WHY.

Stress is at the core of most individuals' healthcare experience. Those who design buildings possess an incredible opportunity to improve life's experiences by reducing an occupant's stress. The hospitality industry makes it its business to transform our hectic lives into a state of tranquility; it has studied lifestyles and knows our wants and desires before we do. Industry researchers inform resort developers who create programs, improve services, and build facilities that will attract our discretionary income. Traveling consumers are continuously realizing the health benefits of incorporating "SPA" into their busy lifestyles, thus increasing their likelihood to spend in these areas.[2] Yet, where else is the need for an improved experience with reduced stress and health benefits more important than in a healthcare setting? A compromised patient seeking medical attention, a worried family member, and an overtaxed clinician trying to administer care and compassion make up a team of most likely candidates for an improved experience makeover. The demand for this outcome is great but documented evidence is slow to get to the design studio. The cycle of innovation for improved clinical practice models and supporting architecture is offset by antiquated mindsets that see the status quo as too difficult to change. There is an anecdote in the industry that references the origin of railroad track dimensions back to Imperial Rome. It is a silly truth that illustrates the magnitude of consequences one pays in design decision-making lead by fear of change. It is in this sad testimony of flawed decision-making that the real need to change the way we design our healthcare facilities is seen. (See Figure 1.4.)

The most compelling reason to build a database of evidence-based knowledge is the economic one. Too many good ideas get missed for fear that an old operational model can't be changed or worse, that the expenditure is too great, so old models are perpetuated in the name of prudent advancement. The way to dispel that fear is to tie the benefit of a capital expenditure to an operational saving of a design detail. In healthcare it is rare that these two parallel accounting mindsets intersect during the design of a building project. This has slowed innovation because the lack of evidence to support a business case for a better building never reaches the board-room table.

The discussion continues to build around how the design process needs to evolve, an evolution that links design more closely to outcomes, and a financial model of a building's lifecycle. It is at that level of scrutiny that this book will address the methodology known as evidence-based design.

Evidence-Based Design

What is evidence-based design? How do you practice this model of design? Will it cost more? Does it require more/different staff or specialized consultants? These are the most common questions being posed by clients and design professionals. Will design practitioners know how to add the appropriate expertise to their teams so that the appropriate rigor is used? Will the studies be valid to truly build a solid base of knowledge? Will academic programs teach this

---

Keyword: Evidence-Based Design

Definition: Evidence-based design is:

- An iterative decision-making process that begins with the analysis of current best evidence from an organization as well as from the field.
- It finds, at the intersection of this knowledge, behavioral, organizational, or economic clues that when aligned with a stated design objective can be hypothesized as a beneficial outcome.

- It does not provide prescriptive solutions, but rather a platform from which to add to an existing base of knowledge or to launch innovation.
- It espouses an ethical obligation to measure outcomes and share knowledge gained for particular design successes and failures, ideally in a peer-reviewed fashion, as is common in academia.

In summary: Investigate • Hypothesize • Continue to Prove or Innovate • Measure and Share

methodology in their pre-professional lesson planning? These are the questions academic and practicing researchers are asking.

The Process

Evidence-based design is a process used to:

- develop and design a new building or renovation project
- bring together a balanced team representing client, stakeholders, and appropriate design disciplines including researchers in the investigation, design, and analysis of a project in an interdisciplinary way
- focus on strategic directives that can lead to improved outcomes through the analysis of past design and facility performance intelligence
- support a proven design detail or inspire an innovative concept hypothesized to improve a stated outcome
- commit to a post-occupancy research project to reveal the success or failure of the hypothesized result
- publish in a peer-reviewed journal.

Interdisciplinary teams typically begin a design process with an investigation of existing conditions. They add to this mix intelligence from the existing facility and from previous projects of a similar nature. Occasionally, there is an effort to gather documented intelligence from similar projects either about design solutions or organizational issues that have been published in peer-reviewed literature. It is in this investigation that the potential for a creative design solution and the level of risk needed to improve a strategic objective or a stated outcome will be revealed. This process does not interrupt the standard phases of design, however, it adds a layer of scrutiny and exploration that triggers greater potential for innovation. Before final decisions are made there exists the possibility of live, simulated, or referential mock-ups (see chapter 4) where pre-measurement of critical features can help assure beneficial outcomes. This process also begins to reveal the need for shifts in culture around new delivery models. A process like this keeps the interdisciplinary team focused on outcomes strategically stated by the project guidelines, but with a global perspective of the industry's most current position on

---

Keyword: Interdisciplinary Team

An interdisciplinary team is balanced representation of all constituencies on a project responsible for the design, building, operations, and use of a facility, with a specific goal to deliver a project within schedule and budget, but more importantly aligned with project goals and desired improved outcomes.

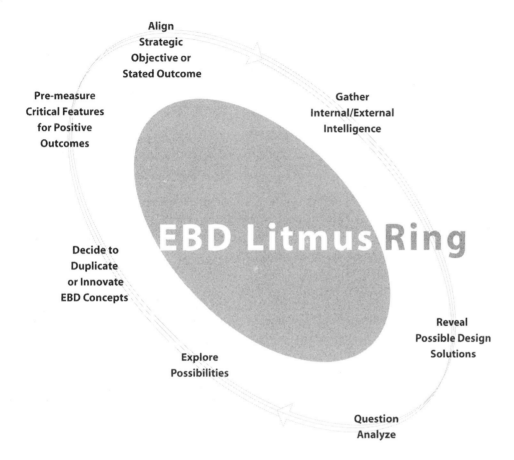

Align Strategic Objective or Stated Outcome

Pre-measure Critical Features for Positive Outcomes

Gather Internal/External Intelligence

EBD Litmus Ring

Decide to Duplicate or Innovate EBD Concepts

Reveal Possible Design Solutions

Explore Possibilities

Question Analyze

Figure 1.5
EBD Litmus Ring: Depicts an iterative process that aligns evidence-based design decisions with an institution's strategic directives after an informed, exploratory and translational design process that uses critical thinking skills. When the alignment does not occur then the concept should be dropped or modified until it does. *CAMA, Inc.*

a particular solution. The process continually forces strategic alignment for the design team as well as the administrative team. (See Figure 1.5.) This Evidence-Based Design Litmus Ring illustrates how critical thinking in an early design phase can push for the option to innovate or stay the course on a common design solution to a particular organizational outcome. It diminishes the fear associated with risky decision-making and empowers leadership to think beyond "Imperial Rome."

The healthcare industry is continually poised to adopt new procedures, such as evidence-based design, that will offer improvement in the areas of quality and safety. Why then are the design professions slow to adopt a practice that will increase the flow of knowledge and the spread of innovation? Is it fear that it will slow a well-oiled machine and compromise profits? I think not. It is this author's opinion that evidence-based design will drive more business to design firms, as they become strategic partners in the improvement of our health delivery system. Let's explore to what degree a firm should be willing to adopt this design methodology.

The Four Components of an Evidence-Based Design Process

There are four basic components to evidence-based design. They are:

1. Gather qualitative and quantitative intelligence
2. Map strategic, cultural, and research goals
3. Hypothesize outcomes, innovate, and implement translational design
4. Measure and share outcomes

The struggle during most projects is when to conduct the various phases or components of evidence-based design and how to use the knowledge gained to better advance design. The current difficulty is that the process is new and firms are backing their way into what they are calling evidence-based design or using the familiar logic of a post-occupancy evaluation. Post-occupancy evaluations (POEs) use the current design methodology and discover where improvement occurred after the project is completed, as opposed to evidence-based design (EBD), which begins the research process in a pre-design phase. This is happening because all team members are not on board from the start—including the client. The ideal is to begin the process with a full interdisciplinary team in place at the start of a project. Let's take a look at how to integrate each of these components into the standard model of design phases.

EBD Component 1: Gather Qualitative and Quantitative Intelligence

It is customary, throughout the process of design, to gather intelligence. Traditionally it is in the programming phase when qualitative and quantitative intelligence shapes a project. This logic is flawed because often a new project is informed with data that references and perpetuates stale models. The process of evidence-based design by nature of its rigorous inquiry suggests an investigation prior to programming that intelligently informs project goals and guidelines. It gives time for consolidated thought processes early in a condensed design schedule. This time allows a team in a broader context to learn and analyze the existing culture of an organization, its strategic objectives, and discovers whether it is a good match for the best solution currently known in the industry or ready for innovative concepts. It is then that a team can wisely approach evidence-based design as a way to forge new roads and explore innovative ways to improve processes in care delivery allowing for new architectural or design models to emerge. For instance, if a project is considering like-handed rooms then the design team would investigate what those who have trail-blazed before them have learned. They would consider improving upon the previous solution by carefully examining the documented studies. (See Figures 1.6 and 1.7.) It is at this point that a team would also understand a board of directors' objective for taking on such a building project or an administrative team's objective to renovate a unit. It is at this juncture where the team learns about existing norms, standards,

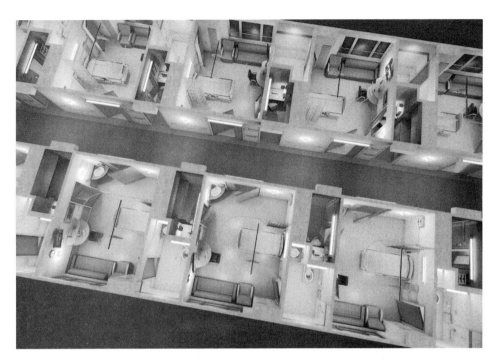

Figure 1.6
Unit design of like-handed room floor-plans. St. Joseph's Hospital (Pebble Project Alumni) is the project that initiated the wild discussion about like-handed rooms very soon after the industry accepted the concept of the single-bedded room. As an innova-tion, it has inherent in its design clues for the next generation of patient room. The hypothesis is that like-handed room designs reduce medical errors and staff stress. The geometry of this plan has spurred creativity in many subsequent nurs-ing unit designs. Studies not complete. *Courtesy of Gresham, Smith and Partners. Ring & Duchateau (Engineering) and CG Schmidt (Contractor).*

Figure 1.7
St. Joseph's like-handed room design also launched the discussion about headwall-based bathrooms. Linked by a common wall, handrails assist in a trip to the bathroom which could produce a reduction in fall rates. Studies not yet complete. *Courtesy of Gresham, Smith and Partners. Ring & Duchateau (Engineering) and CG Schmidt (Contractor).*

Keywords: Qualitative and Quantitative Research

Qualitative research explores the nature of a problem, issue, or phenomenon. It is an unstructured process of inquiry.[4]

Quantitative research explores the extent of a problem, issue, or phenomenon. It is a structured process of inquiry.[5]

and principles that drive an institution's facilities program. It is at the intersection of all of these issues where a dialogue begins about how to structure a research project that will be beneficial to all. The cost and benefit of this exploration needs to be measured[3] as an added service to the traditional contractual model, because the knowledge gained arms a team with greater potential for innovation. Chapter 2 will go into much more detail on this topic. It is, however, important to note that this activity can occur over and over throughout the design process.

EBD Component 2: Map Strategic, Cultural, and Research Goals

It is in the intelligence gathered that a unique body of knowledge specific to a project is amassed. How to make sense of it all is the art of analysis. For an audience attuned to visual tools, a graphic map is a clear and simple way to show all constituencies' goals (see Figure 1.8). It is in this analysis of the collective intelligence that a team will reveal a clear path for project wisdom and the "big idea" or a project's vision will emerge.

Figure 1.8
Map depicting Ohio Health's institutional values and Dublin Methodist Hospital's (Pebble Project) project design clues deduced from a cultural study that informed a new model for healthcare delivery and hence an innovative facility design. This mapping exercise informed the project's big idea to develop a patient-centered culture that embraces humanity and fosters safety. Studies not complete.
Big Red Rooster.

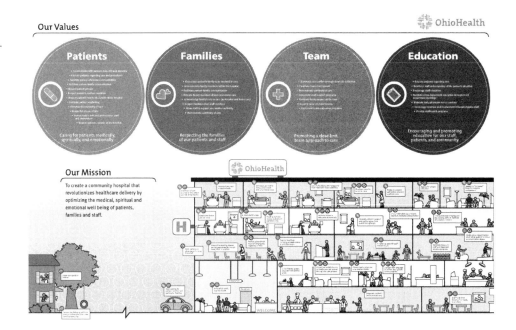

Keywords: Visioning and Deep Dive

Visioning: A creative, interactive set of assignments organized in a retreat format, that results in a forward thinking point of view about a familiar problem. (See Figure 1.9.)

Deep dive: Attributed to the work of IDEO whereby designers, anthropologists, and researchers spend days, sometimes weeks, shadowing people to observe how they behave. The results of this research are often quite different from conventional wisdom.[6]

Figure 1.9 *(left)* Visioning session at All Children's Hospital. Jack designs a room after exploring with other pediatric patients and families what about a hospital makes them happy and what makes them sad. Note: Needles made Jack happy because they keep him well! How can you not listen to such wisdom? The goal from the lessons learned is to reduce patient stress. Studies not yet complete.

Figure 1.10 *(right)* Deep dive, Kim Plavcan takes copious notes at Baystate Health while spending the day on a pediatric unit preparing for a renovation project that will serve as a translational study or a living mockup for a major building project. The hypothesis for the design solution is to improve family-centeredness. Studies not yet complete.
CAMA, Inc.

"Visioning sessions" or "deep dives" (see Figure 1.9) should be conducted to drill deeper into specific topics. These sessions will create new ideas allowing details needed to support the desired behavior to emerge. It is here that the discussion of a research agenda should occur. This discussion should examine the intersection of all strategic initiatives and stated project guidelines. It should consider the desired innovations and transformations that the institution is committed to for a cultural, organizational, and architectural makeover. And it should connect where the brand lies with respect to its promise to patients, community, and staff. Chapter 3 will explore this component of evidence-based design.

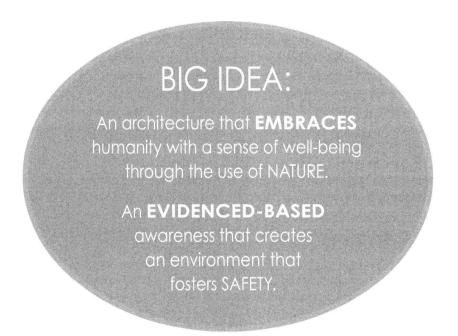

Figure 1.11
It is the "big idea" or project vision that keeps a project and its inter-disciplinary team on point. These statements sum up the design intent. It is here where hypotheses emerge and where project re-searchers see the clues for a research agenda. *Dublin Methodist Hospital (Pebble Project), Karlsberger Architects/ CAMA, Inc.*

BIG IDEA:

An architecture that **EMBRACES** humanity with a sense of well-being through the use of NATURE.

An **EVIDENCED-BASED** awareness that creates an environment that fosters SAFETY.

EBD Component 3: Hypothesize Outcomes, Innovate, and Implement Translational Design

It is in this component of evidence-based design that the clear statement of a hypothesis activates a research project. Although it may not be completely necessary to hypothesize outcomes, it is in the statement of hypotheses that a team engages in the investment of a design intervention. It is in this moment that the design is more than a good solution; it is a means to an end. The importance of a hypothesis lies in its ability to bring direction, specificity, and focus to a research project. It tells a researcher what specific information to collect, thereby providing greater focus.[7] That stated, it is during schematic design that a design team should hypothesize their outcomes. As evidence-based design is being integrated more and more into design practice it has been difficult to get project teams engaged in the process this soon in a project. Ideally, it is here where schematic design can begin to incorporate new and different approaches to problem solving that are informed by and tied to specific outcomes. (See Figure 1.11.)

Design, as we know it traditionally, begins here. Data has been collected and analyzed, goals and guidelines have been articulated, a research agenda is in place, hypotheses have been articulated, and the entire team is on board with clear directives for the project. There are two methods that lie ahead in the evidence-based process—one is to continue to prove that a known outcome will work in your given conditions, i.e.; that single-bedded rooms reduce the spread of

Keyword: Design Hypothesis

A design hypothesis is an explanation of a design intervention intended to produce a desired outcome used as a basis for further exploration.

infection, the other is to take your hypotheses to uncharted outcomes by introducing a new concept where no evidence is present and prove or disprove a hypothesis, i.e., single-bedded rooms that are like-handed reduce medical errors. (See Figures 1.12, 1.13, 1.14, and 1.15.)

Once these design details are presented and approved it is important to do due diligence before installing the concept into a new building. This is called translational design, whereby knowledge from the design studio can be tested at the bedside. It has its roots in translational medicine.

Similarly in design, the safety and effectiveness of a design concept should be tested. It can be tested in the form of a simulated mock-up, whereby all functions shy of the patient's presence can be tested. It can also be tested in a live mock-up where a patient is in a fully operational space, or in a referential mock-up where one portion of a design is tested in an existing setting, often done with equipment testing. In all of these settings, valuable information is gathered and often a design concept is altered and/or tweaked to conform to the culture and operational models of care present in the facility testing the design intervention. Chapter 4 will explore this component of evidence-based design further.

EBD Component 4: Measure and Share Outcomes

Most important in the process of evidence-based design, is the ability to measure results and to share the knowledge gained. The industry has been slow to introduce new concepts because of the lack of knowledge shared. Although many will anecdotally share experiences, carefully documented research on the effects of a particular design intervention is slow to come from the design studio or hospital's facilities department. It is in this measurement that knowledge gained will inspire another team to develop a concept further or abandon the trend and move on. Measurement from hypothesized outcomes using evidence-based design can occur with a team of graduate students or with researchers on staff at a healthcare facility. They need not

Keyword: Transitional Research

"In the translational research setting, statisticians often assist in the planning and analysis of pilot studies. While pilot studies may vary in the fundamental objectives, many are designed to explore the safety profile of a drug or procedure. Often before applying a new therapy to large groups of patients, a small, non-comparative study is used to estimate the safety profile of the therapy using relatively few patients."[8]

Figure 1.12
University Medical Center at Princeton (Pebble Project), HOK/RMJM Hillier/CAMA's study of like-handed canted rooms with bathrooms on the headwall; 249 square feet. The hypothesis is to reduce medical errors and falls. Studies not complete.

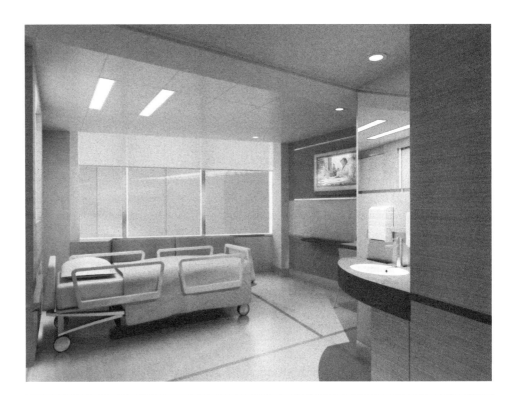

Figure 1.13
University of California Long Hospital, HOK's study of like-handed canted rooms with bathrooms on the headwall. The hypothesis is to reduce medical errors and falls. Studies not complete.

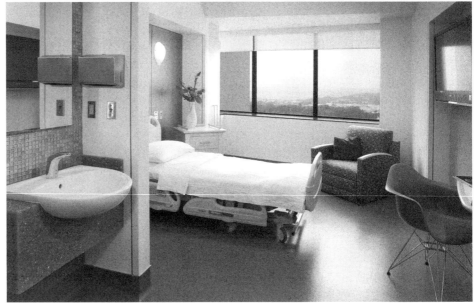

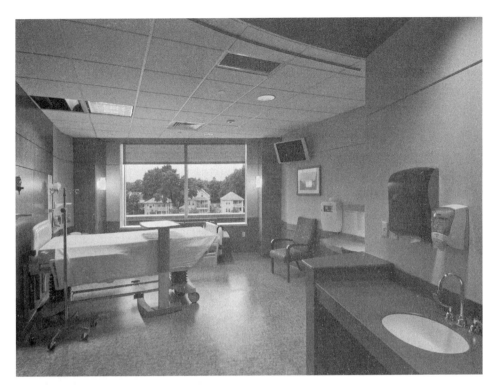

Figure 1.14
Miriam Hospital, HOK/SLAM Collaborative's study of like-handed canted rooms with bathrooms on the headwall; 323 square feet. The hypothesis is to reduce medical errors and falls. Studies not yet complete.
Gregg Shupe Photography.

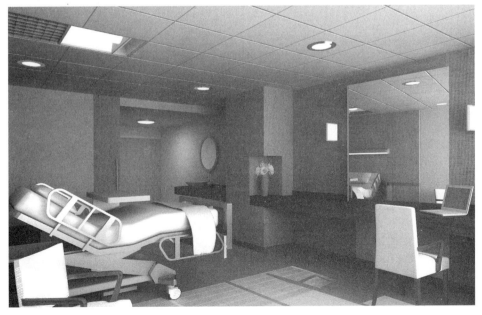

Figure 1.15
HCA Stone Oak, HOK's study of like-handed canted rooms with bathrooms on the headwall; 260 square feet. The hypothesis is to reduce medical errors and falls. Studies not yet complete.

be employed at a design firm—in fact, it may be preferred that they are not for the sake of unbiased conclusions.

The reporting can be done at two different levels of scrutiny. Commonplace with most design professionals is the venue of the professional conference attended by one's peers. Other venues include medically related conferences that offer multidisciplinary audiences of architects and designers, hospital administrators and facility directors, and medical clinicians and patient advocates. The most desired way, however, is to submit research for peer review and, if there are human subjects, to an Institutional Review Board (IRB). This action engages academic partners who may assist in the analysis of the data and help construct the argument for or against the design intervention. It is here where the true contribution to the larger body of knowledge is valued. Chapter 5 will explain more about how to engage or partner in the development of this most important component of evidence-based design.

Table 1.1 Integration of Components of Evidence-Based Design into Standard Design Process

Components of Standard Design	Components of Evidence-Based Design	I Gather Intelligence	II Map Project and Research Goals	III Hypothesize Outcomes Implement Translational Design	IV Measure	Share in Professional Setting	Share in Peer-Reviewed Setting
Occupancy					✓	✓	✓
Construction Administration Mock-Ups					✓	✓	✓
Construction Documents				✓		✓	
Design Development		✓	✓	✓		✓	
Schematic Design		✓	✓	✓			
Programming/Pre-design		✓	✓				

Levels of Evidence-Based Practice

The beauty of the evidence-based process is that engagement in this methodology can occur gradually as a design team adjusts its approach to design solutions. A first step would be to become familiar with the literature that exists. In time, each of the subsequent components to an evidence-based design methodology can be added, exploring a team's comfort zone and willingness to measure and report. It also takes time to convince clients of the benefits of this process. Until comfort with the evidence-based methodology is achieved, it will be a challenge to convince others to engage in this methodology. Another approach to the process, of course, is to subcontract for those services that are unfamiliar. There are new alliances to be made with those obtaining advanced degrees in design and science and incredible opportunities for colleges and universities to develop advanced degrees in design. See Chapter 7, Growth Opportunities for the Design Professional.

Kirk Hamilton, FAIA, empowered all to find a level within the process of evidence-based design that feels comfortable for the project, the team, and the client. In his *Healthcare Design Magazine* article in November 2003,[9] Hamilton articulates how design practitioners can accept this process without much difficulty. A level 1 practitioner requires a buy-in, using past documented studies as a way to inform new concepts and using the knowledge gained as a platform from which to launch new design concepts.

This book's discussion of EBD (evidence-based design) components 1 and 2 falls into Hamilton's level 1 of practice:

1. Gather qualitative and quantitative intelligence
2. Map strategic, cultural, and research goals

In what Hamilton terms a level 2 practitioner he includes everything a level 1 evidence-based designer would do but adds the ability to "hypothesize the expected outcomes of design interventions and subsequently measure the results."

EBD components 3 and part of 4 are engaged in this level of practice:

3. Hypothesize outcomes, innovate, and implement translational design
4. Measure...

Hamilton's level 3 practitioner would again do all that a level 2 practitioner would do but commits to sharing the gained knowledge through articles written in professional journals or lectures given at professional conferences.

The level 4 practitioner goes one step further and submits the found conclusions to a peer-reviewed journal.

EBD component 4 is subdivided into the final two levels of practice:

4. ...and share outcomes. (See Table 1.2.)

Levels of Evidence-based Practice	Components of Evidence-Based Design	I Gather Intelligence	II Map Project and Research Goals	III Hypothesize Outcomes Implement Translational Design	IV Measure	Share in Professional Setting	Share in Peer-Reviewed Setting
Table 1.2 Comparison of Components of Evidence-Based Design to Levels of Evidence-Based Practice							
Level 4 Meet Academic Standards		✓	✓	✓	✓	✓	✓
Level 3 Share Results Publicly		✓	✓	✓	✓	✓	
Level 2 Hypothesize and Measure		✓	✓	✓	✓		
Level 1 Interpret the Evidence		✓	✓				

This graphic maps stages that a design professional, a design firm, or a healthcare facility can use to find their comfort zone for the adoption of evidence-based design practice. If a project requires only known design interventions, then a level 1 practitioner can be contracted to complete the first component of the evidence-based practice. On the other hand, if the envelope is to be pushed to solve a particular safety or quality issue not yet resolved through evidence-based design, then a level 4 practitioner should be engaged who will use all four components of evidence-based design. Chapter 6 will explore these scenarios further by looking in depth at an evidence-based practice model that is currently operational.

Empowering an Interdisciplinary Team

It is easy to see how it takes a variety of skills to achieve a four-level practice. Conducting a project in an evidence-based way is a tall order unless all of the right ingredients are on hand and the right mix of players is in place. A willing and able client who has a clear vision and is willing to empower a team has to be at the forefront of such an approach. This is not just at the facilities level. Boards of directors need to be engaged so that their long view of an institution's future is

Figure 1.16
Interdisciplinary team visioning for the new El Paso Children's Hospital, El Paso, Texas. Design hypothesis is to provide hope and healing in their design. Studies not yet complete.
KMD Architects/ MNK/CAMA, Inc.

aligned with a project's goals. The CEO has to empower all who will have responsibility for the design and construction. Often a CEO is not capable of articulating how corporate strategy gets interpreted into a facility vision. It is here where confusion abounds. It is in the partnership with an enlightened design leader that these shortcomings can be overcome. See Essay 1-1 to learn about "vision keepers." How top administration empowers lower levels of management and establishes a trust-based approach to decision-making[10] can make or break an institution's ability to successfully follow this methodology of design. If a facility manager reports to a higher-level administrator who lives in fear of proposing new concepts to the c-suite, then innovation is squelched. On the other hand, evidence-based design sends these trailblazers into the higher chambers equipped with credible documentation to support an innovation that is directly linked to a strategic outcome. The first part of building a successful interdisciplinary team is the establishment of a solid link with top decision-makers. (See Figure 1.16.)

Clear design team leadership also sets the pace for keeping all parties in the loop, particularly in the early phases of the project. Most healthcare projects have diverse teams who are under tight schedules and budgets, making it easy to slip into a familiar mindset or design silos. These team players all find comfort in executing the design process the way they have

Figure 1.17 *(left)*
Figure 1.18 *(right)*
Culture study conducted by Big Red Rooster for OhioHealth as it prepared to build a new Greenfield hospital—the Dublin Methodist Hospital (Pebble Project). This study drove the early evidence-based design process.

always done so before, making plans and systems almost predictable. The leader may tout an enlightened awareness but the house of cards falls when everyone is not engaged in this process. See Chapter 6 for an example of firm-wide engagement concepts.

Outside consultants are added as needed. It is imperative though to identify who your researcher will be early on. It is in this base of knowledge that you will find the right articles to review, help in the analysis of existing hospital data, and the ability to pose the right questions for significant inquiry. Sometimes it takes a specialized researcher or consulting firm to study the existing and desired culture of an organization to test if the organization is able to make radical transformations and, behave as the new strategic direction intends them to. (See Figures 1.17 and 1.18.)

Make the message clear. It is difficult to transcend from the abstract thinking of design to the analytical mind of the scientist. For those who see in shades of gray the same concept has to be brought into focus in black and white. It is here where a strong graphical approach to documents has to be clear to all who read submitted evidence. Yale University Professor Emeritus Edward Tufte has made information design his life's work. (See Figure 1.19.) The *New York Times* described him as "The Leonardo da Vinci of data." He has authored many books on how to use graphics as a way to clearly present analytical data. For the design team entering into the world of statistical analysis this may be an intriguing way to present your findings to a mixed audience of design and medical professionals.

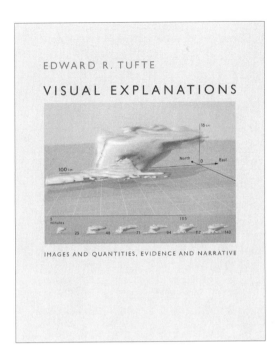

Figure 1.19
Graphical data
presentation skills of
Edward Tufte.
*Reprinted by permission,
Edward R. Tufte, Visual Ex-
planations (Cheshire, CT,
Graphics Press LLC 1997).*

Essay 1-1 Holding to a Clear Vision

Cheryl Herbert, R.N., CEO of Dublin Methodist Hospital, OhioHealth, Dublin, Ohio

The importance of building a multi-disciplinary team focused on the same vision and goals cannot be underestimated. Bringing together the owner, designers, architects, owner's representatives, engineers, construction managers, and even major subcontractors early in a project produces long-term benefits. Sessions during which a consistent facilitator shares the vision, goals, and desired outcomes play an important role in developing a team that will remain steadfast when the going gets tough. "Value engineering" becomes an exercise where, rather than indiscriminately cutting costs no matter the impact on the project goals, everyone works together to achieve the vision and goals in a more cost-effective way. (See Figure 1.20.)

During the design of Dublin Methodist Hospital, the entire project team gathered early in the process for a visioning session as described above. During that 3-hour meeting, the team was empowered to do what was needed to ensure we were successful in our stated goal of "redefining the way patient care is provided." As the owner and project leader, I communicated that the team was to "run until apprehended," meaning I wanted them to

Figure 1.20
Lobby at Dublin Methodist Hospital (Pebble Project), is designed to serve as the community's front door with stress reduction qualities such as an arrival sequence that is customizable and personal, an interior that is blurred with the outdoors, and a gathering space that is full of amenities that distract yet is clear in wayfinding clues for final destination. The design hypothesis is to reduce stress during the arrival sequence. Studies not yet complete.
Photo courtesy Ohio Health/Dublin Methodist Hospital, © 2008. Photography by Brad Feinknopf. Karlsberger Architects / CAMA, Inc. / Big Red Rooster

push the innovation envelope and utilize as many elements of evidence-based design as possible. They were instructed to not let me do anything "stupid" or, in other words, to bring concerns to the forefront sooner rather than later in the project. With that session behind us, the team worked toward common goals. Although budget was a factor, as it is in most projects, decisions were made based on achieving our vision and utilizing evidence-based solutions rather than just making things easier or less expensive to build.

Clear, strong, and consistent leadership was a hallmark of our success. In addition to me, there were others (an architect, a construction manager) who served as "vision keepers." When questions arose that could not be solved by the team, a vision keeper was consulted to make the final call. By limiting decision-making to just a few people, we were assured of consistency even when the construction activity was at its peak and several hundred workers were involved. Each new subcontractor who joined the Dublin Methodist project went through an orientation where the vision and goals were shared, along with an expectation that they would help us accomplish them.

In order to utilize evidence-based design to its fullest, we consulted with The Center for Health Design and became a member of the Pebble Project early in our project. The assistance and resources they provided were invaluable and have been key to our success in building a very different kind of hospital. A consultant usually associated with retail work was brought on board to join the team and help us think in unique ways about the experiences we create for everyone who enters our doors. Being open to hearing from these outside experts and incorporating their work and ideas into our facility has made us what we are today. (See Figure 1.21.)

While not everyone has the luxury we had of building on a greenfield site, there is little that stands in the way of developing a team focused on common goals. One must demonstrate consistency and have the endurance and strength necessary to stay true to the vision when it is challenged, when budget dollars are short, and when issues arise during construction that make it seem next to impossible to achieve all you desire. (See Figure 1.22.)

Throughout our project, it was obvious that evidence-based design helped us keep the team on track and provided rational explanation when we wanted to do things in ways the team had never seen them done. The commitment to this project, built from the very beginning, was tremendous. Our team has much of which to be proud! (See Figure 1.23.)

Keyword: Vision Keeper

A vision keeper is a person or small group of people on the Interdisciplinary Team who hold the team on point and maintain the integrity of the design so that it is always aligned with the project guidelines and developed with the project wisdom.

Figure 1.21
Positive distractions: a respite corner for family and staff just off a nursing unit, which offers a connection to nature and dappled natural lighting—Dublin Methodist Hospital (Pebble Project). The design hypothesis is to improve the family experience and hospital satisfaction ratings. Studies not yet complete.
Photo courtesy of Ohio Health/Dublin Methodist Hospital, © 2008. Photography by Brad Feinknopf. Karlsberger Architects, CAMA, Inc., Big Red Rooster.

Figure 1.22
A patient room design that engages a patient with family and caregivers simultaneously. Physicians are encouraged to consult on the right side of the patient in the family zone. Design hypothesis is to improve communications between staff and families. Studies not yet complete.
Courtesy of Ohio Health/Dublin Methodist Hospital. George C. Anderson Photography, Inc. Karlsberger Architects, CAMA, Inc., Big Red Rooster.

Figure 1.23
Family has been encouraged to become a care partner and must have adequate space to fulfill that obligation. This family zone allows for rooming in, connection to patient and staff, work environment, and access to TV, refrigerator, full bath, and operable window. Design hypothesis is to reduce stress for family care partners. Studies not yet complete.
Photo courtesy of Ohio Health/Dublin Methodist Hospital, © 2008. Photography by Brad Feinknopf. Dublin Methodist Hospital (Pebble Project), Karlsberger Architects, CAMA, Inc., Big Red Rooster.

Drivers for Change in the Healthcare Design Process

In order for change to occur something has to drive it. Often there is more than one variable impacting the field of influence. The need for an evidence-based approach to the design of our facilities is being driven by several factors that are so compelling that the rate of acceptance is occurring rapidly. Change is occurring in the design studio but more importantly the healthcare client is accepting it. Let's take a look at the converging influences.

Healthcare Driver I: A Building Boom

When I started my career in the late 1970s at Yale-New Haven Hospital in New Haven, Connecticut, we jokingly observed that the hospital was really a construction site that administered care to people. Truth is that a healthcare facility, by nature of its complexity and dependence on technology, is always in a state of flux. Current projections are for $45 to $65 billion a year in healthcare construction expenditures.[11] Many drivers are contributing to this construction boom: The physical infrastructure of our hospitals is aging and not suitable for new technologies, labor shortages in all medical fields have redefined care delivery models, operational inefficiencies have undermined safety and quality of service, and cost of care and expectations of delivery from one of the fussiest generations (baby boomers) are misaligned to name a few. As community hospitals give way to larger systems the opportunity also exists to abandon older campuses and move new facilities to more advantageous locations. This phenomenon has given way to an opportunity to build a freestanding new hospital without the burden of a network of antiquated systems.

Essay 1–2 Futurist's Forecast
Ian Morrison, PhD, Healthcare Futurist, Menlo Park, California

The American healthcare industry is in the midst of an enormous construction boom. A confluence of forces has created an estimated $50 billion per annum annual rate of new hospital construction. What caused the boom? Where is it headed? How can we build these new buildings to serve patients and society at large?

What Caused the Boom?

The wave of new hospital construction through the first decade of the new millennium is driven by a number of factors:

- Aging physical plant. The average age of a hospital plant has been increasing steadily over the last several years as hospitals built in the post–World War II period under the Hill-Burton programs reach the end of their useful life. Throughout America, hospitals' boards are forced to make big financial decisions about building brand new facilities or radical renovations of old facilities.
- Operating income meets cheap money. Since the dark days of the Balanced Budget Act of the late 1990s, hospital finances of the top third of hospitals have steadily improved. While not all hospitals are doing well, the strong financial performers have operating income to support large capital projects, whether acquisitions and mergers or new hospital construction. Add this to the historically low-interest and low-inflation environment that the economy has enjoyed over the last several years and you create opportunity for large-scale projects. Whether the operating income strength of these high performers will remain, or money will still be cheap in the future, remains to be seen. Some would point to the vulnerability of many of these capital projects if, for example, Medicare reimbursement rates were substantially reined in.

- Consumer demand for service excellence. As the baby boom ages and their parents go through the cycle of illness, hospitalization, dying and death, there is growing consumer pressure for better healthcare environments. Generations of Ritz Carlton–staying, office-working, affluent Americans have different expectations of their built environment than the Greatest Generation, who worked in factories or drove buses.
- Earthquake preparedness. The State of California has set rigorous standards for earthquake preparedness, causing an enormous explosion in new and replacement hospital construction in the state. RAND estimates that the cost of meeting the standards over the next 20 years may exceed $150 billion, and cause a "baking in" of higher health costs of $1,000 per capita a year. Such estimates are causing regulators to rethink standards and timetables, but nevertheless earthquakes have been a big driver of California hospital construction and a contributor to the almost $1,000-per-square-foot costs to build hospitals in the state.
- Quality and patient safety. Following the path-breaking publications from the Institute of Medicine, quality and patient safety have become central issues on the national health policy agenda. Hospitals have embraced the work of quality improvement and enlightened hospitals are looking for every avenue, including better buildings, electronic medical records, and radical clinical system redesign to improve performance.
- Transparency and accountability for performance. A major sea change in medical care is taking place where hospitals, health plans, and individual providers are being measured on performance and those measures are increasingly being reported to the public. Whether these measures are actually used by consumers to "shop" for hospitals is debatable. What seems clear is that measurement and public reporting puts powerful pressure on healthcare to improve its performance.
- Evidence-based design. It is in this environment that pioneers such as Roz Cama and the Center for Health Design have emerged to bring to the field of health facilities design, the discipline of evidence-based practice. There is good research about elements of new hospital design, that can improve patient satisfaction and health outcomes, and these innovations can be accomplished in a way that doesn't break the bank in the short run, and saves money in the long run. More and more design practitioners are embracing evidence-based design as a means to help healthcare organizations create true healing environments that are safer and higher-performing.

Will the Trend Continue?

The key vulnerability of the hospital construction boom is financial. If Medicare reimbursement rates tighten, if money becomes more expensive, following a collapse in subprime capital markets or global economic events, then this boom may get choked off quite rapidly. But, it seems clear that the top financial-performing hospitals will continue to weather such an economic storm, and indeed further distance themselves from the pack economically. This raises a broader public policy question of whether the built environment for patients is becoming profoundly inequitable, with affluent communities in white suburbs having spectacularly high-performing hospital environments and urban hospitals with large Medicaid and uninsured populations having slowly but steadily decaying built environments.

No matter what, we will have to build or replace our aging healthcare facilities. What the right balance is between ambulatory facilities, acute care facilities, and long-term and home-based healthcare is a much broader question than the scope of this book allows. But what is clear, is that when we build new healthcare buildings of any type, we can and should combine the art of good design with science of evidence-based design to help create better healthcare facilities for the patients, families, and communities they serve. This book can really help design practitioners do that important work.

Healthcare Driver II: Needed Base of Knowledge

In 1997 The Center for Health Design™ in a joint project with Johns Hopkins University conducted a meta-analysis of all research that linked the design of the built environment to a health-related outcome.[12] Of the thousands of studies only 84 met the appropriate academic rigor. It would not be until 2004 that the study would be repeated with a team from Texas A&M, Roger Ulrich, PhD and Xiaobo Quan, Georgia Tech, Craig Zimring, PhD, and Anjali Joseph. These scholars would review and analyze thousands of studies to reveal that a body of knowledge in this field is growing. The study, which was commissioned by the Robert Wood Johnson Foundation and The Center for Health Design, was repeated again in 2008. What was learned from these analyses is that there is rich data pertaining to how the design of the built environment impacts healthcare in certain areas. They are:

- Patient-related outcomes
- Staff satisfaction
- Quality
- Safety
- Operational efficiency
- Financial performance[13]

What becomes evident in looking closely at the amount of qualified evidence is that there is more valid data about patient-related outcomes than staff-related outcomes. This may be because the pendulum of patient-centered care has caused us to neglect seeking answers related to staff issues. As the movement to improve safety and quality of service grows, more evidence-based studies will be conducted and more will be learned about how design plays a role in improving issues related to staff performance and well-being.

Healthcare Driver III: Rapid Developments in Technology

New technologies which drive terms such as wireless, paperless, computer-assisted radiology and surgery, minimally invasive surgeries, digital patient record, flat-screen technology, and bar coding, create paradigm shifts in operational and organizational models which beg for a very different architecture to support these new models of diagnosis, treatment, and care. (See Chapter 6, Evidence-Based Design in Practice.) There exist no right answers at this moment. There is also a bit of skepticism in being a pioneer. Too many new fangled technologies have come down the pike and have failed; so much so that the institution that braved the new world is branded with its failure. Any early adopter stands this risk. (See Figure 2.21.)

Healthcare Driver IV: Quality of Care Initiatives

In 2001 the Institute of Medicine (IOM) highlighted the warts in the healthcare delivery system when it published Crossing the Quality Chasm. The red flag raised was honest and raw. It stated that "Health care today harms too frequently and routinely fails to deliver its potential benefits.[14]" It established six aims for the twenty-first-century healthcare system.

These six aims are adopted by most hospitals and are often presented to design teams to understand in the delivery of design solutions.

Simultaneously, Don Berwick, MD, MPP and the Institute for Healthcare Improvement (IHI) launched a campaign to improve safety in the healthcare systems around the world. On the heels of a "one thousand lives" campaign, where IHI raised the awareness of countless clinicians on how to remember six interventions that could prevent a needless death, IHI has

---

IOM's Six Aims

1. Safe: Avoiding injuries to patients from the care that is intended to help them
2. Effective: Providing services based on scientific knowledge to all who could benefit and refraining from providing services to those not likely to benefit (avoiding underuse and overuse, respectively)
3. Patient-centered: Providing care that is respectful of and responsive to individual patient preferences, needs, and values and ensuring that patient values guide all clinical decisions
4. Timely: Reducing waits and sometimes harmful delays for both those who receive and those who give care
5. Efficient: Avoiding waste, including waste of equipment, supplies, and energy
6. Equitable: Providing care that does not vary in quality because of personal characteristics such as gender, ethnicity, geographic location, and socio-economic status.[15]

Keyword: Evidence-Based Value Engineering

A process by which strategically aligned outcomes, design interventions, construction costs, and return on investment are evaluated based on their value to the overall success of the project. When the principles of EBD become the driving factor, not solely cost, then decision-making is informed by the beneficial outcome and its return on the investment over the life of the project.

launched a "five million lives" campaign, a new initiative to protect patients from five million incidents of medical harm over a two-year period from 2006 to 2008.

The work that The Center for Health Design has done to strategically understand how the IOM's six aims and IHI's campaigns go beyond just an operational model to a design intervention has driven the development of the largest field study research project, known as "Pebble"™. The interconnectedness of so many organizations is putting pressure on hospitals to develop solutions for a better model of care.

Healthcare Driver V: Rising Cost of Construction

In the current economic climate, construction budgets are tight. Budgets are locked in by regulatory agencies and/or boards of directors, all of whom have a fiduciary responsibility to keep the cost of healthcare down. Material and labor costs continue to rise and the design suffers through countless rounds of a process that has become known as the oxymoron "value engineering." A more careful analysis of this dilemma is forthcoming, as projects can no longer afford the delays caused by budget paralysis. It will take an evidence-based approach to find a solution to this chronic problem. Construction management firms are very much aware of the evidence-based movement and need to adopt its concept in connecting capital expenses to operational savings.

Drivers for Change in the Design Professions

Design steeped in the arts evolves over time. Design aligned with a scientific mindset has little time to morph once patrons request it. We just explored the external influences for an evidence-based approach in the healthcare arena, but what external forces will compel the design practices into an evidence-based approach?

Keyword: Trend versus Classic

Design that is influenced by industrial design, the influence of materials and products of the time, is attributed to very recognizable "trends."

Design that is influenced by human behavior is attributed to timeless solutions or "classics."

Design Driver I: Marketplace Demand

No greater force than client demand for a service will spark change. In a 2004 Healthcare Design magazine editorial, I noted the phenomenon of the "Flashpoint," stating that we are all on the same evolutionary path and synapsing at approximately the same rate as our colleagues who are paying attention to the same external forces.[16] Evidence-based design has been evolving in discussions over the last ten years, but in the last two, clients are asking for this service in their "Request for Proposals." It is not always clear that they know what they are asking for, but they are asking. As noted above, the external forces are driving change in healthcare, therefore as this flashpoint is occurring, all consultants need to be on board.

Design Driver II: Need for Knowledge

If a closer look is taken at the need to build a body of knowledge, then it is clear a lot of pressure is on the design community to contribute. It is hard to be in the specialty of healthcare without a social conscience. The Ulrich Zimring study[17] recognizes how much is missing; therefore, the need to defend the right to measure our projects must be strong. Ignorance or laziness can no longer be excuses. Chapter 2 will examine a series of scorecards developed as a tool for this study. Using a five star rating—five being ample evidence to no longer debate the issue, one being little evidence has been gathered and reported appropriately—one should be able to see where the lack of knowledge exists and where design projects can contribute.

Design Driver III: Credibility in the Industry

The next biggest driver for change in healthcare delivery can easily be the notoriety gained by the innovators or early adopters in evidence-based design. Most firms are scrambling to figure out what this means to them, their clients, and their bottom line. There has been more press in significant journals and popular tabloids since evidence-based design has taken hold. Ten years ago, as National President of the American Society of Interior Designers (ASID), I was interviewed by the Wall Street Journal and they were clear that they would not write an article about design unless there was hardcore evidence to prove an outcome. In the last few years, the Wall Street Journal has written several articles about design in healthcare settings. What firm/project does not want that kind of exposure?

Design Driver IV: Justification for Innovation

There exists a multiyear cycle for innovation to occur in healthcare. It can take anywhere from five to nine years for a healthcare design team to come up with a "big idea," develop it, and see it through construction and occupancy. (See Figure 1.24.)

Many projects begin the quest to formulate their guidelines by organizing a tour of the industry's best practices. Conservatively looking back in time, if the projects being visited have been open for a year and it took three years to build them and another two years to design and document, and two more to plan, then what is experienced is an eight-year-old "new idea."

Figure 1.24
Innovation lag time:
span of time from one
project's big idea to
influencing tours. A
potentially nine-year-old
idea informs a new
generation of projects,
demonstrating the lag
time in healthcare's
acceptance of innova-
tive solutions.

That time warp slows innovation and can perpetuate some pretty inappropriate design solu-tions, especially if they prove negative several years after occupancy. Chapter 4 will explore how evidence-based design triggers innovation in more depth.

Building a Body of Knowledge

Sciences that Contribute to an Academic Base

Most of the scientific evidence available to designers and architects about how the design of the built environment impacts human behavior comes from the study of Environmental Psychology. Much less knowledge is available through the sciences of Neuroscience, Evolutionary Biology, and Psychoneuroimmunology. Environmental Psychology is an inter-disciplinary field focused on the interplay between humans and their surroundings. Neuroscience is the study of the brain. Evolutionary Biology is concerned with the origin and descent of a species. Psychoneuroimmunology is a specialized field of research that studies the interactions between social psychology, behavior, the brain, and the endocrine and immune system of the body. There is a need for a post-graduate degree to understand the intersection of these sciences and the influence they have on design, which is to say, only a renaissance mind will capture it all. The dependency on these sciences is being explored in this process of gathering evidence. AIA has partnered with a group of Neuroscientists to truly understand how our brain responds to the environments we design. The work that they are doing needs to inform all projects—which leads to the discussion of knowledge dissemination.

Knowledge Dissemination

The Center for Health Design and the Robert Wood Johnson Foundation have played a sig-nificant role in illuminating the highly regarded studies. Tools to make that knowledge read-ily available are in the works. ASID and the University of Minnesota have developed an online clearinghouse for all research in all specialties in design. InformeDesign, as it is called, pro-vides excerpts from the studies, so at a glance the viewer knows if it is relevant to their design projects. Chapter 2 will look more closely at search engines for literature searches.

Summary

A Call to Arms

World class! How many times have you been requested to design a world-class hospital? A client with that expectation requires a healthcare design consultant at the top of their game who, at a minimum, delivers services that are relevant and create a difference in the marketplace they serve. I was taught early in my career that these characteristics of a service provider either make a brand recognizable or obscure. "Brand," the promise tied to the service you sell, is articulated in your mission statement but also in how you provide clues of that service in your values and in the design of your physical environment. Examine your mission and/or your environment and see what you are promising each and every client you serve. Are you promising world class; are you delivering proven results and better outcomes?

If so, are you:

- analyzing past facility performance, past industry performance?
- hypothesizing improved outcomes as a result of potential design improvements?
- designing to meet industry standards or innovating by designing for new models of care?
- measuring design-driven outcomes?
- sharing the knowledge gained with the industry so it learns from your success and failures?
- partnering with researchers engaged in a peer-review process and then sharing unbiased findings?

If you answer yes, then you are practicing evidence-based design. If not, then let's explore how educational programs, a design practice, a facilities consulting practice, or a healthcare facility can grow and benefit from adopting evidence-based design methodologies, putting you at the top of your game, improving your brand, and delivering world-class quality.

Checklist: Understanding the Shift Toward Evidence-Based Design in Healthcare

1. Definition: Evidence-Based Design is:
   - An iterative decision-making process that begins with the analysis of current best evidence from an organization as well as from the field.
   - It finds at the intersection of this knowledge, behavioral, organizational, or economic clues that when aligned with a stated design objective can be hypothesized as a beneficial outcome.
   - It does not provide prescriptive solutions, but rather a platform from which to add to an existing base of knowledge or to launch innovation.
   - It espouses an ethical obligation to measure outcomes and share knowledge gained for particular design successes and failures, ideally in a peer-reviewed fashion as is common in academia.

Evidence-based design is a process used to:
- develop and design a new or renovation building project
- bring together a balanced team representing client, stakeholders, and appropriate design disciplines including researchers in the investigation, design, and analysis of a project in an interdisciplinary way
- focus on strategic directives that can lead to improved outcomes through the analysis of past design and facility performance intelligence

- support a proven design detail or inspire an innovative concept hypothesized to improve a stated outcome
- commit to a post-occupancy research to reveal the success or failure of the hypothesized result publish in a peer-review journal

2. Components of Evidence-Based Design
   - Gather qualitative and quantitative intelligence
   - Map strategic, cultural, and research goals
   - Hypothesize outcomes, innovate, and implement translational design
   - Measure and share outcomes

3. Hamilton's Levels of Evidence-Based Practice
   - Level 1 Practitioner: Uses past documented studies as a way to inform new concepts and uses the knowledge gained as a platform from which to launch new design concepts.
   - Level 2 Practitioner: Level 1 plus the ability to hypothesize the expected outcomes of design interventions and subsequently measure the results.
   - Level 3 Practitioner: Level 2 plus a commitment to sharing the gained knowledge through articles written in professional journals or lectures at professional conferences.
   - Level 4 Practitioner: Level 3 plus submits the found conclusions to a peer-reviewed journal.

In summary: Investigate • Hypothesize • Continue to Prove or Innovate • Measure and Share

Endnotes

1. Encarta World English Dictionary.
2. Coyle Hospitality 2006 Group Survey, Hotel Online, New York, November 2, 2006.
3. Berry, L.; Parker, D.; Coile, R.; Hamilton, K.; O'Neill, D.; and Sadler, B. Can Better Buildings Improve Care and Increase Your Financial Returns, ACHE, 2004.
4. Kumar, R. *Research Methodology, A Step-by-Step Guide for Beginners,* Sage Publications, London, Thousand Oaks, New Delhi: 2005; p. 13.
5. *Ibid.*
6. Chamberlain, L., Going off the Beaten Path for New Ideas, *New York Times*, March 12, 2006.
7. Kumar, R., p. 73.
8. Carter, R.E.; Woolson, R.F. Statistical Design Considerations for Pilot Studies Transitioning Therapies from the Bench to the Bedside. *Journal of Translational Medicine*, 2004; 2:37.
9. Hamilton, D.K. The Four Levels of Evidence-Based Practice, *Healthcare Design*, 2003; 3:18–26.
10. Berry, L. *Discovering the Soul of Service*, Free Press:New York 1999; 242.
11. Jones, Heather. FMI's Construction Outlook–First Quarter 2007, FMI's Construction Market Forecasts, 2007.
12. Rubin, H.R.; Owens, A.J.; Golden, G. An Investigation to Determine Whether the Built Environment Affects Patients' Medical Outcomes, The Center for Health Design, 1997.
13. Ulrich, R.; Zimring, C. The Role of the Physical Environment in the Hospital of the 21st Century, The Center for Health Design, 2004.
14. Institute of Medicine, Crossing the Quality Chasm, National Academy Press, 2001; p. 1.
15. Institute of Medicine, Crossing the Quality Chasm, National Academy Press, 2001, pp. 39–40.
16. Cama, R. Flashpoints, *Healthcare Design Magazine*, May 2004; 6.
17. Ulrich, R.; Zimring, C. The Role of the Physical Environment in the Hospital of the 21st Century, The Center for Health Design, 2004.

Part II
Yale-New Haven
Hospital, emergency
exam room.
© 2008 CJ Allen/
Salvatore Associates
Architect of Record/
CAMA, Inc.

EVIDENCE-BASED DESIGN METHODOLOGY

"Man is not on earth solely for his own happiness.
He is there to realize great things for humanity."
—Vincent Van Gogh

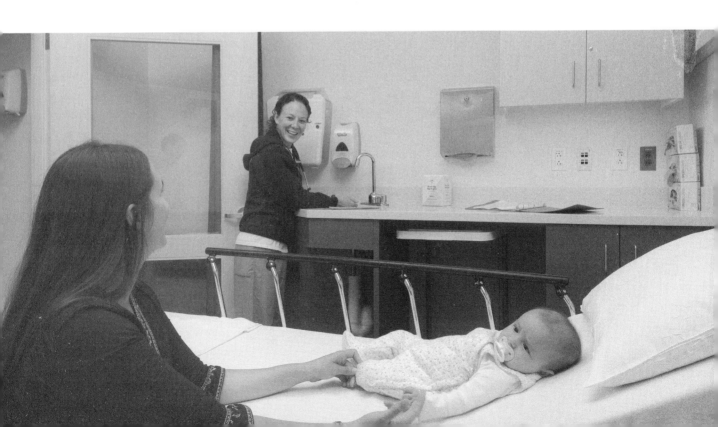

Chapter 2

Step 1: Gather Qualitative and Quantitative Intelligence

"I find that the great part of the information I have was acquired by looking up something and finding something else on the way."
—Franklin P. Adams

This chapter defines the first step in the process. It outlines how an evidence-based practice team is formed and explains how to organize and collect the data needed to formally capture "project wisdom." A researcher and project team members are brought on board for expert testimony. These experts discuss how to gather, interpret, and apply data. A summation of the existing body of knowledge makes a case for the need for more data, particularly in specific areas. This chapter provides a call to arms for practice reform that will move practitioners out of design silos and into a truly integrative process that includes an interdisciplinary approach. A checklist offers the reader a quick reference on the internal analysis and benchmarking necessary to begin.

A baseline from which to launch a research project is needed for all evidence-based design projects. It requires understanding an organization, its culture, strategic drivers, operational protocols, physical plant, etc., as well as the current body of knowledge for its particular project type. Proponents of the evidence-based process have referred to the complexity of the system that keeps a healthcare design project balanced as "the Environment of Care," from the Joint Commission on the Accreditation of Healthcare Organizations. The Environmental Standards Council of The Center for Health Design defined it further and introduced it into the American Institute of Architects Guidelines for Hospital and Healthcare Construction, making it a required component of the functional program.

The project's interdisciplinary team should look within an organization to gather intelligence about the Environment of Care. They should benchmark an institution's projected goals against specific data from evidence-based projects with similar directives for their

respective environments of care. It is in this first step that a research project begins. One does not have to be a researcher to champion this process, but having a researcher on board early in the project clarifies the tasks. How to mobilize an interdisciplinary team is examined, for it is with a broad "group brain" that amazing solutions to design problems reveal themselves about each of the six functional components of the Environment of Care. The evidence-based design methodology is intended to provide a basic framework on which to find a comfortable path to travel. The journey may either build on an existing base of knowledge or

Keyword: Environment of Care

The Environment of Care is made up of six functional components of an organization that contribute to the overall experience of one's care. They are:

1. Concepts
2. People
3. Systems

4. Layout /operations
5. Physical environment
6. Implementation

prove or disprove innovative design concepts that provide a healing outcome for patients, their families, and their caregivers.

This chapter explores four tasks to consider while conducting the first phase of an evidence-based design project:

1. Build an interdisciplinary team
2. Conduct investigations
3. Benchmark against national intelligence
4. Document process

Remember that evidence-based design in this first phase of collecting evidence before design begins is not prescriptive. Each project and its interdisciplinary team will determine how much or how little will be needed for the project's end goal. The steps that follow are intended to be a road map to follow while a new-to-the-game evidence-based team finds its style. Those who design to innovate and achieve uncharted results will hopefully delve into the next phases of research. Find the comfort zone for your institution, firm, and project. Most of all have fun with the process; it is quite an enlightening phase of a building project.

Build an Interdisciplinary Team

An important concept imbedded in evidence-based design methodology is to build an interdisciplinary team. In this chapter it will become apparent that it takes a "healthcare village" to acquire the data needed to develop a full and clear understanding of what comprises the DNA of an institution. How the design team members begin to process all of this data will be explored in the next chapter. Most teams are assembled at the time a project is marketed; as more about the project is revealed, its unique mix of consultants will be identified and added. Table 2.1 is a partial listing of the possible members of an interdisciplinary team. There is a mix of standard design consultants, client representatives, researchers, advocates, and specialized consultants.

Each project team will require a different subset as noted on the following page, but the point is that it is not a small subset that opens the eyes of those planning and designing a healthcare facility. Each representative group plays various roles at various times but in the end it is their collective interchange that contributes to the whole of the project, giving it a clear view. That view, when synthesized, is "project wisdom." How that wisdom informs a project will be explored in the next chapter. It is with this wisdom, if developed carefully, that new and supportive cultures for an institution will emerge. Once a different culture emerges it reveals the need for necessary changes within organizational operations. Designing for these shifts is where innovation is sparked for the planning and design of the new physical plant. It is this kind of transformational thinking that changes organizations and outlasts most of the present team. (See Figure 2.2.)

Table 2.1 Menu for an Interdisciplinary Team				
Design Consultants	**Client Representatives**	**Researchers**	**Advocates**	**Ancillary Consultants**
Architects	Board Members	External Researchers	Patient Advocates	Thought Leaders
Program Managers	Administration	Internal Researchers, often from Nursing or Quality Management	Family Advisors	Industrial Designers
Medical Planners	Clinical Staff		Teaching Hospital Staff (where applicable)	Academic Researchers
Engineers	Quality Management		Community Physicians	Market Specialists
Interior Designers	Facilities		Home Health Associates	Organizational Consultants
Graphic Designers	Development and Foundation		Pastoral Care	Quality Assessment Consultants
Wayfinding and Signage Consultants	Materials Management		Volunteers	Futurists
Lighting Designers	Housekeeping		Donors	
Acoustical Consultants	IT		Institutional Historians	
Landscape Architects	Human Resources		Community	
Specialty Consultants	Marketing and Community Relations			
Construction Managers, etc.	Engineering			
	Risk Management			

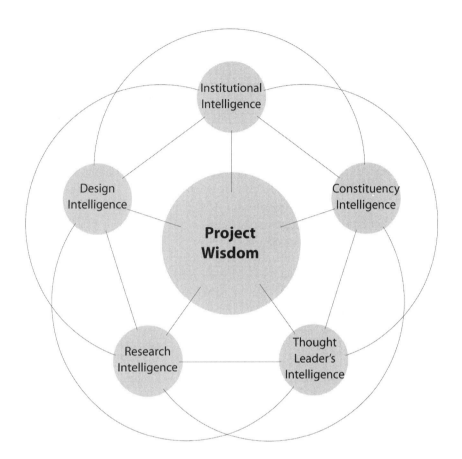

Figure 2.2
Project wisdom: the knowledge gained from the open intercommunication between all members of the interdisciplinary team. Vision keepers are key to the success of this interchange.
(See Chapter 1.)
CAMA, Inc.

Here is where the magic occurs, as it takes the combined efforts of project wisdom to articulate a clear vision that guides the design for an improved future. Chapter 3 will explore the chemistry that allows an interdisciplinary team to work through the steps that lead to visionary design concepts.

Before a team begins its investigations it must establish team rules by creating guiding principles for the project and then design guidelines for the interdisciplinary team. Doing so will establish the way everyone will behave during the exercises of the design process. The vision or "big idea" will come after all of this investigative work is complete.

Keyword: Project Wisdom

Project wisdom is the insightfulness gained after the investigation of internal and external intelligence is discussed and synthesized with an interdisciplinary team. It is what gives birth to the "aha" moments.

Conduct Investigations

Be Curious, Gather Intelligence, Capture Synapses

It is difficult to be in the field of design and not have a sense of current project activity within a particular specialty, as there are many in healthcare. Most designers possess knowledge of firms and/or healthcare facilities that are designing, building or renovating structures. It simply takes access to colleagues, professional associations, marketing professionals, clients, manufacturers' representatives, publications, conferences, webinars, etc., to stay informed. The good news is that most project teams conducting research today publish at various stages in the design process and are also on the lecture circuit. By nature of evidence-based teams being interdisciplinary one should find information throughout the spectrum of healthcare, not just in design publications. Keep a personal database of the who's who in healthcare and more importantly, what knowledge they possess. They may be great interdisciplinary teammates for future projects to expand the breadth of your "group brain" intelligence.

At some level an evidence-based approach cannot begin without a state-of-the-industry analysis. It reveals the possibilities of what can be explored, while clarifying where the potential exists for innovation. Later in the process it helps to place your concepts in the appropriate strata within the broader context of the existing body of knowledge. This base of knowledge is what builds your project and serves as an evidence-based checklist which can be used during the design phases of a project (see flight-ready checklist in Chapter 6).

If cutting-edge knowledge is needed then seek out those who are leading in that area of subspecialty. Do this by finding the "connectors"[1] in the field. Malcolm Gladwell defines "connectors" as those who bring the world together by connecting people to many groups. There are several professional connectors who will work beyond your personal network. Find them through nonprofit associations, through library services or through electronic search engines available at your local university. Gladwell offers many ways to understand the foresight used to move to the next level of innovation in his writings.

Keywords: Guiding Principles and Design Guidelines

Guiding principles set the culture, beliefs, and norms of the interdisciplinary team and clearly articulate the expectations of the project's outcome. They are established early to guide the team as to where the project's baseline will lie. They should also add a clear explanation of the project's measurable outcomes.

Design guidelines create a framework within which the interdisciplinary team will design. The team may follow established institutional standards or may blaze new ground within a stated evidence-based context.

Gather a Facility's Existing Data

The best place to begin on a project is to understand an institution's long-range goals. What is its board of directors' (BOD) vision, both short and long term? How is that vision being used to direct an operational or performance initiative that requires a facility adjustment? Is the institution's administration currently tracking its performance statistics? Do they understand the business case or the return on investment to be made by selecting certain design interventions that align with these initiatives? Is it being communicated? Hence the importance of leadership's presence on the interdisciplinary team while these decisions are being made. These are important dynamics to understand early in a project for the success of an outcome-based design solution.

Many healthcare facilities are undergoing quality improvement measures and may not be aware of the impact needed to improve issues related to safety; timeliness; and effective, efficient, equitable, and patient-centered care (see Quality of Care Initiatives in Chapter 1). It is important, at this phase of a project, to explain the connections certain design features have on these outcomes. There is not a facility today that isn't keeping a scorecard on quality initiatives. Find out which are the most pressing issues within an institution, then search the literature to see who else is solving or has solved for these critical issues. Also find out who is pioneering improvements through your connector network. (See Figures 2.3, 2.4, and 2.5.)

As the healthcare industry goes deeper into understanding customer service, it recognizes it must make cultural shifts within its organizations' human resources. There are wonderful examples of transformed cultures that begin to suggest a different model of care delivery. It

Idea!

Do not toss away those conference catalogs that land on your desk. Take note of who is speaking/publishing and what their topics are. Learn to acknowledge and compile the top five topics being presented. If you do not have the time then train an administrative assistant to do this for you. A trick I learned from a Frank Stasiowski lecture early in my career is to contact the assistants of your top 20 clients or should-be clients and ask which books, magazines, and journals their bosses are reading. Find out which conferences they are attending. Look at the topics being addressed and learn as much as possible about what has already been researched and published in these areas. Use this base of knowledge to formulate innovative evidence-based design solutions where possible. Once a team begins practicing this way it learns that new-found knowledge sends the project research deeper into a subject revealing enlightened design concepts. Each subsequent project begins at a plateau higher than the last because of the wisdom gained. The sooner a team begins the evidence-based process the farther ahead of the pack it is. When seeking consultants it is important to question what innovations those potential consultants are working on. It is in the collection of this intelligence that you build insight on the research the industry or your type of healthcare client is ready for.

Figure 2.3
The University Medical Center at Princeton, Princeton, NJ (Pebble Project): a new replacement hospital being built on a newly developed medical campus. *HOK/RMJM Hillier.*

Figure 2.4
Laguna Honda Hospital & Rehabilitation Center, San Francisco, CA (Pebble Project): a housing and complete continuum of long-term care, housing and healthcare services on a new campus. *© 2008 Anshen + Allen.*

Figure 2.5
Weill Cornell Medical
College/Weill
Greenberg Center,
New York, NY (Pebble
Project) Faculty Practice
Plan: first step in a new
campus for the Medical
School.
*Jeff Goldberg, Esto
photography, Polshek
Partnership Architects.*

is in these new models that a facility must shift as well. See the Weill Cornell Essay later in this chapter. Most of the projects highlighted in this book begin with cultural transformations. The design then adjusts to support these new operational protocols.

Most healthcare institutions measure particular outcomes as a matter of course. These outcomes are generally of interest to an evidence-based design team since they are likely the issues that the institution will be interested in improving. Often the institution is measuring a targeted outcome, but may be reluctant to share knowledge imbedded in patient satisfaction surveys, market share analyses, associate opinions, length of stay statistics (LOS), medical error rates, falls, hospital-acquired infections, drug costs, acoustical noise levels, etc. Early in the design relationship, find out how readily available this database will be. If it is not, then arrange a meeting with the administrator responsible for the design of the project and make evident how relevant this information will be to the development of design interventions that will improve outcomes. It is in the understanding of how to interpret the data contained within these reports that the enlightened "aha" moment will occur.

Essay 2-1
Listening to Patients/Families: A Guide to Getting Started
Mary P. Malone, JD, President, Malone Advisory Services

Designing a new physical environment creates tremendous opportunity and remarkable challenges. The complexities of the space can seem overwhelming; and it must work to produce a wide-range of outcomes. It must be safe, for patients and staff; it must support the operating functions of the organization and, more importantly than ever before, it must be designed to create a healing environment that takes into account the experiences of patients and families.

As a design professional gets started on the process, there are many existing data sources to begin to understand the needs and desires of patients and families. Nearly every healthcare organization uses some type of patient survey feedback tool. Most hospitals now contract with an outside firm to collect the survey data (by phone or mail) and produce data reports for the organization, most of which now contain some type of benchmarking information. Most hospitals are engaged in the process of collecting standardized H-CAHPS (Hospital Consumer Assessment of Healthcare Providers Survey) data of the patient experience that is now publicly reported on the CMS Hospital Compare web site (along with other quality indicators). As of Sept 18, 2008, CMS reported the third public reporting of H-CAHPS data March 2008, July 2008, and September 2008. December 2008 is currently scheduled. H-CAHPS results are available for 2,595 hospitals that voluntarily surveyed and submitted data for patients discharged from January through December 2007.[3]

Most organizations are familiar with the quantitative data—or scores—and design professionals should review the existing information. Many organizations may report overall results; but many others can report more sophisticated information about patient responses to individual questions—and how different types of patients (by gender, age, diagnosis, etc.) respond to the results. Combined with qualitative information (patient/family comments) this information can provide an excellent overview of the current types of experiences being created by the client organization. The comments often provide rich explanatory information—when staff did this behavior, it made me feel this way—illuminating positive and negative elements of the experiences. The surveys also highlight process successes and failures from the patient's perspective—for example, lack of information, waiting time, system bottlenecks, and confusion about aspects of the experience.

The challenge for the design professional is that most patient satisfaction/experience surveys contain little information about the physical environment. Although some (including the H-CAHPS survey) will ask the patient about noise levels and cleanliness; and others include waiting area comfort and ease of wayfinding, for example, most of the surveys do not directly address the physical space. It is not that researchers are not interested in these matters; it is mostly because from the patient/family perspective the physical environment operates in the background of their experiences and the people and processes that they experience end up being more important (in a psychometric analysis of survey findings). To keep the surveys to manageable lengths, many of the physical environment questions are not included.

So, what is a design professional to do? I believe there is incredible opportunity for the design professional to use the information from surveys—as well as from other listening sources listed below—to interpret the data with a designer's lens. One critical issue, though, is that the majority of patients are "satisfied," which means they score in the "top boxes" of most surveys. The challenge is to move the bar from being merely "satisfied" to being completed satisfied (delighted).

Overwhelming the patient/family with survey data and comments reinforces that interpersonal experiences—friendliness/cheerfulness; providing understandable information and updates; respecting not only "patienthood," but "personhood;" providing large doses of empathy; understanding not just the physical elements of disease but the psychosocial, emotional, and spiritual aspects of illness as well—are what matters most to patients and their families (who are increasingly seen as partners of the patient care professionals and not "unwanted visitors"). And, these elements are also on the priority list of things that patients/families would like to see improved.

The patients and families want to trust that they are in a safe place—and in the right place for them to be treated—not just technically; but that everyone on the team is aligned with creating the "best" possible outcome and experience; that all the staff is working together.

Through a designer's lens, then, what are the potential opportunities that can be gleaned from these data sources? Following are just a few suggestions.

- Different types of patients and families (children, older adults, surgical patients, OB patients, newly diagnosed, those coping with chronic diseases) have different types of needs. Sophisticated analysis of the data can help guide the types of improvements that are desired by various groups.
- What are the cues and clues that can be incorporated into the environment that can humanize the experience? How can the space convey that this is a safe place and the right place for this patient?
- How will the physical space support the work processes of the organization to reduce waiting time, or at least provide spaces that minimize the "down time" that patients experience between care events? How will the flow be made to feel more efficient?
- If positive interactions with staff are drivers of positive patient experiences, how can space be designed to create the greatest possibility for staff to create the positive interactions? What processes that allow more face-to-face interaction and better information exchange can be facilitated through the creative design specifications?

Most health care organizations have substantial data available to them regarding the current levels of satisfaction of their patients and families and much of it can be used by a design professional to better understand what is working (or not) in the current environment. Unfortunately, using the data is not as simple as "the survey says x, so I will design y." But that is a fortunate opportunity as well; because using the data requires a more nuanced approached that draws upon the best skills of the designer to interpret the existing experiences and create new environments that help elevate the performance of the organization on multiple fronts.

Following are five additional listening resources for designers. Ask to see if your client will share the following types of information:

- Patient/Family Rounding: Health care organizations often conduct daily rounds on patients to inquire as to various aspects of their stay/visit. Many accumulate this data into databases that can be summarized as to the most common issues that are uncovered.
- Complaint Information Systems: Hospitals usually have a systemic way of gathering and analyzing the most common complaints that are brought to the attention of the organization.
- Patient/Family Councils: Attempting to provide more patient-/family-centered care, many organizations have created councils of and for patients and families to share their experiences. Some are highly formalized throughout an organization—including patients as board members; others may include patients informally sharing their

experiences at unit meetings. Minutes of these council meetings and meeting with council members can provide a rich perspective.

- Focus Groups/Image Surveys: Although the quality can vary widely, marketing departments often use focus groups to learn about the experiences (and desires) of patients and potential patients of the organization. Most marketing departments conduct image surveys every few years of community members (patients and, importantly, nonpatients) that offer a perspective on the organization.
- Mystery Shopping Surveys: Many organizations contract with outside firms to conduct mystery shopping of various types of patient experiences—most commonly in outpatient areas including diagnostics, therapies, EDs, and physician offices. Some organizations conduct these with internal staff and volunteers. Insights from these "shops" can provide another excellent perspective on the opportunities for improvement.

Another important task in the fact-gathering phase is to develop an understanding of the consumer of a healthcare facility's services. Asking who is in its customer base may reveal important variables to consider about physician practices as well as patient needs as stated in the previous essay. There are many clues in market surveys, focus group studies, and slogan development. In most other industries strategic objectives inform marketing campaigns and the subsequent development of facility image. The Weill Cornell "We Care" program is a perfect example of how a strategic directive informed a cultural transformation defined in a marketing program/slogan and influencing the design of a multimillion-dollar building.

Essay 2-2
Weill Cornell Medical College/Weill Greenberg Center
Louis Meilink, AIA, and Richard S. Thomas, AIA

Introduction
The Weill Cornell Medical College launched a series of Strategic Plans in the mid-1990s. The first dealt with critical research needs, faculty, staff, and facilities. The second, Strategic Plan II, which was developed in the late 1990s and implemented from 2001 to 2007, focused on clinical needs.

Like many medical schools, Weill Cornell employs a cadre of more than 700 faculty physicians who teach, care for patients in Weill Cornell's affiliated hospital(s), and conduct clinical practices, primarily in the specialty services. Approximately 1 million ambulatory visits per year occur in their private and "clinic" practices ("clinic" in New York State has a specific meaning tied to hospital facility reimbursement source). The faculty practices are governed by an organization called the Weill Cornell Physician Organization (PO) which provides support services and leadership guidance to the practices.

As part of Strategic Plan II, it was determined that approximately 70 clinical programs needed to expand and/or start and that 15 of them were ideally located in a separate facility designed specifically to serve the most ambulatory, least technologically invasive, most "well" cohort of the college's patients. The need for additional space was demonstrated by the growth of the visits seen in the faculty's existing main ambulatory facility which was designed for 195,000 patient visits per year in 1980 and by 2001 was seeing close to 400,000. The solution to both these programmatic issues was to develop a new facility for the Strategic Initiatives, as the new programs were called, and relocation/expansion of others which fit into the "well" category, followed by a renovation and expansion of the more inpatient-related programs which remained in the existing building directly connected to the hospital. (Other initiatives were located off campus in other Weill Cornell locations.) The building contains 330,000 gross square feet of space of which about 192,000 is departmental, and over 250,000 visits are projected (approximately 1.3 visits per gross square feet—a figure which compared favorably with the use rates of facilities of peer institutions around the United States, but is luxurious for New York).

A series of strategic concepts and a symbiotic confluence of unrelated trends created the planning and design challenges met in the Weill Greenberg Center design. They were as follows:

Weill Cornell: We Care program

For decades, the tripartite mission of the Medical College, like many academic medical institutions, placed patient care last on its list behind teaching and research. Following a series of focus groups and patient satisfaction surveys taken in the late 1990s and early 2000s it was determined that Weill Cornell's satisfaction rates for patients, faculty, and staff, although probably among the best in New York City, were not what the institution wanted in comparison to peers nationally. The Weill Cornell: We Care program, called a "new vision of the patient care experience," included in its principles:

- Making patient care equal to the academic missions of staff and faculty and education
- Embracing best medical practices
- Conducting the practices in a collegial fashion
- Enabling continuous improvement
- Delivering standard-setting performance
- Embracing evidence-based performance

Figure 2.6
On a Manhattan street corner the Weill Cornell Medical Center (Pebble Project) is easily recognizable by its architectural character and its urban-friendly approach. The interior is well organized around a central core with daylighting moving nicely from its center into its interior.
Jeff Goldberg, Esto photography, Polshek Partnership Architects/ Ballinger Architects.

A long list of operational and service changes, developed by the PO, emerged from this program, in particular 46 operational objectives which directly impacted the building design and practice management procedures. They included:

- Working at all levels to respect the patient's time. This led to a commitment to employ an electronic medical record universally and to integrate it with other clinical and business information technology.
- Complete revamping of the new telephone system for appointments, scheduling, and other clinical matters.
- A complete overhaul of the patient check-in/check-out process to focus employees' attention on patient needs at the time of service, not telephone answering or insurance company requirements.

Figure 2.7
Preliminary studies with
Franklin Becker, PhD, at
Cornell University indi-
cated that more attrac-
tive waiting areas are
associated with higher
perceived quality of
care. This translational
study informed the
design of "living rooms"
in the Weill Cornell
Medical Center (Pebble
Project).[3]
*Jeff Goldberg, Esto pho-
tography, Polshek
Partnership Architects/
Ballinger Architects.*

- Sufficient but not excessive numbers of exam rooms to facilitate efficiency, with consult areas included in each room; hotel-like building access with valet parking (very unusual for New York City).
- Clear way-finding both externally and internally (see Figure 2.6).
- Revamped maintenance and housekeeping procedures to keep building clean and neat over time.

Spa Theme: Salus per Aquam (Health from Water)

The Weill Greenberg Center's design was inspired by the "SPA" theme derived from the healing properties of water.

The design team visited spas in New York City to observe their approach to hospitality and service and to study how some of these characteristics might be considered in an ambulatory care facility. The building designs embodied the following key strategies:

- Easy access
- "Living rooms" for waiting with a variety of furniture/seating to provide a warm and comforting environment (see Figure 2.7)
- One-stop check-in at clinical practices restricted to greeting

Figure 2.8
At the core of the building is a multistory, light-reflecting mobile of prisms that are strung to perfect perspective. The work of art captures the attention of all as it is accessible from each floor's balcony and can transform any stressful thought into complete distraction. *Jeff Goldberg, Esto photography, Ray King Studio (artist).*

Figure 2.9
Weill Cornell Medical Center (Pebble Project) physician office located on the perimeter of the building in suites of offices. Physician-to-physician communication will be measured. *Jeff Goldberg, Esto photography, Polshek Partnership Architects/ Ballinger Architects.*

- Exam rooms with separate clinical, family, and consult areas
- Reduced light levels in clinical zones and restriction of overhead lighting
- A feeling of quality and warmth in all materials (elevators, front desk, door handles, toilet accessories, etc.)
- Colors based on water
- Interior finishes and furnishing would be of consistent quality with materials throughout the building, while providing a range of color palettes to avoid everything looking the same
- New York City art and culture: The use of carefully selected and well-placed original artwork to compliment the interior design and enhance the patient experience (see Figure 2.8)

Design and Planning Principles
- All fixed, vertical elements: Stairs, elevator shafts, and telephone and data rooms were located outside of the exam/clinical zone for future flexibility.
- Waiting rooms, conference rooms, public spaces, and offices were placed on perimeter of building to maximize natural light and views (see Figure 2.9).
- Exam rooms designed in clusters of 10 rooms and pods of 5 with shared support.

Figure 2.10
Weill Cornell Medical
Center (Pebble Project)
exam room with net-
worked computers
allowing for consistent
communications.
*Jeff Goldberg, Esto pho-
tography, Polshek
Partnership Architects/
Ballinger Architects.*

- Exam rooms 120 square feet to provide a consult zone in rooms with a desk, computer, and printer.
- MD/administrative offices adjacent to, but not in, clinical zone.
- Branding: Treated steel panels were used throughout the building for identification of major destinations, clinical programs, and donor recognition.
- Inclusion of spa theme and design principles in nonclinical areas.

Technology

Independent of and prior to the development of the Weill Cornell: We Care program, the PO determined that it was important to introduce a systemwide ambulatory electronic medical record (EMR). There are numerous stories of efforts to introduce ERMs at large institutions, some of which have failed in implementation, but the benefits, both financial and clinical, of such systems are widely demonstrated. Accordingly, in the early 2000s a selection of hardware and software, and an implementation plan guiding the faculty through the conversion process, was developed by the PO's information systems office. When it became clear that many of the practices were being relocated, expanded, and significantly changed and that new ones were being created, the PO decided to mandate complete use of the system especially for those practices moving into the new building. This

Figure 2.11
Weill Cornell Medical
Center (Pebble Project)
resource center offering
patients, faculty, and
visitors access to
resources and wireless
communications.
*Jeff Goldberg, Esto
photography, Polshek
Partnership Architects/
Ballinger Architects.*

decision impacted the design of the Weill Greenberg Center in a number of ways—most very positive—such as:

- Provision of computers and printers in each exam room and office, as well as clinical assistant and business stations, all networked together to allow consistent information to be accessed ubiquitously. (See Figure 2.10.)
- Elimination of bulky and space-wasting record rooms.
- Reduction in the unit size of clerical and business stations by virtue of eliminating the tons of paper involved with medical records.
- Elimination of the need to move the record around during the patient visit.

In the pre-EMR era, each practice purchased and maintained its own computers. This led to some confusion when tried to network and became completely impractical when the EMR was introduced. For this reason, as well as logistical simplicity for those practices moving from one place to another, all new computers, all the same and all configured alike, were purchased via the building project and placed in all clinical areas.

The communication system also influenced, and was in turn influenced by, the new processes. Until the move, all phone services were provided by the college's affiliated hospital. When the scope of the new programs was realized it was decided to purchase a whole new system for the college, as the hospital system not only did not have enough remaining capacity but was not structured properly to have the calls according to the PO's practice management standards. The provision of this system benefited the design in a number of ways:

- On-floor communication ability eliminated the need for overhead paging, beepers, "Vocera" phones, or any such accessory system for finding people to, for example, ferry patients to exam rooms.
- The "phone tree" feature allows calls to physicians which formerly were answered by their secretaries or voice mail, to go to others in the practice call centers, so that the number of dropped or missed calls for appointments is minimized. During the phone appointment process all pre-visit registration questions are asked and recorded in the common registration system so that when the patient arrives, the need to have ungainly clipboards and writing surfaces at the reception desks is eliminated. This has cleaned up the desks as well as helped speed the registration process.
- Management records of phone performance encourage quality improvements.

Wireless technology was provided throughout the building. Patients, faculty, and visitors can use their computers in numerous locations without unsightly and dangerous wires dragging along the floor. (See Figure 2.11.)

Technology had negative impacts as well. For example, the Imaging unit was programmed to have both 1.5 and 3.0 Tesla MRIs as well as a PET CT scanner, each of which required extensive and expensive shielding for various things. In one of the "dry" (meaning computer-based) research units in the building, an 85-ton HVAC system separate from the building's had to be provided to cool a room containing numerous servers. And since no one can predict what will come next in technology, large technology rooms—no longer closets—were installed as well as raceways through the building to allow easy installation of wiring in the future.

Operations/Brand/Facility's Alignment

It is easy to see, now that the project is complete, how the Weill Cornell Medical College aligned a cultural shift into a branded program that is reflected in all aspects of its operations as well as its facility design. It is a tall order for most projects because it is often too much to engineer all at once. To align a project in a similar fashion many questions should be asked long before a building project is in sight. Strategically if the opportunity exists to reevaluate an operational model prior to a building project then an interdisciplinary team is on an amazing track. It does, however, have many uncharted waters to navigate. The terrific opportunity is that the Weill Cornell project and others like it that are evidence-based, are committed to

Figure 2.12
Harlem Hospital's five-
story exterior is made
up of fritted glass
façade that features
imagery replicated from
the hospital's WPA-era
murals.
HOK.

measure and share its outcomes. Weill Cornell has taken that commitment one step further by joining an elite group of healthcare facilities in The Center for Health Design's field study Pebble Project, which shares publicly every step of its process to improve their patients' health outcomes. This kind of generosity offers others who will follow keen insight for their future projects. It is in this way that the practice of medicine will improve and the facilities that assist in the administration of care will be developed into a very different kind of environment than is known today.

Cultural Awareness

Answering the question of whom they serve, no doubt led Weill Cornell to the SPA theme. With the right research all projects should be able to determine the cultural needs of their clientele. The design team gains many clues from the base of that knowledge. Knowing what is culturally acceptable or more importantly familiar helps in the journey to eliminate stress. HOK

Figure 2.13
Harlem Hospital's five-story main lobby atrium also provides display space for cultural artwork branding it for its community.
HOK.

Figure 2.14
Ohio Health's rondel acknowledges its Methodist heritage while celebrating its multidenominational faith-based mission. The rondel is displayed proudly in the lobby of the new Dublin Methodist Hospital (Pebble Project). Its icons are exhibited in the design of Dublin's meditative spaces.
Courtesy of Ohio Health/Dublin Methodist Hospital. George C. Anderson Photography, Inc.

Figure 2.15
Uncharted design inter-
ventions: A wayfinding
landmark that offers
more than directional
information. The noted
distances may
empower a frail patient
with the knowledge that
wheelchair assistance is
needed.
*CAMA, Inc. Picture by
Henry Domke, www.hen-
rydomke.com.*

is in the process of designing the Harlem Hospital Expansion project. In order to expand their interdisciplinary team, Jack Travis, AIA, joined the ranks and the results of this awareness provides an environment that "exudes a strong black cultural impact visually and tactilely in the urban planning, architecture and interior of common spaces."[4] (See Figures 2.12 and 2.13.)

Legacy

Understanding an institution's mythology, according to Leland Kaiser, unleashes the clues that are imbedded in the history of an institution. Harlem Hospital took their institutional mythology and made it the centerpiece of their design. It creates a legacy for the community but also creates a more globally recognizable brand of its architecture. How does an institution measure the return on that investment? Some institutions carry their original vision clearly into their future; others lose it for a while and then it resurfaces; and many will never talk about their founders' legacy. (See Figure 2.14.) It makes perfect sense to learn about an institution's founders, their vision for its future, and if there is a link to current strategies. Today many institutions are the result of a merger of two or more community facilities and how these cultures and founding principles are coupled can be an interesting and revealing a place to begin to build a "big idea." It should not create a mold from which no new ideas flow. An institution's mythology should primarily serve as a reference point for why an institution exists and whom it serves. It is interesting to note founding values, and then use them to illuminate the delivery of care in an innovative fashion.

Facility Guidelines

Another layer to peel back in an investigative analysis is an institution's capability or willingness to manage a particular design solution long-term. The Facilities Department is where the knowledge about standards and desired project guidelines exists. Within the evidence-based approach there may be challenges to overcome in a department's rules of application. Be sure to engage these professionals in the interdisciplinary process so their considerations will not cause a design intervention to fail. For example, wayfinding and signage may be within this department's jurisdiction and inability to navigate a facility may be a major complaint on a patient satisfaction report. Solving this "patient dissatisfier" may not be on this department's radar screen. It should, however, become evident in this first phase of evidence-based design, since the investigation will align all components of design with a solution for a particular outcome. (See Figure 2.15.)

Interviewing

Know your customers' customers. In an institution as large as a healthcare facility there are internal customers and external customers—how you gather information from them can reveal very different answers. What you find out can shed new light on a possible design intervention or what might be called an "aha" moment of discovery.

Gatekeepers

The traditional format followed by many design teams is to interview a core group of decision-makers who fully understand a program and are the gatekeepers of a vision for the project at hand. At this level the tone of a project is set and the tolerance for innovation is revealed. Not all projects are intended to innovate. It is for these projects that an evidence-based approach should keep a team from regressing to old familiar methods of designing facilities. The tried, measured, and proven positive design features need not be opened for discussion. See the five-star studies noted in the scorecards in Figures 2.20 through 2.23. The evidence and business case that has been documented for these interventions should dispel any fears and help in the dreaded exercise of non-evidence-based value-engineering. A team that feels strongly about improving a particular outcome through the design of a building program may in fact be willing to be a pioneer. Here evidence-based design can play a role in mitigating risk, particularly in the sharing of ideas with other design teams launching similar innovation in a particular area. An example that comes to mind at this writing is the design of like-handed rooms where, to date, no measurement has proven positive or negative, yet many teams are designing to that end. Enough preliminary work helps to mitigate the risk, but the final success or failure will reveal itself in time. It is in the work of these early adopters where innovation will take place. (See Figure 2.21.)

User Groups

The next level of information gathering comes from what we call staff-based "user groups." These are the interviews where much intelligence is gathered about how an institution is currently operating. Posturing typically occurs here to be sure the long-desired feature for their area is included in the new scheme. How this information is gathered, or more importantly how the questions are asked, is what leads to a better building as opposed to a new and improved old building.

Keep in mind that currently, little past evidence supports what improves staff performance, efficiency, and effectiveness, but many studies are currently on the boards and a growing body of evidence should inform a major shift in the design of staff support areas. This will arm a team with the knowledge to innovate for staff as has been done for patients over the last few years.

Thought Leaders

There is an emerging trend to use thought leaders rather than traditional user groups to help design a facility or unit in a less democratic, more entrepreneurial fashion. This may be formatted as a day for an invited panel of experts to enlighten an interdisciplinary team into a new way of thinking. This discards immediately the need to fix old problems that should never move to the new site. This process does what a good strategic plan tries to achieve—it evaluates internal issues in an unbiased way, while taking a long view into the future of a service or care delivery model by evaluating external possibilities. This method of decision-making seems to be developing among the facilities that are best poised for a rapidly changing future.

Advisory Groups

In the last ten years or so many questions have been asked about how to improve patient- and family-centered care. In 1998 the Picker Institute along with The Center for Health Design developed a tool called An Action Kit: Improving Design Quality and Customer Satisfaction by Assessing the Built Environment. This tool offers a four-tiered strategy for designers and health executives to incorporate patient and family perspectives into the design process. Within the kit are the following tools:

- A videotape featuring the patient's perspective on the built environment
- An environmental checklist focusing on issues of importance to patients
- A survey to access patients' perceptions of a particular built environment
- Focus group priorities to explore patients' perceptions in greater detail

Sessions with constituencies such as family groups, "frequent flyer" patients, and interested community leaders are a way to gather important viewpoints on what satisfies potential users of a facility's services. (See Figure 2.16.) Staging interactive sessions for storytelling or collaging are easy ways to get big issues on the table without having these gatherings turn into gripe sessions.

The Picker Institute offers a comparison of data-collection methods[6] (see Table 2.2).

"People and organizations often organize knowledge concentrically, with the most cherished, vital beliefs at the protected center. At the outer edges are the ideas which the majority rejects. A little closer to the center are the fringes—areas not yet legitimized but not utterly rejected by the center either. Innovation is the center's weakness. The structure, the power, and the institutional inertia all tend to inhibit innovative thinkers and drive them to the fringes. At the social and intellectual fringes, thinkers are freer to let their imaginations roam, but are still constrained by a sense of current reality. The great innovators start at the fringes…"
—Peter Schwartz, The Art of the Long View[5]

Figure 2.16
Patient family advisor collaging to illustrate her desire for a new hospital feature.

Idea!

Before drawings are even available, ask users to describe how they like to work, or more importantly, how they would like to improve an outcome, such as servicing patients efficiently—a very different answer will emerge than if they are asked to critique a plan of a new department. The normal instinct is to reach into the familiar and provide an answer on how to fix the dilemmas that exist in the current delivery model. Once the newly articulated way of working is fleshed out, couple the concepts with the evidence gathered from similar projects. This can now serve as an introduction to a new design concept on how to improve the outcomes that were articulated.

**Table 2.2 The Picker Institute Action Kit for Healthcare Design
Comparison of Data-Collection Methods**

More detail, less generalizability

	Pros	Cons
Casual Observations	No cost	Observer may misinterpret events Observations may not be representative
Systematic Observations	Low cost Unobtrusive Can be done quickly	Observer may misinterpret events Observations may not be representative
In-Depth or Cognitive Interviews	Provides patients' perspective on meaning of events and ways of describing experiences Flexible	Labor-intensive Answers may be difficult to compare
Focus Groups	Provides patients' perspective Allows exploration of complex issues Takes advantage of synergy among patients Elicits different perspectives efficiently Can provide insight into why opinions are held Can help reveal degree or lack of consensus Flexible Appropriate for populations with low levels of literacy	May not be generalizable More expensive than less formal methods
Surveys	Samples are more representative Questions can be standardized Easy to replicate and compare	More expensive Not good for complex issues or exploration of meaning Assumes knowledge of problem and patients' discourse Not appropriate for populations with low levels of literacy

Less detail, more generalizability

Through focus groups with patients and family members, The Picker Institute learned in all cases of Acute, Ambulatory, and Long-Term Care settings that the elements in the environment have a substantial impact on hospital experiences. Eight themes emerged from their study about what patients and family members report that they want from a built environment. The ideal built environment:

1. Is convenient and accessible
2. Is conducive to a sense of well-being
3. Promotes connections to staff
4. Is confidential and private
5. Shows caring for family
6. Is considerate of impairments
7. Facilitates connection to the outside world
8. Is safe and secure

This checklist should be included in a project's design intelligence to measure the quality of all patient experiences.[7]

Visioning Sessions

There are many ways to gather information from the variety of constituencies mentioned above. One very creative way to engage a group is to get them to think out of the box. Creating a visioning session should be tailored to your particular need. Easy steps to follow are:

- Find an inspirational place to elicit the best ideas. If possible conduct the session in an area away from the work environment that is free from interruption. Find a place that relaxes and soothes where ideas can flow freely. Ideally, have access to outdoors. Transform the space in which the team(s) will work; provide toys, food, and a variety of implements to express oneself. Make the environment "healing."
- Establish ground rules whereby no idea is a bad idea as it may spark brilliance in another participant.
- Be sure all are engaged. Know going in who the naysayers are or who the silent participants are so that all engage equally and freely. Dispel negative thoughts with good facilitation skills.
- Develop ice-breakers that unclench folded arms and elicit giggles so it is understood that this is a way to think at 30,000 feet and hope that the concepts that will emerge at the end of a session will reveal possibilities hidden in a tightly closed chamber of their brains.
- Be a good facilitator and do not lead with your ideas. Listen carefully, as these sessions will reveal inspiration.

Figure 2.17
An Imagineer badge created for a visioning session with the Yale-New Haven Hospital Laboratory Medicine Staff.

- Begin with an overview that puts the exercise into context. Get members of the board, core group, users, community, and the design team involved so the breadth of involvement is clear at a high and low level. Make it inclusive. Compose your subteams politically, so they are diverse, allowing for enlightenment at all levels.
- Set goals for the session so you have an idea of an end point.
- Develop exercises that lead to revelations about those goals.
- Break the group into smaller, more manageable groups. Ideally, give them similar yet different problems to solve.
- Begin with issues lists. Be creative in how they report. Will they use images, words; will they report, collage, create a song, or tell a story?
- Create an innovative reporting structure for each team; have them select a leader or team of leaders.
- Set time limits. Have your team keep an eye on their progress so that they stay on track. Give them 10-, 5-, and 2-minute warnings.
- Have a record keeper armed with camera, audio or video recorder, flip charts, or whatever works best for your final deliverable and then sum up at the end of each interval.

- Reward the participants with something memorable that they will keep as a reminder of their role in the development of the project. (See Figure 2.17.)
- Gather and keep all materials produced for an interim report that the design team will analyze for the next stage of design development.

It is in these sessions that all constituencies of an interdisciplinary team can be involved. This process maintains the need to give all a voice but not necessarily a vote. It manages potentially a closed-minded team of care providers from derailing a strong vision to innovate while allowing them to participate in the visioning. It also begins to lay the groundwork for cultural transformation, which all teams should begin prior to moving onto a new unit. It shows teams ways of thinking outside of the box. Visioning can also brings to the surface deep-rooted concerns that can be addressed long before the move. These concerns aired in a positive environment, might even enlighten a positive design change.

Shadowing or Deep Dives

The best way to understand the pros and cons of an existing model of care is to observe it first hand. Depending on the data being collected, a note pad, camera, and tape measurer can be the best tools for recording and understanding why the status quo is broken. Walking around, poking in and out of spaces or just standing still and observing an area and the people in it will reveal a whole host of interesting thoughts about why something is not functioning properly. Most designers are trained to observe and see possibilities after careful observation. Possible solutions will build from this shadowing exercise. In today's environment, though, it takes a savvy team to interpret a model that uses old tools into a new model for radically different technologies or care delivery models. (See Figure 2.18.)

It is in all of these fact-gathering exercises that the unique character of a project will reveal itself. There are many similar initiatives that healthcare facilities today are focused on, but few can address them all. By taking deep dives different cultures will get to a different place in the exploration of a new solution. That is the beauty of this phase of evidence-based design. It is not just the search of past academic studies; it is in the analysis of all gathered intelligence that the innovation for a particular project is revealed.

Benchmark Against National Initiatives

How does this collected data stack up at a broader level? It would be difficult to be even the smallest community-based healthcare facility and not know where the analysis of its data stands in the scheme of national healthcare. *US News and World Report* ratings are noticed and touted by all entities who pass their rigor. Look in the lobbies of those ranked and you will find a framed page from this annual report highlighting the institution. It will not be long before healthcare organizations notice their design interventions are tracking on a national level. The Pebble Project gets a tremendous amount of press; partly because of the

Figure 2.18
Direct observation of
a lab tech at work at
Yale-New Haven
Hospital.

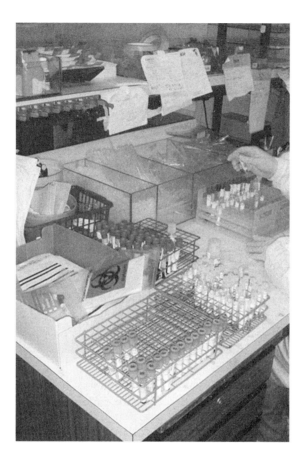

Center's marketing efforts but mostly because of the new ground being explored through design. In fact, just recently Zagat teamed up with Anthem Blue Cross and Blue Shield to reveal a new online survey tool that will allow consumers to share their physician experiences with others. Known as the "wildly popular burgundy bible," *Zagat Survey* is the world's most trusted source for information about where to eat, drink, stay, and play[8] and yes, now heal! Consumers will be able to review their doctor visits online based on:

- Trust
- Communication
- Availability
- Environment

The review will be available in certain markets nationwide.

Figure 2.19
Creating market loyalty.
Women make most
healthcare decisions
for their families.

It is amazing that the Environment is being recognized. This base of knowledge will give more credence to certain design strategies as healthcare facilities become more competitive within their market. There is more than local competition going on; there is competition within Centers of Excellence for national and even international patients. That competition goes both ways as more foreign institutions compete at a price point spawning a new business known as medical tourism. Using evidence about how to design the most effective facility may be a bargaining tool to create market loyalty. The Obstetrics Departments learned that early in the 1980s. (See Figure 2.19.)

Record the Intelligence Gained in Your Internal Investigations

Before a literature search is conducted one must have an idea of the areas to study. Do an analysis of the internal intelligence gathered at any point in the project. Record and analyze the high points of the project's strategic drivers, the project vision if stated at this phase of the project, internal metrics, and desired design interventions. It is in this analysis that the hypotheses or the topics to search for will reveal themselves. As you go through the design process you will continue to discover new topics. Determine a method to keep track of the intelligence captured and share that knowledge with the team. This analysis keeps the team on point and the continual review keeps the "flashpoint" imminent. (See Figure 2.20.)

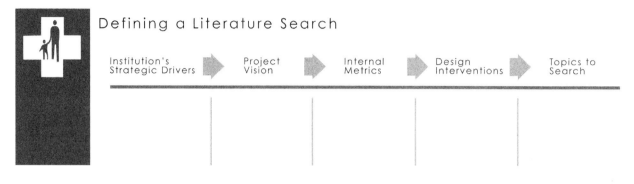

Defining a Literature Search

Institution's Strategic Drivers → Project Vision → Internal Metrics → Design Interventions → Topics to Search

Figure 2.20 (above) Defining a literature search: The topics to search must be narrowed down to reflect the key drivers of a project where improved outcomes have the most impact.

Conduct a Literature Search

Once the key issues to be researched are articulated, the core research team should develop a strategy for seeking the needed base of knowledge. Identify how ambitious the effort will be to seek out studies. Articulate a finite number of issues to be researched. This process can occur throughout the design of the project as questions and new concepts emerge. Then set a strategy for a deep dive into a knowledge base. It is during this process where the decision is made to be an innovator or a laggard or somewhere in between. (See Figure 2.21.) You may innovate in one area but follow in others. It becomes obvious where all team members are on board and review the findings together.

Tools are continually developing that will help find the most pertinent studies in the field at large. Visit The Center for Health Design's website, www.healthdesign.org, and look under Resources and you will find one list of Websites and Blog Links. This will begin any search in building the base of current knowledge from which to launch an intelligent investigation. (See Figure 2.22.)

Figure 2.21 Rogers Adoption/ Innovation Curve.

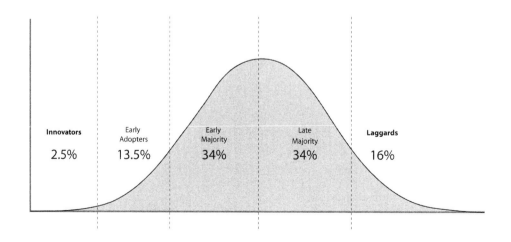

Innovators	Early Adopters	Early Majority	Late Majority	Laggards
2.5%	13.5%	34%	34%	16%

Figure 2.22
www.healthdesign.org:
The Center for Health
Design's website is an
invaluable tool and a
great place to begin a
search.

www.pubmed.com (PubMed) and www.medline.com (MEDLINE) are online sources for articles from clinical authors. Google's "Scholar" feature provides another search engine that combs journals and literature.[9] If the task of doing a search is daunting, then contract a researcher or an intern to assist in ferreting out important hard-to-find data. It may be possible to establish a relationship with a local university's graduate students looking for a semester project. An organization may also have an appropriate person on staff who can be assigned time on a project. Most healthcare facilities have professionals who are good statisticians and know how to conduct research.

There is an art to conducting a search and a good librarian may become the most valuable member of your team at this juncture. There is a language associated with the material that is available—become familiar with it so your requests are clear. A glossary of Library and Information Science is building on Wikipedia.

Literature searches can be done a number of ways; it depends on your access to search engines. Knowing what to search is difficult, but is not as hard as it used to be. One useful tool is a product of the Ulrich and Zimring study[10] of 2004 repeated in 2008[11]. This study identifies all current viable research that falls within the realm of improving outcomes within the healthcare built environment. Ulrich and Zimring take this base of knowledge and organize it into four categories of research:

1. Reduce stress, improve quality of life and healing for patients and families
2. Reduce staff stress/fatigue, increase effectiveness in delivering care
3. Improve patient safety and quality of care
4. Improve overall healthcare quality and reduce cost

These four categories of research are then subdivided into the specific issues the research papers studied. These specific issues are given a five-star rating, five stars meaning the evidence is so compelling that the issue need no longer be debated; one star meaning little evidence is available to support the design intervention. These scorecards become valuable tools at this stage of a project in helping to identify what a project might like to learn more about. They begin to frame the evidence needed to proceed in your investigative process. (See Figures 2.23 through 2.26.)

Listed below are a few links that create connections to a foundation of knowledge that will trigger new links.

www.cfah.org The Center for the Advancement of Health translates to the public the latest evidence-based research on health, healthcare, prevention, and chronic disease management, with an emphasis on how social, behavioral, and economic factors affect illness and well-being.

www.gghc.org Green Guide for Health Care provides the healthcare sector with a voluntary, self-certifying metric toolkit of the best practices that designers, owners, and operators can use to guide and evaluate their progress toward high-performance healing environments.

www.informedesign.org InformeDesign is a resource and communication tool for designers. Research summaries are added weekly.

www.familycenteredcare.org The Institute for Family Centered Care provides leadership to advance the understanding and practice of patient- and family-centered care in hospitals and other healthcare settings.

www.ihi.org Institute for Healthcare Improvement is a source of energy, knowledge, and support for a never-ending campaign to improve healthcare worldwide.

www.uwm.edu/dept/iae/research University of Wisconsin-Milwaukee Institute on Aging & Environment promotes research, scholarship, and service concerning environments for older persons, particularly those suffering from cognitive impairments.

www.anfarch.org Academy of Neuroscience for Architecture supports studies workshops and university-based educational programs designed to explore research that "bridges" neuroscience and architecture.

www.researchdesignconnections.com/blog The Research Design Connections Blog is a forum to discuss recent research of interest to designers.[12]

**Reduce stress, improve quality of life and
healing for patients and families**

Reduce noise stress	☆ ☆ ☆ ☆
Reduce spatial disorientation	☆ ☆ ☆ ☆
Improve sleep	☆ ☆ ☆ ☆
Increase social support	☆ ☆ ☆ ☆
Reduce depression	☆ ☆ ☆
Improve circadian rhythms	☆ ☆ ☆
Reduce pain (intake of pain drugs, and reported pain)	☆ ☆
Reduce helplessness and empower patients & families	☆ ☆ ☆
Provide positive distraction	☆ ☆ ☆
Patient stress (emotional duress, anxiety, depression)	☆ ☆ ☆ ☆

THE CENTER FOR
HEALTH DESIGN

Figure 2.23
Scorecard 1: Reduce
stress and improve
quality of life and heal-
ing for patients and
families.

**Reduce staff stress/fatigue, increase
effectiveness in delivering care**

Reduce noise stress	☆ ☆ ☆ ☆
Improve medication processing and delivery times	☆ ☆ ☆
Improve workplace, job satisfaction	☆ ☆
Reduce turnover	☆
Reduce fatigue	☆ ☆
Work effectiveness; patient care time per shift	☆ ☆ ☆
Improve satisfaction	☆ ☆ ☆

THE CENTER FOR
HEALTH DESIGN

Figure 2.24
Scorecard 2: Reduce
staff stress/fatigue and
increase effectiveness in
delivering care.

Figure 2.25
Scorecard 3: Improve
patient safety and
quality of care.

**Improve patient safety and
quality of care**

Reduce nosocomial infection (airborne)	☆ ☆ ☆ ☆ ☆
(contact)	☆ ☆ ☆ ☆
Reduce medication errors	☆
Reduce patient falls	☆ ☆
Improve quality of communication (patient → staff)	☆
(staff → staff)	☆
(staff → patient)	☆ ☆ ☆
(patient → family)	☆ ☆
Increase hand washing compliance by staff	☆
Improve confidentiality of patient information	☆ ☆ ☆

THE CENTER FOR
HEALTH DESIGN

Figure 2.26
Scorecard 4: Improve
overall healthcare
quality and reduce
cost.

**Improve overall healthcare quality
and reduce cost**

Reduce length of patient stay	☆ ☆
Reduce drugs (see patient safety)	☆ ☆
Patient room transfers: number and costs	☆ ☆ ☆ ☆ ☆
Re-hospitalization or readmission rates	☆
Staff work effectiveness; patient care time per shift	☆ ☆ ☆
Patient satisfaction with quality of care	☆ ☆ ☆ ☆ ☆
Patient satisfaction with staff quality	☆ ☆

THE CENTER FOR
HEALTH DESIGN

Figure 2.27
Cover of handbook for
Baystate Health's
Master Facilities'
Visioning Session.
*Steffian Bradley
Architects/CAMA, Inc.*

Document Process

It is vitally important at this first stage of a project to record the process and capture a team's mindset, an institution's awareness, and an industry's pulse on the topics that this design project will push and pull on. (See Figure 2.27.) This record will create a baseline from which you will measure growth within the team and their thoughts about design solutions. Because this is an iterative process the team will cycle back to this component of evidence-based design many times. New ideas will be born and further intelligence will be gathered. With a large enough team this base of knowledge recorded correctly will save someone additional steps later on. This is the time in the process to know where your research project will fare in the broader base of knowledge. The team should be able at this point to articulate what theories exist in the broader base of knowledge and where there are gaps. The next component of the process will illustrate more clearly the road map for the design phase of a project. It is on the path we follow in the next chapter that the decision to innovate or not will be made easier.

Summary

Gathering intelligence is a significant step in the planning of a design and ultimate research project. It is what sets the tone and keeps a team clearly focused on the original vision for the project. Learn to be a good investigator and build this process into the way you start every project. Use the following checklist for gathering intelligence. Share the data collected often with the entire team.

Checklist: Gathering Internal and External Intelligence for an Evidence-Based Project

1. Build an Interdisciplinary Team
   - At the start of a project identify who will have representation on the team. Be sure there is adequate representation from the design consultants, thought leaders and researchers, institution's leadership, staff, and stakeholders.
   - Recruit evidence-based leadership for your team, firm, and facility.
   - Build the right team of subconsultants after you have completed some of the work below.
   - Insist on an interdisciplinary (inclusive) approach.
   - Systematically adjust all mindsets within the firm and institution to accept this design methodology.
2. Conduct an Investigation
   - Establish guiding principles and design guidelines
   - Create a database of who's who in industry doing evidence-based design. Get to know them.
   - Create a log of useful weblinks that will keep you informed on current trends.

- Keep a file of major healthcare industry issues, articles, conferences, lectures, webcasts, etc. (library cataloging).
- Study institutions that have transformed cultures along with their facilities.
- Know the "Business Case" of similar type facilities (ROI for similar design programs).
- Analyze the current snapshot of the industry and see what is and what can be.
- Find the "connectors" in the industry that will help you get to the next level of knowledge.
- Collect data from the existing facility about:
  - Legacy, medical firsts, historical significance to a community (for merged facilities especially)
  - Strategic drivers
  - Project vision
  - Quality initiatives
  - Cultural shifts needing to occur
  - Internal metrics (performance measures)
  - Customer base and their concerns. Create a matrix of their socio/economic statistics and record specific needs.

- Marketing programs, slogans. Know which programs are being promoted and what promises are being published.
- Know the institution's brand for image development.
- Ability to manage new concepts. (Learn who the gatekeepers are, engage them early and transform them into champions.)
- Conduct visioning sessions and deep dives. Learn what the desires and wishes are for a new building program from leadership, staff, patients and families, community and thought leaders.

- Start with an evidence-based lecture to readjust mindsets and to see a new future.

3. Benchmark Against National Initiatives
   - Analyze internal intelligence.
   - Conduct a literature search.
   - Create a list of design interventions with proven outcomes and a list of where the gaps exist (use Ulrich/Zimring scorecards).
   - Decide to stay a common course using the knowledge gained from the proven studies or to innovate by diving deeper into the topics that have minimal measurement.

4. Document Process

Endnotes

1. Gladwell, M. *The Tipping Point*, Little, Brown and Company: 2000; pp. 38–41.
2. http://www.hcahpsonline.org/executive_insight/default.aspx
3. Becker, F.; Douglass, S. The Ecology of the Patient Unit: Physical Attractiveness, Waiting Times and Perceived Quality of Care, *Healthcare Design*, November 2006.
4. Kliment, S.; "Jack Travis, FAIA on Black Identity." *AIArchitect*, Vol 14, November 2, 2007.
5. Schwartz, P. *The Art of the Long View*, Currency Doubleday, 1991, 1996, p. 69.
6. Center for Health Design & The Picker Institute, Consumer Perceptions of the Healthcare Environment: An Investigation to Determine What Matters, 1998.
7. Picker Institute, Action Kit: Improving Design Quality and Consumer Satisfaction by Assessing the Built Environment, CHD, 1998.
8. Reuters 2008, Anthem Blue Cross and Blue Shield in Ohio Launches Health Survey Tool, Tuesday, January 8, 2008.
9. Hamilton, D.K. "In Search of Evidence", *Health Facilities Management*, 2007; 8:21–24.
10. Ulrich, R., Zimring, C. The Role of the Physical Environment in the Hospital of the 21st Century, The Center for Health Design, 2004.
11. Ulrich, R.S., Zimring, C.M., Zhu, X., DuBose, J., Seo, H., Choi, Y., et al, A review of the research literature on evidence-based design, Health Environments Research & Design, 2008, 1:3:61-125.
12. The Center for Health Design, www.healthdesign.org/resources/weblinks.

Chapter 3
Step 2: Mapping Strategic, Cultural, and Research Goals

> "Some men see things as they are and ask, "Why?"
> I dream things that never were and ask, "Why not?"
> —Robert F. Kennedy

Step 2 begins with positioning a project toward greatness by defining value-driven leadership. Using the project wisdom gathered in the first step the interdisciplinary team will define the "project's vision" which is mapped by identifying the right project drivers needed to inform the design process. It is here that the first discussion of a research agenda occurs, keeping the design and research team focused on the vision.

Now that information has been gathered from a variety of sources and the project's intelligence clearly organized, the data collected has to be synthesized into a project vision and ultimately into research goals. At the intersection of the data collected are clues for the project's design drivers that will reveal a road map for research. It is in the interpretation of these intersecting points that the uniqueness of project vision will emerge. (See Figure 3.2.) It takes value-driven leadership skills in order to facilitate this open exploration without fulfilling a selfish desire. It is the charge of the interdisciplinary team to mold wisdom into a vision that guides through to the completion of a remarkable facility designed to improve measurable outcomes.

The interpretation of "project wisdom" into a project vision requires careful coordination and value-driven leadership. It starts with the role project leadership plays in engaging an interdisciplinary team and keeping them on point. Typically this may not be recognized as a part of the evidence-based design process. When it is, a perfect storm exists for creating the vision. Correctly sharing project wisdom will position a team to a higher level of thinking, taking it from a mediocre level and driving it to greatness. It is at the core of this thought process that the real questions/synapses of a project will emerge. Specifically in this chapter

Figure 3.1
Grass spray.
Picture by Henry Domke,
www.henrydomke.com.

the following topics will reveal a clear road map to evidence-based outcome-driven design solutions:

1. Positioning a project toward greatness
2. Defining project drivers/improved outcomes
3. The art of mapping a vision
4. Establishing a research agenda

Positioning a Project Toward Greatness

Embedded in evidence-based design are some very important concepts about project success. One very significant piece is the creation of the interdisciplinary team, defined in the previous chapter. The second is value-driven project leadership; and the third is in the articulation of a strong project vision linked to research goals.

> "Sessions during which a consistent facilitator shares the vision, goals, and desired outcomes play an important role in developing a team that will remain steadfast when the going gets tough."
> —Cheryl Herbert, R.N., CEO of Dublin Methodist Hospital, Dublin, Ohio (see Herbert Essay in Chapter 1).

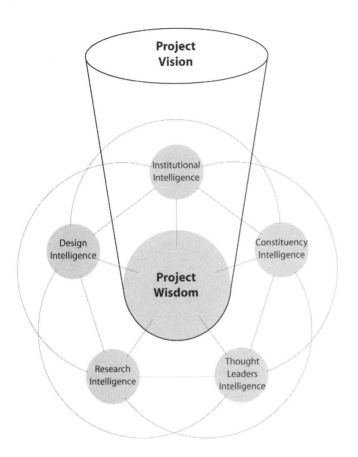

Figure 3.2
Project vision: A stated view of what is to be upon project completion. The inspiration for a vision comes from project wisdom and, in an evidence-based design project, is articulated into a measurable outcome. CAMA, Inc.

Good projects happen often, great projects happen infrequently. Good leadership on major building projects is exhibited often, extraordinary leadership comes rarely. It is extraordinary leadership that warrants the effort of an evidence-based approach, especially when the goal is to innovate and succeed. An extraordinary leader must:

1. Select the right interdisciplinary team for the project
2. Possess value-driven leadership
3. State a clear project vision
4. Use evidence-based design principles
5. Focus on outcomes

"Good is the enemy of great."[1]

— Jim Collins

Keyword: Project Vision

A project vision is a stated view of what is to be expected upon project completion; an inspiration that is clearly articulated and informs all design decisions. It is the project's "big idea". In an evidence-based project it is always linked to measurable outcomes.

There is no question that the success of a great project rests with the right team players. Resistant members of a team typically revert back to familiar methodologies that foster silos. Communication stops and mediocrity reigns. It is here where a poor team player will call upon their existing body of knowledge to do as they have always done before, instead of working with the "group brain" of the interdisciplinary team to forge new possibilities. Great leadership as stated below keeps poor players off the "bus" but when not possible keeps them on point and prevents them from reverting back to the familiar.

So what kind of leadership does it take to masterfully deliver a great project? During the course of my tenure with The Center for Health Design, I have had the honor of serving on the board with Leonard Berry, PhD, distinguished professor of marketing at Texas A & M. In his book *Discovering the Soul of Service,* Dr. Berry illustrates how values-based leadership requires an interdisciplinary team effort. (See Figure 3.3.) His study outlines the context through which value-driven leadership plays a role in defining the culture of an evidence-based project.

Value-Driven Leadership

1. Strategic focus is about knowing an institution's core values or, as Dr. Berry points out, "the definition of your business." For a project's interdisciplinary team it is in the initial internal investigation that this should be clearly articulated. (See Chapter 2.) Many projects today find different ways to phrase "advancing medicine" as the definition of their business. At an early "Pebble" meeting, Sandra Bennett Bruce, CEO, at Saint Alphonsus

"First who…then what. We expect that good to great leaders would begin by setting a new vision and strategy. We found instead that they first got the right people on the bus, the wrong people off the bus, and the right people in the right seats—and then figured out where to drive it. The old adage 'People are your most important asset' turns out to be wrong. People are not your most important asset. The right people are."[2]

—Jim Collins, *Good to Great*

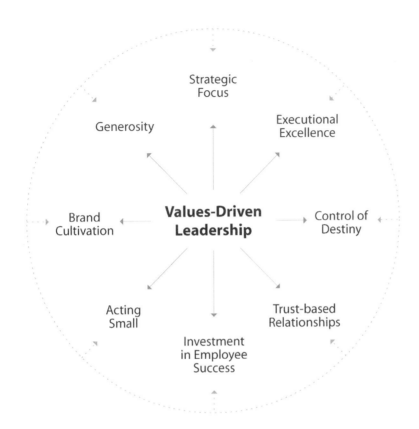

Figure 3.3
Drivers of sustainable
success in a service busi-
ness also inform the suc-
cess of an evidence-
based project.
*Leonard L. Berry,
Discovering the Soul of
Service (New York, The
Free Press, 1999), p. 17.*

Regional Medical Center, Boise, Idaho, said her institution chose to use evidence-based design and become a Pebble Project because strategically they fully understood what it meant to advance medicine—it was "advancing healing" that they were in search of answers to. At the core of their value system is a vision for healing. In Dr. Berry's mindset, Saint Al's has defined their business in the terms of fundamental customer needs, which is an enduring path to follow. This project vision is clear because it has proven design interventions that are quite measurable. For the interdisciplinary team it sends a

"What came from intensive study of truly outstanding service companies
is the most exciting discovery of my research career to date:
The drivers of sustainable success in labor-intensive service businesses
are common across different business."[3]
—Leonard Berry, *Discovering the Soul of Service*

Figure 3.4
The project vision
at Baystate Health
speaks to executional
excellence.

Figure 3.4
The project vision at Baystate Health speaks to executional excellence.

signal that those evidence-based design interventions that are aligned with this measurable outcome for healing must be considered for this project, and any that may trigger an innovative concept may be worth the risk since they are in complete strategic alignment.

2. Executional excellence is paramount in a labor-intensive service business. It relies on the quality of the performers, which is integral to the quality of the customers' experiences. It is at this stage of a project that an interdisciplinary team should map the patient, family, and staff experience to fully understand where the paradigm shifts need to occur in the delivery of service and hence the kind of design needed to support those shifts. (See Chapter 2.) (See Figure 3.4.) Berry's first rule of execution in his sample firms is to hire excellent people to fulfill company strategy. In the project's evidence-based intelligence it is then imperative to identify the needs of these exceptional employees and not dumb the facility down for the poor performers no matter how high up the chain of command

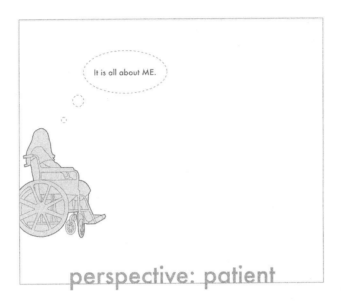

It is all about ME.

perspective: patient

Figure 3.5
Most patients will tell you that when being cared for it is all about them. How will you customize your project to design for each individual's needs within your design solution? More research is needed.

they sit. It will require an investigation in the literature to see what allows great teams to perform at the top of their game, what kind of work environments support those behaviors, and what tools and resources need to be at hand. There are many studies outside of the healthcare specialty that address workplace performance and can offer great clues on how to support workplace activities that will lead to executional excellence.

3. Control of destiny requires staying focused on the customer—according to Berry it is largely attitudinal. In most services purchased today it is all about the customer, so how can healthcare be all about each patient, one at a time? (See Figure 3.5.) Customization is a new trend in product delivery—my iPod has different songs than yours because I have customized mine to my preferences. How then is that level of service expectation delivered in a healthcare facility? Researching design interventions that allow a caregiver to spend more time at the bedside when needed, yet allowing for privacy when not, may bring an interdisciplinary team to a very different design solution of a nursing unit. If the solution is new then it will have no available evidence to show the level of risk. The team will have to decide if the project can bear the responsibility for an innovation or forego the risk and solve for a tried and true operational model. Cheryl Herbert's mantra on her project was "Run until Apprehended!" She empowered team members to reach for innovation with an evidence-based safety net. Leadership instills the values that offer a team clear direction for a project's intended destiny.

4. Trust-based relationships, according to Berry, characterize the sustained success of a company. It is important to note that in an evidence-based approach to the design of a healthcare facility the interdisciplinary team must operate on a basis of trust. How many times

Figure 3.6
A staff respite area
within the Jay Monahan
Center for Gastro-
intestinal Health at New
York Presbyterian
Hospital/Weill Cornell.
Guenther 5 Architects.
© Adrian Wilson,
© Frederick Charles.

Figure 3.6
A staff respite area within the Jay Monahan Center for Gastrointestinal Health at New York Presbyterian Hospital/Weill Cornell. *Guenther 5 Architects. © Adrian Wilson, © Frederick Charles.*

have you seen a request for a brilliant solution squelched because those midway up the chain live in fear of seeking approval? A design concept based on an evidence-based solution that has been proven elsewhere helps to mitigate the risk when proposing its use. Of course, in an evidence-based solution the team always includes decision-makers at the top. If the solution is truly innovative, and no conclusive evidence exists to support it yet some evidence leads to a strong indication that it might succeed, then the team should proceed in a trust-based fashion. The evidence-based process then supports the success of the team and in time its solution may sustain the success of the newly developed operation.

5. Investment in employee success is a sign of a great service company. Companies that invest in employee success typically reinforce core values, motivate, promote personal development, and professionalize the service delivery role. The pendulum in healthcare has swung so far toward patient-centeredness that little data exists to improve the work environment for healthcare providers. It is paramount that the body of knowledge be built to improve staff work and provide replenishment zones. In the Dublin Methodist Hospital mapping exercise, the stress level of the emergency medical staff was discussed. On a busy or critical shift, an employee may not be able to leave the unit for a meal break let alone for a coffee break. It was decided that a ten-minute replenishment break would offer the best possible solution. It required carving out space along the perimeter of the building to provide a respite space where a staff member could sit in a comfortable chair, put up their feet, look outdoors, call home, or plug in an iPod for a short break. No evidence pointed to the success of this kind of design intervention but it was well worth the risk to develop a new design concept and find out if the design team's hypothesis was right. The risk was taken because if proven correct it would do a world of good for a harried staff member and ensure the success of their performance through the rest of a hectic shift. (See Figure 3.6.) Cost of adding a staff respite room: $35,000; cost of an alert caregiver: Priceless! (See the Business Case in Chapter 5.)

6. Acting small allows for personalized care. This value-driven leadership quality empowers not only managers, but also frontline staff to function within the context of an institution's core values while providing services that support a vision. Supportive design features are developed from the clues gathered in visioning with those frontline workers who share their unique care interventions delivered within the subcultures on each of their units. Solutions can be slightly different on similar units, but must be connected to the whole. The design team has to be careful not to design for any one individual who may be gone by the time a project is complete. The interdisciplinary team has to understand that at the core of the intention is a feature that adds special value to the bigger picture. The innovation may be in how to add flexibility to the plan for future change. By virtue of an interdisciplinary decision-making process the design feature should never be misaligned if it is tested using the evidence-based Litmus Ring (see Figure 1.5). Success comes in finding design interventions that are linked to the overall vision. If the design detail offers variation to a standard it may be prime for a research study, providing the cultures are not so drastically different from each other.

7. Brand cultivation is about exceeding a customer's expectation for an experience. For example, Ritz Carlton has a system in place on the Dublin project dubbed as "The Ritz Handoff."

Figure 3.7
The "Ritz Hand-off"
adapted for the Dublin
Methodist Hospital
(Pebble Project). Perches
are available as touch-
down stations that allow
greeters to rove and
provide visitors a much
more welcoming experi-
ence. Is this kind of
greeting a patient satis-
fier? The study is not yet
complete.
*Rendering courtesy of
Karlsberger, Architect of
Record. CAMA, Inc./
Big Red Rooster.*

Customization: The Ritz Handoff

Chicago—The instant a cab pulls up to The Ritz Carlton–Chicago, Mark Farrell lunges to open the taxi door, takes charge of an overnight bag, and welcomes this unannounced guest by name. How did he know it? "I peeked at your luggage tag," the doorman says with a grin.[4]

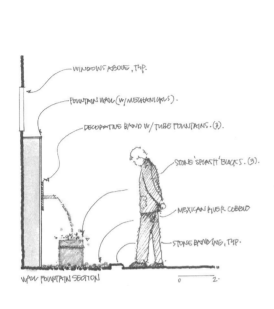

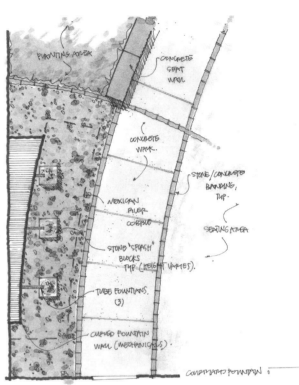

It was on the Dublin Methodist Hospital project that the interdisciplinary team, while trying to discern what would make an exceptional arrival experience, referenced the practice Ritz Carlton masters so well. It led to the elimination of the reception desk in the lobby. Roving greeters are placed at the entrance to more nimbly approach patients and families on a more immediate and personal level. (See Figure 3.7.) Will this cultivate a brand for the Dublin Methodist Hospital? Time will tell, as the Dublin Methodist Hospital is committed to measuring the outcome of this bold move.

8. Generosity is a success sustainer in a labor-intensive service company according to Berry. In healthcare, generosity can be defined a number of ways but responsibility to its community is one sure way. How will a project connect to its community? Provide for the community it serves? There are unique design possibilities to explore for every project. Great civic buildings of the past provided the community with grand public spaces. Most healthcare administrators today are concerned with the appearance of too much money being spent in their public spaces. This shift in thinking has allowed for more attention to detail in patient areas, yet the front door is a prime opportunity to welcome the community into one's facility as a Wellness Center. Celebration Health in

Figure 3.8
Detail of a segment of a walking path along the Dublin Methodist (Pebble Project) Campus. Thirteen special gardens are planned throughout the building and around the campus. Studies not yet complete.
MSI- Landscape Architects.

Florida has a fitness center—front and center—available to its staff, patients, and community. What a wonderful pronouncement to being a health center. Many other facilities are positioning resource centers and cafes at the main lobby as a way to offer families a diversion but also to be a public resource to the community. With the advent of the healing garden, walking paths are emerging as great respite zones for patients, families, and staff, but also for the community. Imagine if the great gardens of a community were located on a medical campus because the evidence shows a strong connection to nature promotes health and healing. (See Figure 3.8.)

The leadership qualities noted above are what Len Berry refers to as the soul of service. For those who have been on great teams, these qualities are recognizably what makes a team perform beyond expectations. They are empowering because the team's purpose is clear and every effort is harmonized toward one end goal. The lessons here were intended by Berry for operational leadership but, as illustrated, work as well for the performance leadership needed for an interdisciplinary team to design a world-class healthcare facility.

Defining Project Drivers/Improved Outcomes

Like the evolution of the "Ritz Handoff" concept to the design of a lobby without a reception desk, informed concepts for designing a better environment need time to develop and should follow the rigor of the evidence-based design Litmus Ring (see Figure 1.5). In so doing, project drivers can be linked to improved outcomes. To get to that point, all of the investigative work in the evidence-based process that has been collected to date has to be critically interpreted in order to articulate project drivers that will improve a building's performance. This, in an ideal project schedule, is where schematic design begins. (See Table 1.1.) It is here where you identify "project drivers."

Assessing all of the data collected is a daunting task, especially at the beginning of a project when wish lists are long. Questions present themselves about making changes in existing culture, operations, and facilities design. An additional search of the literature with a narrower focus may reveal inspiration for a transformational design solution. The investigation may help to determine exemplary facilities to tour. Deep dives are most beneficial at this stage of a project to reveal another layer of intelligence about why a culture exists and how the design of the space can improve the tasks performed. Let's take a closer look at how to draw clear expectations for the design of your research study and the design of your project.

Keyword: Project Driver

A project driver is a design intervention that is linked to a specific outcome that becomes apparent after the internal and external intelligence is analyzed.

Many design teams approach this task slightly differently. Some are more rigorous than others in maintaining a clear understanding of the data collected in the design process. See Figure 6.3 for a look at Anshen + Allen's "Flight-Ready Checklist,"—a way to keep ever present all of the evidence-based principles that should be applied to the project. A hand-book is another easy tool to capture and disseminate the most important information for the project at hand. It keeps the entire team properly informed. Handbooks can be updated as more information is collected as well as continually edited so that the message is clear and the data pertinent to the phase of design at hand. The documentation should even include early visioning sessions such as those captured by Baystate Health in Springfield, Massachusetts, which revealed a pictogram of current and desired patient, family, and staff perspectives for a new ICU. (See Figures 3.9 and 3.10.) These tools keep interdisciplinary teams focused on their original goals. Progress through the rest of the design phases moves smoothly because all have participated and own a clear understanding of the decision-making.

A handbook may also contain the summation or definition of the outcomes expected. The Baystate Health interdisciplinary team boiled down their internal analysis to six action-able project drivers. (See Figures 3.11 and 3.12.)

The first project driver was about staff "teamwork" and "communication." The Baystate Health interdisciplinary team looked at the evidence and set out to achieve one of the insti-tution's guiding principles to transform patient care by managing the flow of work. The evi-dence-based Litmus Ring came into place—see Figure 1.5.

1. Strategic Objectives Stated
   Baystate Health's Strategic Master Planning Guidelines were reviewed and stated a need for a state-of-the-art environment that:
   • Fosters innovative approaches
   • Supports efficient delivery of care
   • Meets six IOM aims (see Chapter 1)
   • Enhances multidisciplinary practice care, teaching use of technology
   • Enhances the experience
   • Fosters a healthy work environment
2. Intelligence Gathered
   Internally: (see Figures 3.9 through 3.12)
   Externally: The following supporting studies were revealed in a literature search.
   • Transforming the work environment for nurses: This study links nurses' skills at monitoring patients' health and symptoms to improved clinical outcomes, and sug-gests their vigilance is an important defense against errors.[5]
   • Transforming care at the bedside (TCAB): Studied the strongest concept in decen-tralized nursing, care at the bedside. It cites four drivers for success in the efficiency of care.

Figure 3.9
Visioning boards from
Baystate Health; current
patient perspective of
the ICU and CCU.
*Steffian Bradley
Architects/CAMA, Inc.*

- Safety and reliability: Care for patients who are hospitalized is safe, reliable, effective, and equitable.
- Care team vitality: Within a joyful and supportive environment that nurtures professional formation and career development, effective care teams continually strive for excellence.
- Patient-centeredness: Truly patient-centered care on medical surgical units honors the whole person and family, respects individual values and choices, and ensures quality of care.
- Increases value: All care processes are free of waste and promote continuous flow.[6]

Figure 3.10
Visioning boards from Baystate Health; ideal patient perspective of the ICU and CCU.
Steffian Bradley Architects/CAMA, Inc.

- What Matters Most to Patients:
  - Facilitates connection to staff
  - Is conducive to well-being
  - Is convenient and accessible
  - Is confidential and private
  - Is caring for family
  - Is considerate of people's impairments
  - Is close to nature[7]

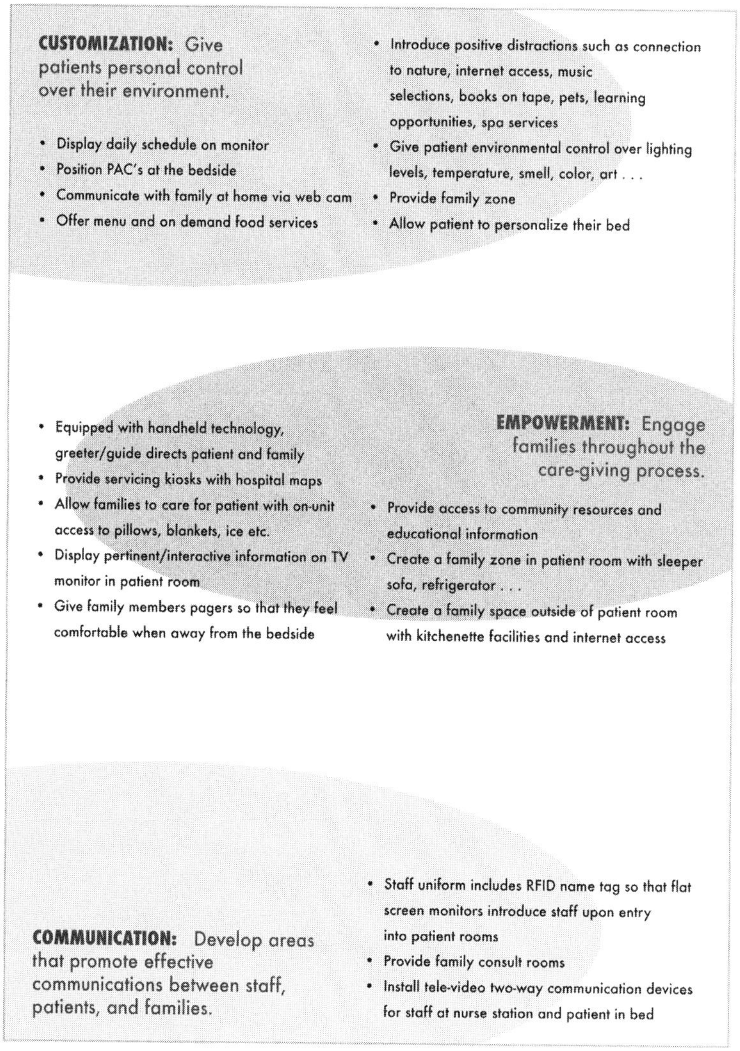

Figure 3.11
Final analysis of
Baystate Health's vision-
ing that revealed project
drivers.
*Steffian Bradley
Architects/CAMA, Inc.*

CUSTOMIZATION: Give patients personal control over their environment.

- Display daily schedule on monitor
- Position PAC's at the bedside
- Communicate with family at home via web cam
- Offer menu and on demand food services

- Introduce positive distractions such as connection to nature, internet access, music selections, books on tape, pets, learning opportunities, spa services
- Give patient environmental control over lighting levels, temperature, smell, color, art . . .
- Provide family zone
- Allow patient to personalize their bed

- Equipped with handheld technology, greeter/guide directs patient and family
- Provide servicing kiosks with hospital maps
- Allow families to care for patient with on-unit access to pillows, blankets, ice etc.
- Display pertinent/interactive information on TV monitor in patient room
- Give family members pagers so that they feel comfortable when away from the bedside

EMPOWERMENT: Engage families throughout the care-giving process.

- Provide access to community resources and educational information
- Create a family zone in patient room with sleeper sofa, refrigerator . . .
- Create a family space outside of patient room with kitchenette facilities and internet access

- Staff uniform includes RFID name tag so that flat screen monitors introduce staff upon entry into patient rooms
- Provide family consult rooms
- Install tele-video two-way communication devices for staff at nurse station and patient in bed

COMMUNICATION: Develop areas that promote effective communications between staff, patients, and families.

- Toward More Time at the Bedside:
  - 30 percent of nursing time at bedside
  - Remainder of time doing documentation, retrieving medications, and other tasks
  - 1 mile traveled every hour
  - Study goal to increase time at bedside to 90 percent through materials management redesign and improved retention[8]

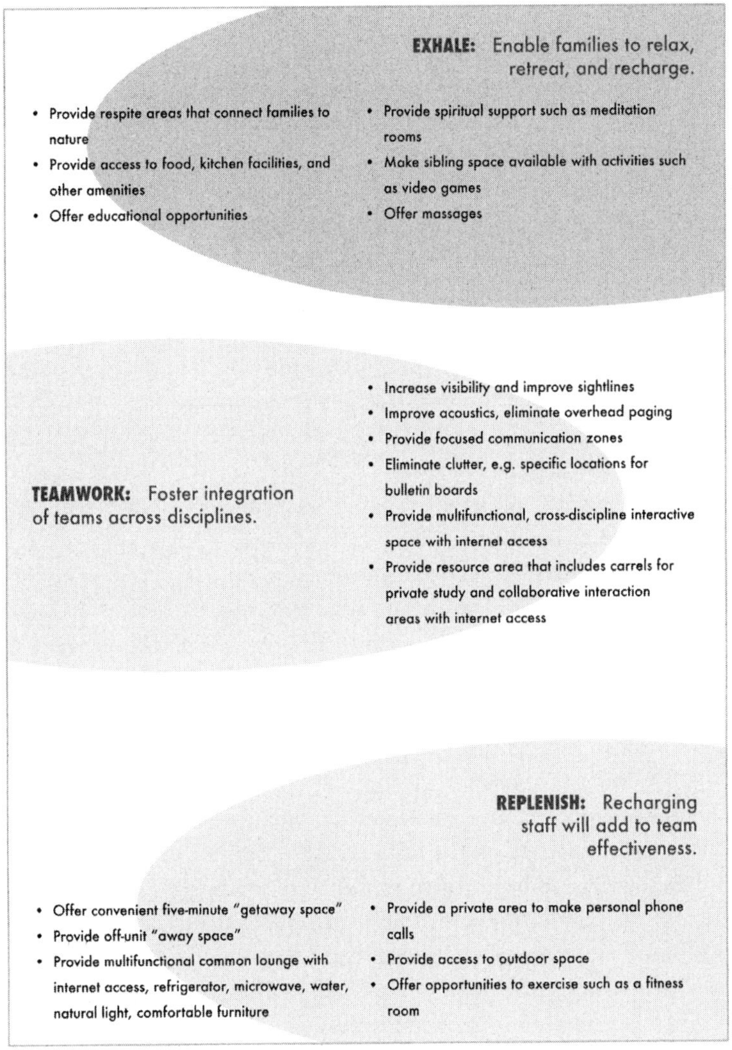

EXHALE: Enable families to relax, retreat, and recharge.

- Provide respite areas that connect families to nature
- Provide access to food, kitchen facilities, and other amenities
- Offer educational opportunities

- Provide spiritual support such as meditation rooms
- Make sibling space available with activities such as video games
- Offer massages

TEAMWORK: Foster integration of teams across disciplines.

- Increase visibility and improve sightlines
- Improve acoustics, eliminate overhead paging
- Provide focused communication zones
- Eliminate clutter, e.g. specific locations for bulletin boards
- Provide multifunctional, cross-discipline interactive space with internet access
- Provide resource area that includes carrels for private study and collaborative interaction areas with internet access

REPLENISH: Recharging staff will add to team effectiveness.

- Offer convenient five-minute "getaway space"
- Provide off-unit "away space"
- Provide multifunctional common lounge with internet access, refrigerator, microwave, water, natural light, comfortable furniture

- Provide a private area to make personal phone calls
- Provide access to outdoor space
- Offer opportunities to exercise such as a fitness room

Figure 3.12
Final analysis of Baystate Health's visioning that revealed project drivers.
Steffian Bradley Architects/CAMA, Inc.

3. Reveal Possible Design Solutions by Redefining the Work Environment
   • Nursing/in-room consult: At patient bedside, access to technology, patient family, work zone, sink and hand-washing

- Work zone/Perch: Outside patient room(s) available to colleagues, family, with technology and visual access to patients
- Touchdown/Pod: Available workstation access to technology, acoustical privacy, place for off-unit staff to stash carry-ons, sit/stand options, leave clear when finished or leaving the unit
- Collaborative/war room: Confer with team members (away from patient), access to technology, acoustic privacy, single/multiple monitor(s), visual access to unit
- Consult room: Family care team conference: Quiet room for staff and family
- Off-stage workroom: Mix of work/conference tables and individual carrels that may be open or assigned, with technology access and phone; may contain library reference
- Private workspace/cocoon: Alone time, phone privacy, confidential, concentration, personal issues, work surface, acoustical privacy
- Document task area shared: Computer/workspace, phone, technology; locked files, storage
- Document task area: Desk, phone, technology, locked files, storage, 2- to 3-person conference space
- Monitor station: Position and access as necessary; technology and phone
- Resource center: Shared manuals, reference, technology access
- Lounge: Coffee, refrigerator, microwave, counter, cabinets, table(s) and chairs, lounge chairs, marker/bulletin board, lockers if necessary, phone
- Replenishment area: Lounge chairs, view to nature, room-darkening option, phone, music, soft lighting

4. Question and Analyze

   In interdisciplinary discussions the pros and cons of these work environments were explored and developed further for the Baystate culture. (See Figure 3.15.) With this knowledge in hand design studies were conducted that would later inform the layout of the core of the unit. This evidence-based transformation defines a very different work environment than what would have come from a non-evidenced-based team. It is here where the result of the initial research manifests into an "aha" moment.

5. Duplicate or Innovate and Premeasure Critical Features

   Baystate, through the work of SBA Architects, has been a pioneer in the on-stage /off-stage concept of work environments. The initial design was implemented in the D'Amour Cancer Center (see Chapter 4) and fueled the confidence in the team's design concepts and investigative intelligence to move forward.

6. Align with Strategic Objective

   With that level of confidence in the process, the design implementation for this type of nursing unit passed the evidence-based design Litmus test.

This type of analysis helped CAMA, Inc. in the development of our "Perch/Pod" concept. It began several years ago on a project at Yale University where Linda Lorimer, Secretary of the University, in a description of an efficient work environment referred to a "Perch." This transient work environment was supported by the research at the time being conducted by the American Society of Interior Designers (ASID) on workplace performance.[9] The study identified five key components to creating a productive work environment:

1. People performance
2. Designed environment
3. Workflow
4. Technology
5. Human resources

The study concluded that in order for a work environment to be productive it must offer:

1. Access to people and resources
2. Comfort in one's surroundings
3. Privacy
4. Flexibility of the environment

Several years ago in the pursuit of a more efficient ICU work environment at All Children's Hospital, St. Petersburg, Florida, an ICU physician and nurse described an ideal intensive care work environment and the Perch/Pod concept was born in a healthcare application. In a day, the whole hospital was abuzz and all units wanted a Perch/Pod arrangement. The concept is as follows: If the primary clinical care station ideally moved to the bedside, as supported by the research cited for the Baystate Health project, then the next best place to conduct one's work would be just outside the room—ideally across the hall where one would "perch" with greater visibility of multiple rooms yet have access to colleagues in the core of the unit. At ends of the unit would be located "pods" where those not permanently assigned to a unit would light upon a work surface in a stand/sit scenario for electronic access and interaction with colleagues. The perch is assigned to nurses on duty, the pods are for all who report intermittently on the unit. The pods are available on a first-come, first-served basis, but are relinquished at the completion of their occupants' duties on the unit. This concept was embraced at the Dublin Methodist Hospital where measurement of its effectiveness is underway. (See Figure 3.13.)

CAMA, with Heery Architects, is exploring an alternate concept for nomenclature, including the perch, for ambulatory use at the Medical College of Georgia Cancer Center. At this institution, a study will be conducted to examine a patient's stress level when clinical treatment areas have less clinical names. The perches, or nurse stations, will be called "libraries." (See Figure 3.14.) All waiting areas will be called "commons;" the major link between the waiting area and exam treatment area will be called the "gallery" and is treated

Figure 3.13
Perch/pod at the
Dublin Methodist
Hospital (Pebble Project)
located just outside the
patient room, allowing
for visual access and
communications with
medical staff. Note
access to daylight
within core of the unit.
Studies not yet com-
plete.
*Courtesy of Ohio
Health/Dublin Methodist
Hospital. © 2008.
Photography by Brad
Feinknopf. Karlsberger
Architects/CAMA, Inc.*

as such. Exam rooms will be located in "suites" and each suite will be named after a Georgia flowering tree, i.e., the "Magnolia Suite," or "Palmetto Suite." Infusion will be called the "garden," as it looks out on and has access to a planted terrace. The lobby and all ancillary

Storytelling: An Ideal Day of Cancer Treatment

"Once upon a time in a far-away land I was diagnosed with cancer. I was taken to a room where I experienced absolute serenity while receiving a massage
and being able to think about my upcoming treatment.
I was taken by yacht to a beautiful island where I was
serenaded by island birds and insects and my senses
were tickled by the scent of the tropical flowers. The
rippling, trickling water flowing over the rocks soaked
my senses where I didn't experience nausea. All the
staff was eager to please and assist me through every
step of my journey. I was greeted by a warm genuine
smile through each phase of my treatment. I was given
an opportunity to choose where I wanted to receive my
treatment. I could choose meditating alone or celebrating with a group. We were offered tantalizing nour-
ishment and refreshments that were pleasing to the
eyes as well as palate. When it was time to leave I
wasn't rushed and was given time to collect myself and
given first-class service and transportation to my next
destination."

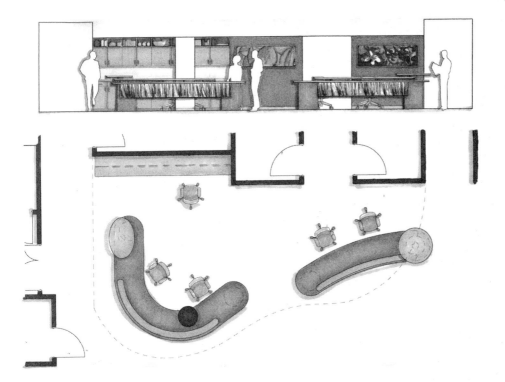

Figure 3.14
"Perch" or "library" at
the Medical College of
Georgia Cancer
Center.
*Heery Architects/CAMA,
Inc.*

support areas will be called the "marketplace." These names of spaces were a direct inspiration from a visioning and storytelling session that was conducted with a very engaged patient and family advisory team along with administration, clinical staff, design and construction management staff—truly interdisciplinary. The preceeding is a delightful fairy-tale description created at the session of an ideal day of cancer treatment— it is a written summation of the group's wishes and desires for an ideal care facility.

Medical College of Georgia has perfected this inclusive model of patient and family advisory group guidance like no other team I have experienced. The evidence-based results are developing with ease and are truly of an innovative scale. At an Anthropology Conference I spoke at recently, I was told that changing the perception of care by changing the nomenclature of clinical spaces would be a study of interest well beyond the design fields. I was invited to speak about the interpretation that the Dublin Methodist Hospital's Big Red Rooster Cultural Study used in the design of its evidence-based facility. The design fields have yet to learn of the far reaches of this new discipline called evidence-based design.

Like most evidence-based ideas, this concept then pushes the next level of logic, which begs for the redesign of the core of a nursing unit. If the staff work zones become more efficient then the core must also become more efficient. The idea of improving workflow and

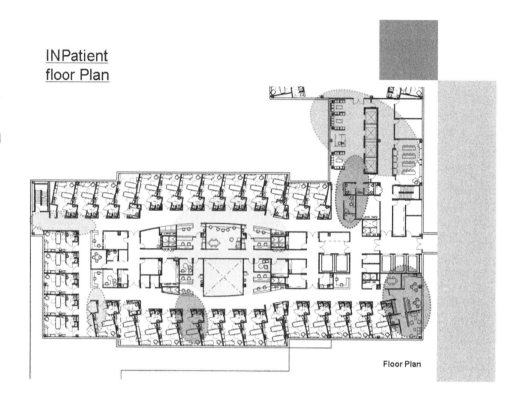

Figure 3.15
Schematic plan development for Baystate
Health. Note different
variation of Perch/Pod
with on-stage/off-stage
materials management
capability. Also note
variation of like-handed
room where access to
view trumps like-handedness throughout the
unit.
*Steffian Bradley
Architects/CAMA, Inc.*

**INPatient
floor Plan**

Floor Plan

making it transparent to patients and families forces an analysis of materials management and its flow on and through a unit. At Baystate Health, this on-stage/off-stage concept has been incorporated with the Perch/ Pod concept and is currently in the planning stages for their new expansion project. (See Figure 3.15.)

Project Driver: "Direction and Diversion"

I am most proud to share a meaningful and far-reaching story about a visioning session that revealed a powerful cue about project drivers. I was facilitating a parents' group meeting at Hasbro Children's Hospital in Providence, Rhode Island, where a mom stood up and said what she wanted most in her new hospital was "direction and diversion—get me to where I have to go and make me forget why I am going there." This was a major project driver at Hasbro Children's Hospital. Under Bruce Komiske's value-driven leadership Hasbro later did a "Post Occupancy Evaluation" of the building project and as a result of the design interventions saw a 25 percent increase in patient satisfaction scores.[10]

It is in the review of the project wisdom that the identification of project drivers or articulation of outcomes becomes apparent. Using the evidence-based design Litmus Ring the drivers are validated or dropped. How to implement these drivers into great design ideas is where the art of mapping comes into play.

The Art of Mapping a Vision

> "Most of us aren't very good at perceiving reality as it is.
> Most of what we 'see' is shaped by our impressions,
> our history, our baggage, our preconceptions."[11]
> —Peter Senge

Mapping is an exercise that begins in the schematic design process. Those who took Drawing 101, will remember the surprise experienced in the exercise of drawing with your less dominant hand. You had to link what your eyes were telling your brain to the activity of your hand. The dominant hand has a mind of its own and draws from an internal base of knowledge, or what it thinks the eyes see. The use of the less dominant hand requires much more information and the drawing emerges shaky but much truer to the subject being drawn. Such is true with a "mapping" exercise. Design teams can typically draw most healthcare spaces using an internal base of knowledge. Synthesizing collective intelligence or project wisdom, on the other hand, requires much more effort yet reveals a strategically aligned picture of a project's design direction well beyond the team's internal base of knowledge. Take that project wisdom and add to it an exercise of predicting outcomes, and new possibilities emerge. Realization of those possibilities allows ideas to emerge that will provide cues for the design of a unique plan.

Idea!

Create a retreat for the interdisciplinary team. Begin with a recap of all intelligence gathered. Using that project wisdom, envision the possibilities of an ideal experience from the arrival sequence to procedural operations to contemplative moments for patients, families, and staff. Do the same for outcomes related to safety, quality, and stress reduction. Record what the team visualizes onto a schematic plan showing just where and how those experiences can manifest themselves into new design ideas. If the team gets stuck then have an inspirational tool. During the Dublin Methodist Hospital Project's mapping exercise the team watched the Andy Goldsworthy film "Rivers and Tides."[12] Let ideas come from all directions and see what emerges. Then record the ideas for each area of the building, creating a map by marking up plans with indications. Then take the sum total and express it as a "big idea" for the project or what is commonly known as the "project vision." Let it guide the design process.

Figure 3.16
Baystate Health project
driver's map for new
nursing units.
*Steffian Bradley
Architects/CAMA, Inc.*

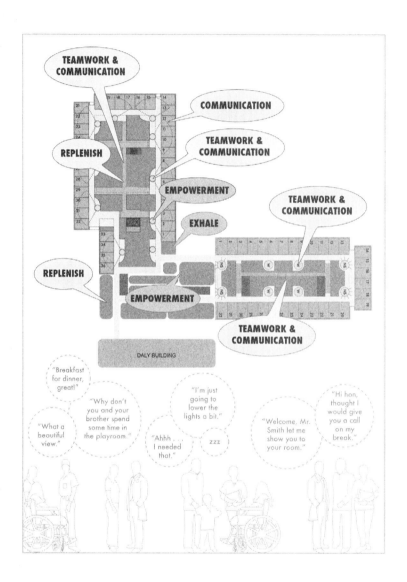

The schematic phase of the design process is where the project is defined. Defining a design intervention according to its outcome is the essence of the data collection phase of evidence-based design. The synthesis of all of the collected information is an art (See Figure 1.19.) but once the project's wisdom is articulated into a map it makes the design team's job easier. Hence the importance of mapping exercises. (See Figures 3.16 and 3.17.)

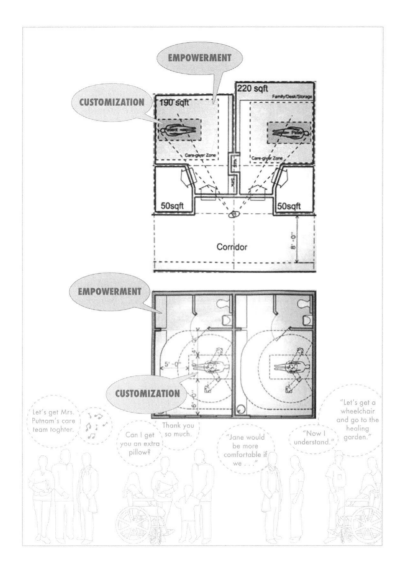

Figure 3.17
Baystate Health's proj-
ect driver's map for new
patient room studies.
*Steffian Bradley
Architects/CAMA, Inc.*

Mapping is about articulating project wisdom within a plan that is aligned with the project vision. It is less about *how* to design and more about *why* to design. It speaks to the behaviors of all of those who will experience the building through their work or process of healing. It has to be patient-centered, family-focused, and staff-supportive. A map reveals clues to new or informed design solutions. (See Figures 3.19 through 3.23.) It is from here that a project's designs can be developed further with the intended outcomes clearly articulated.

Patient-Care Delivery Model

IDEO, DePaul Health Center for SSM Health Care

SSM Health Care approached IDEO with a vision to develop a new patient-care model at the DePaul Health Center that will ultimately provide the foundation for improved services. Realizing that hospital services influence the well-being and care of people, DePaul aspired to provide innovation for a comfortable patient experience. To achieve this, IDEO explored the hospital's space usage, technology, services, and staffing and then developed design concepts for a new patient-care delivery system.

IDEO worked onsite at DePaul's facility to fully research the opportunities for innovation. By brainstorming, observing, interviewing, and actually living as a DePaul patient, IDEO visually "mapped" the patient-journey process. The map documented DePaul's procedures from patient check-in to recuperation. Visualizing the journey helped IDEO identify current challenges, such as moments of confusion, and helped DePaul recognize that these moments were "translation points" where new designs could have significant impact. IDEO created 3-D blueprints that illustrated solutions for new systems, technologies, and space implemented within the existing DePaul environment. (See Figure 3.18.)

IDEO provided DePaul with a framework to create its new patient-care delivery model and developed concepts to support the new model. In addition, IDEO worked closely with a cross-functional team from DePaul to prototype and begin testing some of the design solutions. By learning the basic steps of process innovation and receiving a rough implementation plan from IDEO, DePaul can now further refine and actualize the design concepts. By employing multiple, small-scale innovations, DePaul can deliver improved patient-care delivery services.

Establishing a Research Agenda

At some point the decision will be made as to whether or not a project will measure its outcomes. Not all projects qualify for research, but if they do there are several questions to ask before making that decision.

Figure 3.18
DePaul Health Center
map of the patient jour-
ney process. It maps
the journey from check-
in to discharge identify-
ing project drivers.
© IDEO.

ARRIVAL EXPERIENCE
BLUR INSIDE/OUTSIDE
Exterior landscape and architecture will connect
through to the interior.
Conscious of impairment/age: need to graciously
accept the failure to negotiate a large facility.
Benches and wheelchairs available at entries.

Figure 3.19
Dublin Methodist
Hospital (Pebble Project)
project driver for the
arrival experience.
*Karlsberger Architects/
Big Red Rooster/
CAMA, Inc.*

ADMISSION
A rover/greeter will acknowledge arrival and check
status for admission.
Perches will be available as a home base.

If further processing is necessary, patient will be invited
to a **private area** where admission will be processed
electronically.

From there the patient is **escorted or directed** to the
next destination. This will be complete with the
necessary tools and/or an alert to my next greeter as in
"The Ritz Handoff."

Figure 3.20
Dublin Methodist
Hospital (Pebble Project)
project driver for the
admission experience.
*Karlsberger Architects/
Big Red Rooster/
CAMA, Inc.*

Figure 3.21
Dublin Methodist
Hospital (Pebble Project)
project driver for the
emergency experience.
*Karlsberger Architects/
Big Red Rooster/
CAMA, Inc.*

EMERGENCY EXPERIENCE

Me

An emergency experience is "all about me."
I am sick, injured, and I want care now! When I
arrive I need a **point of embrace**. There
needs to be an **immediacy** to that greeting. I need
communication about what's next. Security
is transparent!

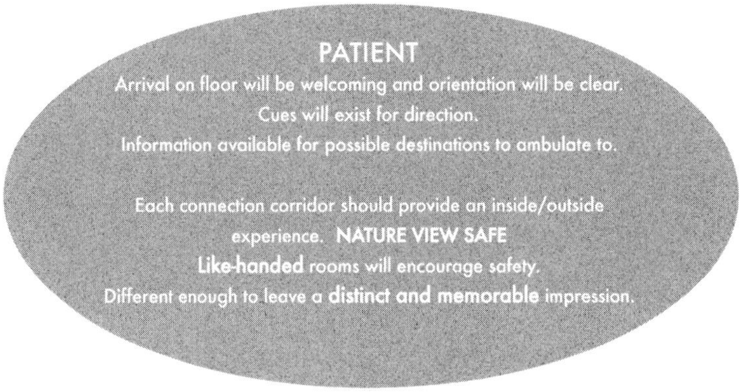

Figure 3.22
Dublin Methodist
Hospital (Pebble Project)
project driver for the
patient experience.
*Karlsberger Architects/
Big Red Rooster/
CAMA, Inc.*

PATIENT
Arrival on floor will be welcoming and orientation will be clear.
Cues will exist for direction.
Information available for possible destinations to ambulate to.

Each connection corridor should provide an inside/outside
experience. **NATURE VIEW SAFE**
Like-handed rooms will encourage safety.
Different enough to leave a **distinct and memorable** impression.

Figure 3.23
Dublin Methodist
Hospital (Pebble Project)
project driver for the
staff experience.
*Karlsberger Architects/
Big Red Rooster/
CAMA, Inc.*

STAFF
Operating in a frenetic environment,
they need to **exhale.**
Provide a 10-minute spa, a place to
replenish without distraction.

1. Is the project aiming for improved clinical, organizational, or economic outcomes?
2. Will the testing of these outcomes contribute to the larger body of knowledge within the healthcare industry?
3. Is the institution already measuring these potential outcomes? If not, is a qualified researcher available to work on the project?
4. Is there adequate baseline data?
5. Are there resources to follow through with a valid study?
6. Is there interest in publishing?

If the answer is yes to any of the above questions, then it would be wise to explore the research topics the project presents. At this stage do not narrow the focus, but know that your baselines are in place. Once mapping exercises or subsequent schematic drawings are complete then a research agenda can be explored. It is now when a true researcher can evaluate the potential for building on an existing body of knowledge or launch a new innovation. All collected data is looked at to see if the baseline is clear. An analysis of your literature search places you in the proper strata of contribution to the industry. This discussion will push an institution to see if the supporting culture and organizational operations can support or need to be modified to support a new concept. An investigation of similar business cases will identify the return on the investment of the design solution. More will be revealed on the financial returns of an evidence-based project in Chapter 5.

Move the Team to New Insights

It is here when the push and pull occurs. By engaging a researcher you create new insights for the project but also for the industry as a whole. It is useful to write a preliminary research proposal. The following essay shows the thought process used by Craig Zimring, PhD of the Georgia Institute of Technology in determining research possibilities for the Dublin Methodist Hospital just after schematic design was completed.

"More than a set of skills, research is a way of thinking and examining critically the various aspects of your day-to-day professional work; understanding and formulating guiding principles that govern a particular procedure, and developing and testing new theories for the enhancement of your practice."[13]

—Ranjit Kumar

OhioHealth Dublin Hospital Preliminary Research Ideas
Preliminary Report
Draft for review and discussion: June 26, 2005, Craig Zimring, PhD,
Professor of Architecture, Georgia Institute of Technology

Overview

This is a summary of research ideas that resulted from a meeting on June 24, 2005 with OhioHealth Dublin Hospital president Cheryl Herbert and the design team from Karlsberger architects and CAMA, Inc. The team seeks to rethink design, and how design can facilitate culture and work process change to make the hospital much safer and more supportive of positive experiences by patients, family, and staff. They seek to create a research program that will thoroughly evaluate the project and will make a substantial contribution to healthcare design. They are also committed to The Center for Health Design and the Pebble process and are eager to contribute to those as well.

The team evolved five packages that seemed to reflect the team's goals, and I have proposed a sixth, after looking at the Big Red Rooster report on culture.

I have devoted some space to suggesting principles for the research program that might apply to Pebbles more generally. Also, these ideas will need to be simplified and focused. It is more than a brainstorm list but far short of a plan. In the spirit of full disclosure it also includes some specific comments that reflect my own research interests and those of my colleagues.

Background

OhioHealth is developing a new general hospital in Dublin, Ohio, a rapidly growing suburb of Columbus. This will be the first completely new hospital in central Ohio in over 20 years. The first phase, scheduled to open in fall 2007, will include 94 beds with the expectation that it will eventually grow to 200 to 300 beds. The first phase includes some 290,000 gross square feet, including shelf space.

A visionary and values-oriented president, Cheryl Herbert, who is pushing her design team to "Run until apprehended," drives the project. The consultant team, Karlsberger Architects, CAMA, Inc., and others, have responded by providing an innovative design process and an innovative design that are driven by the focus on values such as:

- Caring for patients medically, spiritually, and emotionally
- Respecting the family of our patients and staff
- Encouraging and promoting education for staff, patients, and community
- Promoting a close-knit team approach to care

These values have led to an ongoing process where internal advisory groups, consultants, and the design team constantly interrogate existing assumptions about work process, culture, and design to question how work process, culture, and design can be rethought to make patients safer and improve the experience of patients and family. This process has led to both refinements of the existing state-of-the-art, such as providing variable acuity rooms with generous natural light and appealing views, and to innovations in healthcare such as providing operable windows and eliminating the traditional admissions area and functions in favor of roving greeters who will provide personal service to patients and visitors.

One of the many impressive aspects of this project is its commitment to objective and unvarnished evaluation and a willingness to share lessons learned both within OhioHealth and with the healthcare industry. The team shares a view that this project can have a role in helping the industry move toward a patient- and family-oriented model that is much safer than that of other new hospitals. After spending a day with the team as part of the Center for Health Design Pebble Program, I am inclined to agree.

The following is a preliminary set of suggestions about establishing a research program. It will need to be refined and further focused.

The Outline of a Research Program

Principles for the Research Program
- Build on the experience of other Pebbles. (See Figure 3.24.) For example, we know that other Pebbles have studied:
  - Infection rate
  - Nurse turnover
  - Transfers
  - Falls
  - Errors
  - Workload index
  - Nurse back injuries
- Extend key research findings
  - Natural light reduces pain, drug use, length of stay
  - Noise levels impact patient and staff stress, patient length of stay, and likeliness to return within three months
  - Interruptions and poor lighting increase medication errors
  - Ample and well-located sinks increase hand-washing compliance
  - Others
- Use national benchmarks and methods where available, such as those listed below, and use common measurement methods, populations, exclusions, etc. However, in each case we will need to ask: Which are most likely to be influenced by design?

- Which are already collected by OhioHealth or can be collected at modest cost?
- Which are of most interest to OhioHealth?
- AHRQ Quality Indicators:
  http://www.qualityindicators.ahrq.gov/downloads/psi/psi_guide_rev3.pdf
- JCAHO Core Quality Measures http://www.jcaho.org/pms/core+measures/
  candidate+core+measure+sets.htm#ICU%20Core%20Measures
- The Leapfrog Group Hospital Quality and Safety Survey
  http://www.leapfroggroup.org/for_hospitals
- National Quality Forum
  http://www.qualityforum.org/txhospmeasBEACHpublicnew.pdf
  http://www.qualityforum.org/
- IHI 100K Lives Campaign
  http://www.ihi.org/IHI/Programs/Campaign/
  - Deploy rapid response teams
  - Deliver reliable, evidence-based care for acute myocardial infarction
  - Prevent adverse drug events (ADEs)
  - Prevent central line infections
  - Prevent surgical site infections
  - Prevent ventilator-associated pneumonia
- Consider both process variables (such as hand-washing compliance) and outcome variables (such as infection rate)
- Provide good measures of environmental variables known to be linked to safety, quality, and experience such as light and noise levels, air quality, etc.

Research Program Packages

On June 24 we discussed a five-part research program, and I am suggesting a sixth (Work Process and Culture): (1) Documentation; (2) Business Case; (3) Safety Case; (4) Patient-and-Family Experience Case; (5) Work Process and Culture; and (6) Risk Reduction.

Documentation

1. Create a strategic plan and timeline that provides a road map and milestones for documentation and for key presentations and publications
2. Document vision and process. While the team is intact and enthusiasm is high I strongly suggest:
   a. Document the key programmatic choices and why they came out the way they did. For example:
      i. What options were considered about room size and layout? What were the final choices in terms of quantitative dimensions as well as type of layout (such as same-handed rooms, outboard bathrooms, etc.)?

    ii. Repeat this process for lobby/entry/coffee house, ICU, pharmacy, family activity areas, etc.

  b. Create a video of key participants, site, events, and key materials (early and revised plans, etc.)

  c. Create a timeline of actual events and decisions; this will fade quickly in people's minds

  d. Gather and archive all materials: interim and final plans, models, programs, etc., and create high-quality, high-resolution professional digital copies

3. Create and disseminate products:

  a. A list or description of the key programmatic drivers and final choices:

    i. Area per bed

    ii. Net-to-gross ratios

    iii. Quantities and proportion of area devoted to different functions, and especially to patients and families

    iv. Patient rooms sizes and other key space-planning drivers

    v. Other drivers that a healthcare facility or consultant might use for initial planning and costing

  b. Provide an article suggesting a new process

  c. Help create a structure for The Center for Health Design's website documenting the Pebbles

Business Case

1. Document all costs and time, and especially any that are over and above traditional costs for a high-quality facility in an affluent suburb:

  a. All costs for consultants or staff time

  b. Construction costs

  c. Maintenance and operations

2. Document financial benefits using measurements from Fable Hospital and others. Dublin has an opportunity to be one of the first real fable hospitals.

  a. Turnover

  b. Falls

  c. Infection

  d. Errors

  e. Transfers

  f. Market share

  g. Philanthropy

  h. Others?

3. Other balanced scorecard (BSC) issues from the OhioHealth BSC. Note: It is worth a discussion to look at this BSC and ask which measures are likely to be affected by design.

Safety Case

There is an opportunity to use Dublin as the first step toward the potential of a 100 Safest Hospitals in the World campaign. Safety here applies to both patients and staff. I suggest several strategies. Some of the aspects of the business case can be reframed as part of the safety case. In the business case, the emphasis is on financial impacts; in the safety case it is focused on safety outcomes.

1. Build on the experience of other Pebbles. (See Figure 3.24.) For example, we know that other Pebbles have studied:
   a. Infection rate
   b. Transfers
   c. Falls
   d. Errors
   e. Nurse back injuries
2. Extend key research findings
   a. Interruptions and poor lighting increase medication errors, especially in the pharmacy
   b. Ample and well-located sinks increase hand-washing compliance
   c. Others
3. Use national benchmarks and methods where available, such as those listed below.
   a. AHRQ Quality Indicators:
      http://www.qualityindicators.ahrq.gov/downloads/psi/psi_guide_rev3.pdf
   b. JCAHO Core Quality Measures http://www.jcaho.org/pms/core+measures/candidate+core+measure+sets.htm#ICU%20Core%20Measures
   c. The Leapfrog Group Hospital Quality and Safety Survey http://www.leapfroggroup.org/for_hospitals
   d. National Quality Forum
      http://www.qualityforum.org/txhospmeasBEACHpublicnew.pdf
      http://www.qualityforum.org/
   e. IHI 100K Lives Campaign http://www.ihi.org/IHI/Programs/Campaign/

Patient and Family Experience Case

Improving the patient and family experience is a key goal of this project, including providing more personalized service, providing engaging and meaningful experience as an alternative to waiting, positive distraction, and giving patients and families more meaningful control and choice for patients.

- Press Ganey scores. (Note: Georgia Tech is working with Emory to link Press Ganey scores to individual environmental characteristics by analyzing scores by room number and location, and this could be extended here.)

- Conduct a space syntax analysis of the circulation system of this hospital in comparison to other benchmark cases;, and test predicted patterns of movement and interaction
- Observe how families spend their time, in comparison with other facilities
- Collect family and patient stories and "critical incidents"
- Have volunteer OSU students attempt to find their way through the hospital, in comparison with other similar-sized facilities
- Measure time spent by staff giving directions
- Create new measures of patient and family centeredness

Work Process and Culture

The Dublin team is working to create a hospital that will be excellent, will have enjoyable and well-functioning teams, will be relaxing and comfortable, and will be healthful. The team sees the hospital design process as a way of evolving the culture and work processes that allow these to occur. Some suggested measures are:

- Press Ganey scores
- Staff support from observation or questionnaire:
  - Staff absenteeism
  - Time spent at the bedside
  - Staff time spent in transfer
  - Staff time spent collecting supplies or other materials
  - Staff stress, gathered using standard questionnaires or catecholamines (a simple swab test of stress hormones)
- Observation of teaming activities
  - Where does teaming go on in Dublin versus comparison hospitals?
  - How much time is spent in team activities?
  - To use Steelcase's terms, what is the information persistence for different kinds of information in Dublin versus others? What kinds of information are present in the environment versus electronically versus in staff's personal records?

Risk Reduction

An innovative facility such as Dublin carries the potential for great benefit but also the risk of failure when attempting new strategies. There are several ways to reduce risk:

- Model the key functional systems and their interactions using simulations and computer modes. Georgia Tech has developed several modeling methods of particular relevance:
  - Modeling mold risk and HVAC (Professor Godfried Augenbroe: Godfried Augenbroe godfried.augenbroe@arch.gatech.edu)

- Modeling the interactions between lighting, HVAC, noise, air quality, and functional systems such as circulation and work flow (Professor Ruchi Choudhary ruchi.choudhary@coa.gatech.edu)
- Make the mock-up evaluation process as formal as possible within time and space constraints, using scripts that include demanding processes and procedures such as transfers, codes, bedside procedures, etc.
- Ask skeptical observers to suggest potential failure scenarios, such as leakage around the operable windows, low census, staff cut-backs, etc. Attempt to anticipate these failures, and put in place an active monitoring system once the project opens with an "environmental rapid response team" with the resources and authority to correct problems.
- Plan on a "quick response survey" 3 to 6 months after occupancy, where staff and patients can report on their experience working and living in the space and plan on some contingency funds to correct any misfires.

This essay gives insight on a number of outcomes impacted by design and worthy of exploration through project research. Dublin Methodist Hospital is a Greenfield hospital that has reinvented many standard healthcare design features by nature of its evidence-based approach to design. The administration is committed to The Center for Health Design's Pebble Project and has launched a number of these research agendae following its opening in January 2008. Watch for published reports as they should emerge at the same time this book is released.

Summary

Most project teams miss this component of evidence-based design to synthesize and carefully map project drivers. It is the basis of a level 1 evidence-based practitioner. It is here where a project benefits from thoughtful insight offering at a critical moment the opportunity to work with an institution on operational or cultural shifts that a new design concept will support. Later in the project it becomes burdensome and may prohibit a great design idea from being accepted. The knowledge gained through the literature search provides some security helping to balance the risk necessary to innovate. The next chapter will explore that exciting phase of the evidence-based design project.

Checklist: Mapping Strategic, Cultural, and Research Goals

1. Positioning a Project Toward Greatness
   - Select the right interdisciplinary team
   - Establish value-driven leadership
     - Strategic focus
     - Executional excellence
     - Control of destiny
     - Trust-based relationships
     - Investment in employee success
     - Acting small
     - Brand cultivation
     - Generosity
   - State a clear project vision
   - Use evidence-based principles
   - Focus on outcomes
2. Project Drivers/Improved Outcomes
   - Document project wisdom
     - Handbook
     - Flight-ready checklist
   - Identify project drivers
   - Review against guiding principles
   - Conduct additional literature searches
   - List possible adjustments to organizational culture or operational protocols
3. The Art of Mapping a Vision
   - Create a retreat for mapping project drivers
   - Scenario plan for all areas within a plan
   - Provide inspiration
   - Synthesize all project drivers into one big idea or project vision
   - Articulate by mapping project drivers on a plan
4. Establishing a Research Agenda
   - Determine if a research project exists
   - Identify areas of measurement
   - Note current areas of measurement
   - Assess baseline data
   - Identify resources for valid studies
   - Identify publishing opportunities
   - Benchmark area of study
   - Review similar business cases
   - Write a preliminary proposal

Endnotes

1. Collins, J. Good to Great, HarperCollins Publishers, 2001; p. 1.
2. Collins, p. 13.
3. Berry, L. Discovering the Soul of Service, The Free Press, 1999; p. 16.
4. USA Today, Service with a Style, January 25, 2008, 2D.
5. IOM, Keeping Patients Safe, Transforming the Work Environment for Nurses, 2004.
6. IHI Innovation Series, Transforming Care at the Bedside, 2004.
7. Center for Health Design & Picker Institute, Consumer Perceptions of the Healthcare Environment: An Investigation to Determine What Matters, 1998.
8. Janecek, J. Toward More Time at the Bedside, Johns Hopkins Nursing Magazine, Spring 2003; Vol. 1, No. 1.
9. American Society of Interior Designers, Productive Workplaces: How Design Impacts Productivity: Expert Insights, ASID, 1998.
10. Komiske, B. Designing the World's Best Children's Hospitals, Images Publishing, 2000.
11. Jaworski, J. Synchronicity, The Inner Path of Leadership, Berrett-Koehler Publishers, 1998; p. 8.
12. Riedelsheimer, T. Andy Goldsworthy's Rivers and Tides, 2001.
13. Kumar, R. Research Methodology, A Step-By-Step Guide for Beginners, Sage Publications: 2005; p. 2.

Chapter 4
Step 3: Hypothesize Outcomes, Innovate, and Implement Translational Design

"New discoveries in science…will continue to create a thousand new frontiers for those who still would adventure." —Herbert Hoover

In step three, the real reason for evidence-based design unfolds. Without the proper foundation, innovation is just a good guess. Design professionals have been easily trained to use an intuitive approach. That intuition is based on an internal database of successes and failures. In an evidence-based approach, innovation is based on an evolving database of many others' successes and failures. Although all risk is not mitigated, it is minimized.

This is also the most creative step in that new concepts evolve from the critical thinking that takes place in synthesizing the collected data. The hardest part is to hypothesize the desired outcome. A safety net exists in the ability to test before the actual project is completed through the use of mock-ups or early renovation projects. It is here where hypothesized outcomes can be measured and design ideas translated into a final project solution.

Also in this chapter, experts who have conducted such studies and have adjusted designs for more favorable outcomes offer insights on their completed work.

To design is to adventure! The charge of the designer is to answer a need, solve a problem, and improve the status quo. In order to do so one must investigate the need, clearly state the problem, articulate a desired outcome, possibly implement prototypes, and be accountable through completion. Some solutions are tried and true and others are innovative. As design problems are approached in an evidence-based way one must be clear that the desired outcome is articulated in measurable terms. As noted in the last component of the evidence-based design process, engaging a researcher early in the process helps to formulate appropriate questions. Let's explore the following four parts of this phase of an evidence-based project:

Figure 4.1
Manus Island tree snails.
Picture by Henry Domke,
www.henrydomke.com.

1. Hypothesize Outcomes
2. Design for Improvement: Dare to Innovate
3. Build Mock-Ups: Translational Design
4. Share the Process

Hypothesize Outcomes

Hypothesizing an outcome is not necessarily the sole property of a research project. It is what designers do every time a design decision is made. In a conventional design process a design team anticipates that all of its pre-design research and inherent base of knowledge and experience will be adequate in solving for a posed dilemma. A level 1 evidence-based designer will embellish a baseline with a more rigorous level of investigation adding critical thinking to conventional practice after evaluating peer-reviewed studies. At level 2, the stakes go up; one must hypothesize the outcome of intended design interventions to be followed by measurement of the outcomes where an assumption may be proven or not.

What is a design hypothesis? Where and when does one hypothesize within the context of a design research project?

By hypothesizing or stating a design intention (Geboy), an interdisciplinary team is proposing that the interpretation of project wisdom or all data collected—both internal and external—will:

1. Inspire the team to an "aha" moment creating a *clear* project vision
2. Identify the *right* project drivers
3. Spark the inspiration for a *measurable* design intervention (tried and true or truly innovative)
4. Support the *positive* behavior or culture of the intended user in a building that is three to four years out for the lifecycle of the design

Risky business!

Using Ranjit Kumar's logic an evidence-based design team will hypothesize in order to bring the following to a design research project:

- Clarity, from project wisdom
- Specificity, from project drivers
- Focus, from design intention

That said, the formation of a "design intention" (Geboy) or "research hypothesis" sets a research project in motion. Like the evidence-based design Litmus Ring (see Figure 1.5), a hypothesis allows a team to question a design intervention's purpose and to re-adjust its course as needed. The process of critical thinking may reveal additional thoughts that require additional inquiry, hence the iterative process referred to in the definition of evidence-based design. Here the articulation of your design intervention will distinguish itself by either having a known link with a documented outcome or having to innovate or improve a behavior

Keyword: Design Hypothesis

A design hypothesis states the direct relationship between a design intervention and a desired outcome used as a basis for further exploration and measurement.

A hypothesis is a tentative assumption made in order to draw out and test its logical or empirical consequences.[1] *Merriam Webster*

"Hypotheses, though important are not essential for a study... Hypotheses are important for bringing clarity, specificity and focus to a research study. A hypothesis is a speculative statement that is subject to verification through a research study."[2] Ranjit Kumar

"Semantics are important to the process of moving from research to design hypotheses, too. Although most designers are familiar with the scientific notion of hypothesis, my preference is to put the hypothesis concept into design context—more design than science. That's why I prefer the terms proposition, or even better design intention."[3] Lyn Geboy, Kahler Slater

Figure 4.2
Clarian Health—Riley
Hospital for Children
balcony rail details that
include hypothesized
parent-proof height,
child-like distractions,
and maintenance-free
materials.
Michael O'Callahan photography, KMD/CAMA, Inc.

Design Hypothesis: Safe, Distracting, Maintenance-Free Balcony Rail Design

An example of how a hypothesized outcome drove a design intervention came from an interdisciplinary team effort at Riley Children's Hospital in Indianapolis. The architectural plan had a multistory entry that required a balcony rail. In the gathering of internal intelligence there was tremendous concern from the clinical staff about children being at risk of a fall due to the actions of foolish parents trying to balance their child on that rail. Code requirements did not seem to satisfy the team and a literature search came up empty, so the wisdom that came from the internal analysis focused the design intention. The design hypothesis called for a rail that engaged a child at their level, that was safe, easily cleanable, and would discourage parents from setting their child on the top of the rail. A simulated mock-up was built

to test the hypothesis. (See Figure 4.16.) A formal study did not take place, but no incidents of injury have been reported and children seem to enjoy its geometry. (See Figure 4.2.)

The design intervention was to set the height and angle of the rail so as to discourage parents from balancing a child on its cap. In addition the supports had to engage children and allow them to peer through the opening in the rails, but disguise fingerprints on the glass. The design is self-explanatory with an affordable diachroic glass insert, which created an interactive color-changing diversion as children passed reinforced the theme of movement, a constant in this multispecialty clinic. (See Figures 4.3 and 4.4.)

Figures 4.3 and 4.4 Clarian Health—Riley Hospital for Children illustrating child engagement and human-scale safety considerations. *Michael O'Callahan photography, KMD/CAMA, Inc.*

through speculation in uncharted waters. How will you know what to hypothesize? I asked that of Nick Watkins, PhD.

Essay 4-1
Comprehensive Healthcare Requires Comprehensive Evidence-Based Design Research

Nicholas Jay Watkins, PhD, Director of Research, Cannon Design
Julie Lawless, PhD student, University of Kansas, School of Architecture

Consider the Context

If evidence-based design (EBD) research shoulders its way onto your desk, it is because forces in healthcare are challenging entire infrastructures to boost quality across all aspects of healthcare delivery. In an ongoing effort to reward quality over quantity, the Centers for Medicare & Medicaid Services (CMS) will reimburse hospitals based on a variety of performance criteria including patient-centered care, adverse events, cost efficiency, and infection rates.[4] Simply put, hospitals that can validate their performance through solid research will earn money.

Other forces prompting a growth in evidence-based research in all aspects of health-care delivery include but are not limited to:

- Emerging Types of Healthcare Settings
- A Consumer-Driven Market
- Aging Consumers
- Advances in Information Technology
- Translational or "Bench-to-Bed" Research
- The Nursing Shortage Crisis

The above forces entrench EBD research in a larger context than most of us think when reading a study of the therapeutic benefits of a window view of nature (Ulrich) or patients' perceptions of waiting rooms (Becker).

The healthcare industry needs a panoramic lens by which to frame and capture the wide context of its increasingly comprehensive services and criteria. For healthcare designers, the lens has to be comprehensive enough to frame a specific project within the scope of the client's operations and lifecycle costs. Simultaneously, the lens should frame external forces like CMS reimbursement requirements. For example, a designer might ask an EBD researcher how to demonstrate to a client that a configuration of centralized and decentralized nursing stations contributes over the long-term to staff retention and fewer medical errors. Another question might be whether a rural or urban site would allow for improved patient accessibility, additional patients for clinical trials, and increased opportunities for psychiatric patients' integration back into the community.

Comprehensive Facility Evaluation: It Can Be Done

Evidence-based design research that accompanies programming and schematic design offers a panoramic lens by which to assess EBD's contribution to an organization's performance. EBD researchers can evaluate a facility's design based on a variety of criteria stipulated by the client and government agencies. Challenges to the development of such evidence-based design research include the tension between designers' and researchers' expectations for EBD research, designers' and researchers' differing standards for EBD research, and the gaps in communication among patients, staff, administrators, and designers. A comprehensive facility evaluation conducted at pre- and post-occupancy resolves these challenges.[5] To illustrate the benefits of comprehensive facility evaluation (CFE), we will turn to a recent example from research of comprehensive cancer centers.

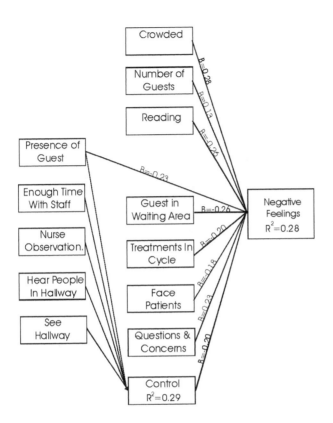

Figure 4.5
Path-analytic model of patients' responses from one chemotherapy treatment area. Contrary to the researcher's, clients', and designers' expectations, the more often chemotherapy patients faced each other during a session, the less negative feelings the patient experienced. The more patients felt they had (1) social support from having a guest present; (2) spent enough time with staff; (3) been observed by nursing staff the entire session; (4) heard people in the hallway the entire session; and (5) seen the hallway the entire session, the more control they felt. Consequently, the patients had fewer negative feelings. Other factors (not pictured) contributed to less control. Since results came from a study of one chemotherapy area, they should not be generalized to other chemotherapy treatment areas.
Image created by Nicholas Watkins.

Case Study: Research of Comprehensive Cancer Centers

Comprehensive cancer centers consolidate the continuum of cancer care from prevention to survivorship into one destination. The National Cancer Institute stipulates that a comprehensive cancer center houses patient services, research (e.g., basic, clinical, population sciences), and engages in community outreach.[6] Patients and scientists benefit from innovative clinical trials and interdisciplinary care teams. Another benefit of specialty hospitals like cancer centers might include higher quality. One study of specialty orthopedic hospitals found a 40 percent lower risk of patients developing post-surgical complications compared to patients in general hospitals.[7]

In an effort to understand how, if, and what design elements contribute to an effective comprehensive cancer care setting, researchers at Cannon Design have undertaken a CFE of multiple comprehensive cancer centers. Findings to date have informed programming and schematic design of future centers. Post-occupancy evaluations will evaluate the

Figure 4.6
Design of a chemother-
apy area informed by
evidence-based design
research. Question-
naires, interviews, and
focus groups were used
to design a chemother-
apy area with a family-
friendly waiting area.
Sliding screens afford
patients privacy when
desired.
*Illustration by Cannon
Design.*

performance of these centers according to National Cancer Institute and other industry criteria. Topics of interest have included:

- The experiences of patients including those differing by age, ethnicity, stage of cancer, diagnosis, treatment pathways, number of guests, and reason for choosing the cancer center.
- The impact of an interdisciplinary team of staff and various treatment spaces (e.g., radiation oncology, chemotherapy area) on workflow, patient outcome, and adverse events.

A CFE can measure the direct and indirect impact of a facility's design and operations on a variety of outcomes. For a specific example, I will illustrate the use of CFE to evaluate the responses of patients receiving treatment in the chemotherapy treatment area of a comprehensive cancer care center. (See Figure 4.5.)

A key finding from a study of one client's chemotherapy treatment area included the importance of a "socio-petal" chemotherapy treatment area that reinforces face-to-face interactions among patients who share rooms and staff.* Performed during the programming of a cancer center, this research and testimonies from patients revealed that patients received social support from or enjoyed the mere presence of other patients when sharing a chemotherapy room or bay. Thus, the designers and the client saw the importance of including communal chemotherapy rooms or bays. Additional statistical analyses revealed how many patients should belong to a bay or room. Surprisingly, the availability of a window view and direct exposure to daylight did not have a direct impact on patients' negative feelings. Additional analyses will explore how patients differ in their chemotherapy experiences by ethnicity, diagnosis, and number of prior visits. (See Figure 4.6.)

Summary

Evidence-based design research can measure relationships among several aspects of healthcare. There are several forces that contribute to the growth of EBD research. A comprehensive facility evaluation approach can capture the wide scope of the forces in one image. Research of a client's chemotherapy treatment area demonstrated how a CFE approach can inform programming and schematic design.

* Exploratory factor analysis of the patients' responses to the State-Trait Anxiety Inventory revealed that several items loaded strongly onto one factor called "Negative Feelings." Items included but were not limited to anxiety, nervousness, worry, confusion, and strain.

Timing is everything. Doing investigative work and mapping research goals early in a project allows for a hypothesis to be articulated as design begins. (See Table 1.1.) This clearly is a critical stage in the development of an evidence-based project. Truth be known, most project teams don't begin to discuss research agendae until after design development. The design development phase will change as more teams become comfortable with the process. Conducting external investigations (from literature searches) seems to fit comfortably into the conventional design process but given the pressure of speed that most projects are operating under, even the firms sworn to the evidence-based process are slipping into the familiar practices. Unless a team is prepared to redesign after design development is complete, it is important to incorporate the first steps of evidence-based design, having hypotheses in place at the end of schematic. By doing so early in the process:

1. A researcher can be engaged to recommend ways to articulate a hypothesis that leads to a clean study.
2. A baseline of data can be collected from within the client organization to support a post-occupancy study.
3. The need for additional information about an existing body of knowledge can be articulated.
4. Additional members can be added to the interdisciplinary team if needed, e.g., an acoustician to develop a baseline of noise for a hypothesis that will require measurement of noise levels in the new space.
5. A determination can be made to prove a known outcome or venture toward a solution that is truly innovative.

Figure 4.7
A nurse station built around the paper chart, at Yale–New Haven Shoreline Medical Center. As electronic medical records emerge, more distributed stations will evolve like the perch (see Figure 3.13).
Salvatore Associates Architect of Record/CJ Allen Photography/CAMA, Inc.

The next chapter will discuss in greater detail the role of the researcher within the interdisciplinary team.

Design for Improvement: Dare to Innovate

So much changes in the time it takes to design and build a healthcare facility that it is almost impossible to predict what might be relevant for a project that will not be occupied for many years. By nature of this time lapse a design team must think futuristically, for at the risk of building a better old building they must innovate. It is in the evidence-based process that innovation can be grounded in the security of an informed process where a certain amount of rigor replaces an educated sense.

Design innovation is a term often associated with industrial design or the design of machinery or objects. Architects and designers design new concepts into buildings all of the time, but these new concepts morph at such a slow pace that it is impossible to notice them as being different. How many times have you had an "aha" moment thinking it was truly an original idea and some time later you notice your great original idea is incorporated into another team's project? We are all being influenced by the same factors and we are all wired to respond similarly. As they say, "great minds think alike." Actually, we are all being primed by the same external influences. It seems as new products come to market they change lifestyles and behaviors. This leads to new and different practices of operation for routine tasks, e.g., stopping at AAA to get a Trip Tik™ is no longer necessary if you have access to a GPS. The new product then needs a new environment in which to operate. Automotive dashboards change; map pockets disappear. (See Figure 4.7.) The fields of architecture and interior design need to have rapid influence on product development. As evidence-based

Technological Influences Toward Changes in Workflow

When facing a new user group that looks like they have never participated in a design charrette, I ask a provocative question which changes their reference point from designing a better old solution to designing a new evidence-based innovation.

I simply ask how many have ever been involved in the renovation or new construction of a kitchen. Ninety percent of them will typically raise their hands. I then state the evidence-based intelligence about how to successfully design an operational kitchen. Evidence shows that there is a direct relationship between the positioning of the sink, refrigerator, and stovetop in the meal preparation area and one's efficiency.[viii] If a kitchen is truly about cooking, and not for show, then this triangle is a very important tool in the successful design of the space. In the old paradigm the traditional refrigerator, or what I call the "big box," incorporates all cold storage, crispers, icemakers, and freezer space. The problem is that the refrigerator serves many other functions and by placing it in this meal preparation triangle it interferes with the convenient flow for other activities like easy access from the kitchen table (which in most American homes today is no longer directly in the meal preparation area) for beverages, ice, and condiments, or ease of access to the microwave for

leftovers, etc. Manufacturers have now deconstructed the big box into refrigerated components and drawers creating a more efficient model of cold storage. This allows for the crisper to be directly adjacent to the sink, the beverages and condiments adjacent to the dining table, the leftovers adjacent to the microwave, and the traditional "big box" refrigerator can now be placed in the mudroom or garage for what I call the just-in-case-of-a-snowstorm supply of sustenance. If the business case is to be made on how first costs can be justified for new and expensive equipment, one must look at the value of one's time spent running around the work zone and realize that by deconstructing one piece of equipment a more efficient model emerges offering an incredible return on one's investment, typically called "the business case" (see Chapter 5, Step 4: Measure and Share Outcomes).

This story usually resonates with most in the group and immediately opens up the possibilities for discussions about how new and future technologies may offer an innovative solution to designing their space, creating a different paradigm on how to work effectively and efficiently. It makes the leap from designing a better old building to new and innovative solutions.

practices take hold, new environments for improved human behavior will evolve requiring new products to support changed operational models. The firm IDEO and other industrial design teams operate in that mode of thinking now. Rarely are industrial designers invited to the healthcare interdisciplinary design team. The two are seen as different marketplaces. But should they be? Chapter 7 will address the healthcare industry's need to pull innovation of product into our evidence-based environmental design solutions.

A new conference, "X3," will open in June, 2009. It will address this very phenomenon of how technology drives changes in workflow and hence the design of the built environment. The success in true innovation is to anticipate the technology that will allow the change that evidence-based design drives.

Creativity is needed to drive innovation. Daniel Buros, in his book *Technotrends, How to Use Technology to Go Beyond Your Competition*, offers five keys to unlocking creativity:

1. Observation

   Observe and see what you have not seen before. Spend some time and take a fresh look at familiar objects or tasks.

2. Incubation

   Immerse yourself into a problem, idea, or dream consciously seeking a result. Then back off from deliberate attention in order to allow your thoughts to mix with other elements that are present below the level of consciousness.

3. Intuition

   People who use their intuition draw conclusions based upon what they see as a pattern. The ability to recognize these patterns is directly related to the breadth and depth of their experience. Those who have the greatest exposure to a variety of experiences are better able to discern meaningful patterns.

4. Emotion

   The stronger the emotion the more we generate new creative solutions.

5. Stimulation

   The most gifted creators are constantly exchanging information and ideas with others.[9]

In evidence-based design, observation occurs during "deep dives," incubation occurs while assessing gathered intelligence or "visioning," intuition is used in "mapping" exercises, emotion is expressed in the "vision," and stimulation occurs in "measuring and sharing."

Buros offers ways to use creativity to help us see what might be. He identifies in a book written in 1993 "technologies that exist for products and services not yet on the shelf but available for the innovator who wants to invent the future."[10] It is an interesting approach, looking at the tools now available to invent the next iteration of a more fulfilling life. He goes on to suggest that one should "give your customers the ability (to do what they can't do, but would have wanted to do, if they only knew they could have done it).[11]

Figure 4.8
University Medical Center at Princeton (Pebble Project) takes the like-handed room, incorporates all previous projects' improvements and adds canted geometry, allowing for greater visibility out of the window from the bed.
HOK/RMJM Hillier/CAMA, Inc.

There is a challenge in taking this approach in healthcare. The industry is typically slow to suggest change because of the inherent risks, particularly the unknown costs. Budgets are tight and expenditure for change so infrequent that the guarded answer is to err on the side of certainty. The next chapter will explore "the business case" for the justification of an evidence-based design decision.

The cost issue aside, change generally requires adjustments to the entire Environment of Care (see Chapter 2) which makes innovation complex. As previously noted, the principles of evidence-based design are more likely to encourage innovative solutions. Add critical thinking with the entire interdisciplinary team present and new concepts certainly emerge. New concepts are likely to trigger innovative project drivers. The difference in the noted process is that an innovative project driver may never have been tested so literature searches may not produce helpful results. An innovation, however, like any other design intervention should be hypothesized in measurable terms. These innovations should absolutely be mocked-up and tested before a final installation occurs. For instance, designing a like-handed room in order to reduce medical errors is still in the category of innovation. It has not been measured and reported as of this writing. (See Figure 4.8.) The problem of safety at the bedside has only partially been thought out in terms of the mechanics of what drives human

Keyword: Design Innovation

Design innovation occurs when a burgeoning need is recognized and a successful solution is developed.

error. There is much work that lies ahead to compensate for the few innovations that have occurred in the last eight years. All teams embracing this yet-to-be-proven design intervention should follow the protocols the Institute for Health Improvement (IHI) is recommending in order to find clues for future improved design developments. The design professions have caught up with an industry that has been slow to address change and can now join together to help lead reform.

In his book *The Art of Innovation*, Tom Kelley of IDEO states that their approach to innovation is part golf swing, part secret recipe. The secret formula is actually not formulaic; it is a blend of methodologies, work practices, culture, and infrastructure. In shorthand, IDEO has five steps to their methodology:

1. *Understand* the market, the client, the technology, and the perceived constraints on the problem.
2. *Observe* real people in real-life situations to find out what makes them tick; what confuses them, what they like, what they hate, where they have latent needs not addressed by current products and services.
3. *Visualize* new-to-world concepts and customers who will use them.
4. *Evaluate and refine* the prototypes in a series of quick iterations.
5. *Implement* the new concept for commercialization.[12]

The IDEO methodology, like Buros' keys for creativity, offers insights on how to use evidence-based design for the development of new concepts. One must not just go through the motions but become a student of the merits of adjusting a design process, own its philosophy, and re-educate a profession about the great opportunities that lie ahead.

The Pebble Project has introduced us to a generation of projects whose participants are willing to explore, discover and share a better way to deliver care, in a word—innovate. They all seem to begin with a redefinition of culture. In the work at The Dublin Methodist Hospital, Weill Cornell Ambulatory Care, and many that are following, culture is addressed first. A group from the Massachusetts General Hospital and the Massachusetts General Physicians Organization has emerged to share the hardest questions asked about the delivery of an ambulatory care practice for the future. Without physical space they began their quest with an exploration of an ideal experience for patient and provider. In an interview with Nicola Majchrzack, MPH, and Brad Seamons, AIA, I asked about their journey.

Massachusetts General Ambulatory Care Practice of the Future

The Mass General story is an ideal model for innovation because it is solidly rooted in the efforts of a small committed group. They explained that the current root of the crisis is in the inability to attract physicians to the practice of primary care. This has created a shortage of primary caregivers and as such is a problem that must be solved for their community. Dial back three to four years ago and a core group of all of the right people got together to look

Figure 4.9
Transformation is part of
a natural cycle.

at what a new model of care could look like. This exercise split the group into two factions one termed the "space ship" mindset, or let's blow-up everything we know and start from scratch, and the other the "staircase" mindset or let's take a look at the redefinition of a model one step at a time. This latter group ultimately wore itself down to a small interdisciplinary handful of physicians, nurse practitioners, and administrative and patient advocates. They organized a multiday retreat with IDEO and the following emerged: The retreat developed into a scenario-planning exercise that invented a cast of characters with specific challenges that needed to be overcome. The group brainstormed, developed the care journey, storyboarded the journey, and built a prototype. What emerged were eight major paradigm shifts in the ambulatory care model with implications for the design of a new Environment of Care.

Paradigm shifts:

1. Current focus on sickness would change to a focus on health and life balance
2. Shift from event-based healthcare to continuous healthcare
3. Evolve from static experiences to iterative experiences
4. Less directive communication and more collaboration
5. Move from individual experiences to team-based experiences
6. Instead of patient going to treatment, the treatment would go to the patient
7. From one size fits all to mass customization
8. From obscurity to transparency

"We will design the ambulatory care practice that delivers ideal care in the ideal environment to optimize outcomes for all."[13] (See Figure 4.9.)

The implications for the design of the new Environment of Care include:

1. Design solutions that address a person's lifestyle, family history and experience—not just symptoms
2. Design healing solutions that support patients' needs anytime, anywhere
3. Design solutions that provide the ability to continuously measure and adapt to patients' providers' goals over time
4. Design solutions that allow for dialog among care staff and with patients and their families
5. Design solutions that involve multidisciplinary teams where appropriate
6. Design solutions that consider the patient as the center (instead of medical staff or location)
7. Design solutions that allow for efficiency but also for personalized experiences
8. Design solutions that allow staff and patients to easily see and use necessary information and process at all times.

This project is now beginning to develop its physical manifestation. They will clearly venture down a path others have not been down and should develop an innovative physical model to match their cultural transformation. They are committed to follow an evidence-based methodology of design as they have signed on as a Pebble Project. If you are developing an ambulatory project, watch for their interim reports. As a Pebble Project, they will be generous in sharing knowledge gained.

Innovation through Improving the Experience

In 1998 Joe Pine and Jim Gilmore wrote the book *The Experience Economy*. Their premise is that:

- Companies stage an experience when they engage customers in a memorable way.
- Experiences are events that engage individuals in a personal way.
- To enter the Experience Economy one must first customize services.
- Success relies on picking the right people to play the parts.
- When you customize an experience you change the individual.
- What people really want from an experience is transformation.
- Nothing is more important than the wisdom required to transform customers.[14] (See Figure 4.10.)

Interior designers take note: The work of transforming experiences has not been carefully documented and measured. There is much innovative work to be done in the healthcare arena to transform customers' experiences. Joe Pine is a founder, with Gary Adamson and Mark Scott, of Starizon—an experience design firm—where they recognize how important this transformation is in healthcare.

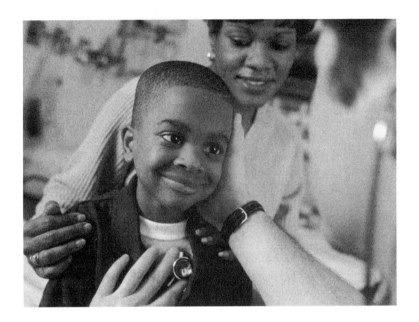

Figure 4.10
"It's all about me!" Memorable experiences that are customized to the individual become transformational.

Each year the Center for Health Design and *Healthcare Design Magazine* along with Starizon present "The Discovery Award" recognizing those companies that are leaders in experience design and offer the best examples for others to follow. In November of 2007, the award was given to Baystate Health's D'Amour Center for Cancer Care in Springfield, Massachusetts. The project was judged on:

1. Harnessing the power of an operational theme
2. Personalizing the experience for each customer
3. Designing on-stage and off-stage areas for employees
4. Casting and rehearsing the employees
5. Instilling the company way through inspiration

Although this project was designed and constructed before the concept of evidence-based design was clearly defined, it re-invented its culture using similar practices and as such has a changed care-delivery model, developed a new architectural model and has documented improved outcomes. It has also become the benchmark for future building within the Baystate Health System which is a strong proponent for an evidence-based approach.

Essay 4-2
Changing the Cancer Treatment Experience

Linda Haggerty, AAHID, Steffian Bradley Architects; Amy Starling, Former Administrative Director, Baystate Health System; Wilson Mertens, MD, Medical Director, Cancer Services, Baystate Health System

Baystate Health System's (BHS) D'Amour Center for Cancer Care is located in Springfield, Massachusetts, and is a three-story, patient-centered oncology facility that has revolutionized the way care is provided to cancer patients in the region. It has 64,000 square feet of space and consolidates the services of the Baystate Regional Cancer Program conveniently under one roof. The facility's service includes advanced imaging, therapeutic and information technologies, and is driven by a model of care that is patient-centered. (See Figure 4.11.)

Prior to board approval, a new administrative team was established with the goal of creating a truly integrated cancer program. Initial steps included focus groups with referring physicians and practices as well as patients past and present, with results presented to cancer program clinicians and administrators. Key causes of dissatisfaction were addressed; processes reviewed; and enhanced supportive care approaches, based on well-evidenced clinical approaches (such as standardized treatment, side-effect prevention, and management) were instituted and made transparent to patients, leading to fewer hospitalizations and an increase in ambulatory cancer care.

Subsequent to board approval, administrators, physicians, support staff, patients, community members, the architect, and the contractor embarked on a planning process that included:

- facility site visits for the purpose of peer input
- definition of current processes, capabilities, and volumes
- identification of the potential for future growth
- investigation of new technologies and treatment paradigms
- patient focus groups and retreats
- evaluation of the appearance of current facilities, including lack of integration, from the patients' point of view
- learning how other industries handle change and defining themselves from a customer experience perspective.

It became clear that Baystate would re-engineer every aspect of interaction with their patients and institute major change.

A series of retreats were scheduled and facilitated by Starizon, an experience consultant. A diverse group whose first task was the development of an identity and theme for the cancer center attended the retreats. Starizon used skits to point out old behaviors, and focused the group on outside market trends and patient expectations.

The retreats discussed all aspects of cancer treatment: the individual's needs versus family needs; surviving cancer, a patient's journey back to health, facing insurmountable odds; physical and psychological struggles; and the bonds that develop between cancer patients and their caregivers. Out of these retreats emerged a re-engineering process, working from the bottom up and top down. It also became apparent that change would be difficult but welcome. Included in the process was the development of a theme:

> "Partners on your journey to well-being."

In order to create the experience and execute the desired ambiance, the treatment process was separated into what the patient sees and what isn't necessary for them see. In each phase of treatment there would be "off stage" events and "on stage" events.

After the first retreat and initial brainstorming, a core group of individuals broke into subteams to thoroughly examine the patient path and staff workflow. Existing processes

Figure 4.11
The Discovery Award Winner 2007: Baystate Health System's D'Amour Center for Cancer Care.
Steffian Bradley Architects.
© Robert Benson.

were mapped until an improved flow was envisioned prior to schematic design commencing. (See Figure 4.12.)

Teams were created to design the facility's functional areas; SBA architects and interior designers attended these meetings and engaged in a dynamic process that incorporated concepts developed at the patient provider level. A committee tasked with overall design integration, to ensure that functional level requests were appropriate in terms of budget, technology support, and compliance with the theme, reviewed these. Each area of facility design was presented to patients and or cancer patient advocates for validation and additional suggestions. (See Figures 4.13 and 4.14.)

Tandem to this effort a small group toured other cancer treatment facilities to obtain important feedback and investigate alternative patient care approaches.

Indirect lighting, in the form of light coves and dropped ceiling planes, highlight areas of patient and staff interaction. Natural and indirect lighting work together to articulate the patient's way to and from the living room and into the treatment space. In corridors, borrowed light from translucent glass walls; curved compact fluorescent slots; and artistic, backlit glass panels provide dramatic illumination. Effective lighting and short travel distances eliminate the need for most conventional signage. In addition, daylight utilization, motion and light sensors, and a programmable digital lighting system increase the center's energy efficiency. (See Figure 4.15.)

As evidence of success the center met five-year projections within only five months of opening, and a fourth linear accelerator, originally intended for future installation, was brought online simultaneously with the rest of the project to meet demand. The center has attracted patients throughout New England because of their focus on patient-centered care, advanced treatment technology, and quality staff. The improvements in workflow and communication allow staff to work more efficiently and patients are saved the trouble of multiple visits. Staff turnover is 2 percent and staff report high levels of satisfaction with the efficiency of their work environments.

Most important, though, are the results of patient satisfaction surveys: prior to the opening of the facility, Baystate's cancer program's key patient satisfaction metric (percentage of patients rating overall care "excellent") ranged between the 75th and 85th percentile of ambulatory facilities. Since the opening, the program has consistently been rated above the 90th percentile, with four consecutive quarters at the 100th percentile.

Future Opportunities for Innovation

It is amazing how quickly an innovation in one region can impact projects nationwide as well as globally. Projects are being marketed across community borders and many administrators are asking for the latest innovation because it was published in a professional journal or even

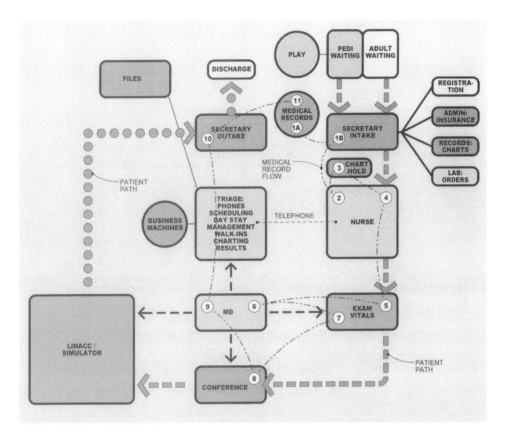

Figure 4.12
To begin planning, an oversight group and subcommittees were formed to address specific patient areas. There was a strong tendency to develop forums along departmental lines which were defined by physician specialty. However, patient therapy requires an integrated approach and in order to remain in accord with our theme, functionality from the patient perspective was the primary determinant of committee structure and membership.
The D'Amour Center for Cancer Care— © Steffian Bradley Architects.

the *Wall Street Journal.* As families and clinicians relocate from these innovative providers their baseline of expectation has been raised and the demand grows exponentially. When they show up in your focus groups they will offer insights not presented before and, if evidence-based, then the margin of risk for innovation closes while the opportunity for improving the services within healthcare is elevated. Where are we at the time of this writing? The best barometer is to watch the Ulrich/Zimring scorecards. (See Figures 2.3 through 2.6.) Researchers have found that those studies with four or five stars have enough evidence linking environmental factors with an outcome and are highly recommended for use in designs. Those with three stars, however, have relatively fewer studies and more measurement is needed; and those with two or fewer stars indicate that research is highly encouraged. It is here where innovation is likely to occur. It is recommended that if you would like to be able to publish in an area that will draw attention to your project then be sure to have at least one of these deficient areas show up in your research agenda. Based upon the 2004 study of factors with three stars or less, the following opportunities exist:

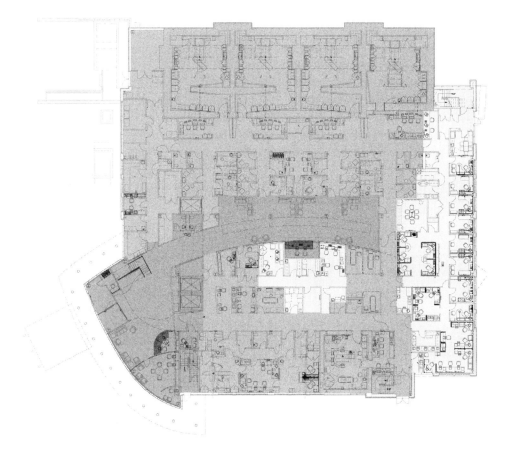

Figure 4.13
First floor, noting on-
stage patient experi-
ence and off-stage staff
zone.
*The D'Amour Center for
Cancer Care. © Steffian
Bradley Architects.*

Reduce Stress, Improve Quality of Life and Healing for Patients and Families
• Reduce depression
• Improve circadian rhythms
• Reduce pain (intake of pain drugs and reported pain)
• Reduce helplessness and empower patients and families
• Provide positive distractions

Reduce Staff Stress/Fatigue, Increase Effectiveness in Delivering Care
• Improve medication processing and delivery times
• Improve workplace, job satisfaction
• Reduce turnover
• Reduce fatigue
• Work effectiveness; patient care time per shift
• Improve satisfaction

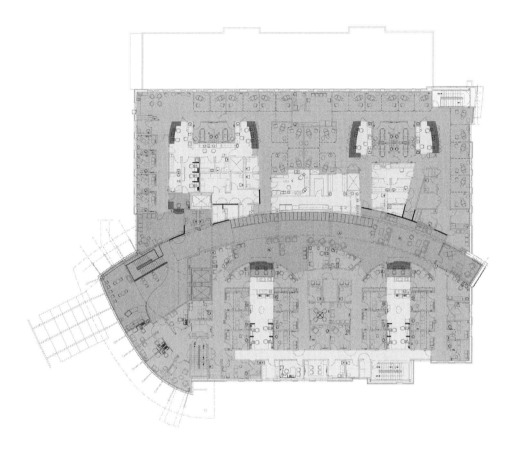

Figure 4.14
Second floor, features multi-disciplinary clinical team space directly from exam rooms, central family area, and infusion suite with private and group spaces.
The D'Amour Center for Cancer Care. © Steffian Bradley Architects.

Improve Patient Safety and Quality of Care
• Reduce medication errors
• Reduce patient falls
• Improve quality of communication (patient to staff)
• Improve quality of communication (staff to staff)
• Improve quality of communication (staff to patient)
• Improve quality of communication (patient to family)
• Increase hand-washing compliance by staff
• Improve confidentiality of patient information

Improve Overall Healthcare Quality and Reduce Costs
• Reduce length of patient stay
• Reduce drugs (see Patient Safety)
• Re-hospitalization or readmission rates
• Staff work effectiveness; patient care time per shift
• Patient satisfaction with staff quality

Figure 4.15
Daylighting used thera-
peutically, experien-
tially, and sustainably.
*The D'Amour Center for
Cancer Care. Steffian
Bradley Architects, ©
Robert Benson.*

There is much yet to be proven. Think tanks need to be formed around each of these topics so that the billions of dollars being spent on construction today are spent wisely and
improve the quality of care for decades to come. Watch for the 2008 scorecards and renew
this list, assign it to project teams, and create incentives to pay attention to these solutions.
The opportunity to innovate on projects just beginning is exciting!

HAND WASHING

Figure C-4
Access to hand-washing sink is hypothesized to decrease the spread of infection. Studies are not yet complete.
Yale–New Haven Hospital Children's Hospital Emergency Department.
© 2008 C.J. Allen. Salvatore Associates/CAMA, Inc.

Figure C-5
Exam room sink on a 45-degree angle is hypothesized to improve hand-washing compliance thus reducing the spread of infection while fostering better staff-to-family communications. Studies are not yet complete.
Yale–New Haven Hospital Children's Hospital Emergency Department.
© 2008 C.J. Allen. Salvatore Associates/CAMA, Inc.

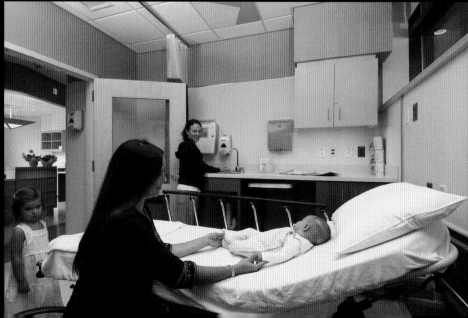

REDUCTION OF FALLS

Figure C-6
The 1999 landmark Ann Hendrich study proved that the relationship between the bed and the bathroom had a direct impact on the reduction of falls. A double leaf door was installed to increase the size of the opening so two could pass through comfortably and safely. Study indicated a 75 percent reduction of falls.
Clarian Health Cardiac Comprehensive Critical Care Unit at Methodist Hospital (Pebble Project) Dan Francis, Mardan Photography, BSA LifeStructures/Maregatti.

Figure C-7
Simulated mock-up room that illustrates the next level of innovation to the private room based upon critical evidence-based thinking that places the bathroom on the patient's headwall with an accessible handrail hypothesizing further reduction in falls. The mock-up supported the placement of the bathroom on the headwall but disputed the double leaf door at this location. Studies are in progress.
OhioHealth Dublin Methodist Hospital (Pebble Project) Jason Meyer/Feinknopf.Karlsberger/CAMA, Inc.

KE-HANDED
OOMS

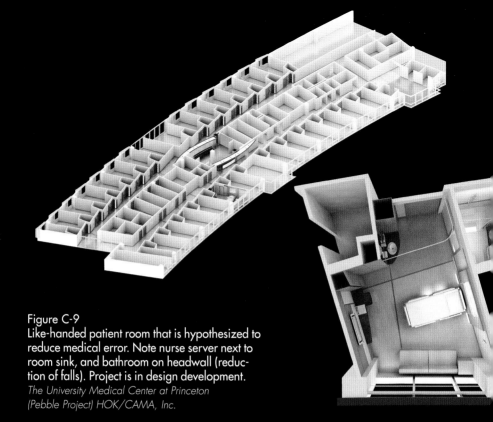

igure C-8
esign of a like-
anded room nursing
nit that has informed
ew geometries creat-
g the canted room
fering better views
ward nature hypoth-
izing a shorter
ngth of stay from the
oger Ulrich landmark
udy.   Possibility
xists to study the
pact of the nurse
rver on the number
 distributed nurse
ations currently at a1
 12 ratio, compared
 the standard
erch" at 1 to 4.
oject is in design
evelopment.
e University Medical
enter at Princeton
ebble Project),
OK/CAMA, Inc.

Figure C-9
Like-handed patient room that is hypothesized to
reduce medical error. Note nurse server next to
room sink, and bathroom on headwall (reduction of falls). Project is in design development.
The University Medical Center at Princeton
(Pebble Project) HOK/CAMA, Inc.

igure C-10
ivate patient room
omotes patient-cen-
red privacy; room-
g-in promotes con-
ection to family;
eadwall and footwall
ectronics provide
stomization; like-
andedness promotes
fety; hand-washing
nd clinical zone at
e door reduces
read of infection and
omotes timely and
ficient care. A live
ock-up will be
searched for a trans-
ional confirmation of
e plan's effectiveness.
e project is in design
evelopment.

STAFF EFFICIENCY

Figure C-11
Perch/pod distributed care stations hypothesizes more efficient delivery of care creating more primary care time for nursing at the bedside, also offering quick touchdown spaces or pods for ancillary staff. Note light wells in the center of unit. Studies not yet complete.
Courtesy of OhioHealth Dublin Methodist Hospital (Pebble Project), © 2008 photography by Brad Feinknopf.
Karlsberger/CAMA, Inc.

Figure C-12 *(far left)*
Decentralized nursing offering direct observation into two rooms at once—commonly used in intensive care units with private perch across hall.
American Family Children's Hospital at the University of Wisconsin Hospital and Clinics. © Ballogg Photography Inc., Chicago. HDR.

Figure C-13 *(left)*
Nurse servers located immediately outside patient rooms provide convenient access to supplies for nurses while roll-out writing surfaces allow for instant charting. More investigation is needed about this method of materials management's contribution to nursing efficiency.
American Family Children's Hospital at the University of Wisconsin Hospital and Clinics. © Ballogg Photography Inc., Chicago. HDR.

CONNECTION TO NATURE

Figure C-14
The blurring of indoors and outdoors is successful with large windows and natural materials. Although the patient does not have a direct view out the window, the awareness of daylight can be hypothesized to improve satisfaction levels and promote healing.
Community Hospital of the Monterey Peninsula. HOK.

Figure C-15
When a view of nature is not available, the interior design can simulate the qualities of the exterior. The whimsy of this interior courtyard plays on the senses.
St. Mary's Hospital Winter Garden. Don Kerkof/Imagewerks Studios, Kahler Slater.

Figure C-16
If one recognizes that Mother Nature has a successful formula for the design of a stress-free environment (see Chapter 7), then one begins to appreciate the organic design of the lobby of Credit Valley Hospital.
Peter Sellar, KLIK photography, Farrow Partnership Architects.

CONNECTION TO NATURE

Figure C-17
Healing gardens have become popular because of the known healing qualities of nature. In addition, they offer respite and distraction for staff and families and for patients who can ambulate or view gardens through windows.
Healing garden just off of Sentara Williamsburg Regional Medical Center's Chapel. Photo © VanceFox.com, HDR.

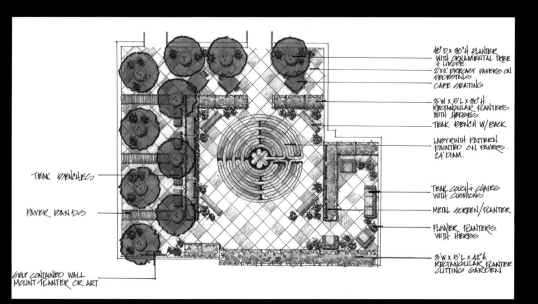

Figure C-18
Rendering from landscape architects of the surgical waiting rooftop meditative garden. The labyrinth offers a way to pass time and focus worried thoughts in a positive way. Quiet, tucked-away options for reflectance are also available, yet connected by doorway to the main surgical reception area.
Studies not yet complete.
OhioHealth Dublin Methodist Hospital (Pebble Project), MSI Landscape Architect.

DAYLIGHTING

Figure C-19
Clerestory and full-wall glass panels flood the lobby of OhioHealth Dublin Methodist Hospital with daylight-ng. The view out through the clerestory helps in wayfinding and orientation as one sees one's final desti-nation. Studies not yet complete.
(Pebble Project) photo courtesy OhioHealth, Dublin Methodist Hospital, © 2008 photography by Brad Feinknopf, Karlsberger/CAMA, Inc.

Figure C-20
Daylight floods waiting areas but also spills as it is borrowed into cor-ridor and adjacent spaces. Note the dif-erence in the quality of the space with the shadows cast. Spaces with a strong connec-ion to nature often blur interior and exte-rior materials.
San Juan Regional Medical Center. Hedrich Blessing, Steve Hall Photographer, Kahler Slater.

Figure C-21
Most healthcare facilities have many interior spaces that are devoid of natural lighting. When possible plan an interior to capture a long view down a corridor to draw light patterns into the space. Again, the use of natural materials reinforces the connection to nature's variability.
Jay Monahan Center for Gastrointestinal Health, © Adrian Wilson, © Frederick Charles, Guenther 5.

Figure C-22
Daylighting is not always easy to capture but when the value of its power is understood then it supports the effort to capture its stress-reducing qualities. In areas like radiation therapy it takes a special effort to bring natural light into a space.
University of Medicine and Dentistry of New Jersey, New Jersey Medical School, University Hospital Cancer Center. © Woodruff/Brown Photography, RMJM Hillier.

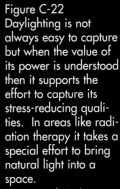

Figure C-23
Moving infusion patients toward windows in one study "did not have a direct impact on a patient's negative feelings" but sharing the experience with a neighboring patient did. (See Essay 4-1.)
Stony Brook University Medical Center. Photo by Björg Magnea, Cannon Design.

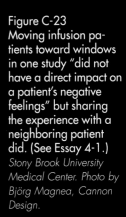

POSITIVE DISTRACTIONS OR RESOURCE CENTERS

Figure C-24
True to the Planetree ideal of empowering patients and their families through education, a Planetree Health Resource Center at Sentara Williamsburg Regional Medical Center.
Photo by VanceFox.com, HDR.

Figure C-25 *(below)*
Family Library at Martha Jefferson Hospital Outpatient Care Center.
Hedrich Blessing, Steve Hall Photographer, Kahler Slater.

Figure C-26 *(right)*
Resource Center at Jay Monahan Center for Gastrointestinal Health.
© Adrian Wilson,
© Frederick Charles.

CULTURE

Figure C-27
WPA Murals imposed on the exterior skin of facility creating a neighborhood land-mark and promoting a community's legacy.
Harlem Hospital Center. HOK.

Figure C-28 *(below left)*
Creating a sense of pride in place through referencing a cultural legacy at the Alaska Native Medical Center.
Courtesy NBBJ, © Assassi Productions.

Figure C-29 *(below)*
Iconography that is decorative as well as symbolic of the culture of the community Alaska Native Medical Center serves.
Courtesy NBBJ, © Assassi Productions.

SUSTAINABLE

Figure C-30
Healthcare projects that consider the health of the earth as well as their occupants make logical sense. Public Corridor Chapel, University Medical Center of the Rockies.
Joel Eden Photography, Heery.

Figure C-31
Designed around the thermal comfort of its occupants this multi-story space changes the perception of a clinical treatment into a transforming experience.
Patrick H. Dollard Discovery Health Center, David Allee photography, Perkins + Will.

COOPERATIVE AND LONG TERM CARE

Figure C-32
Off the edge of a New York City streetscape is the entry into the headquarters of The American Cancer Society that also serves as the entry to its respite care "Hope Lodge."
SLCE/CAMA, Inc.

Figure C-33
Linden Ponds dining room creating a long-term care experience that is driven by the current markets. As generational expectations change, so will the design of these facilities. What will the Baby Boomer Generation expect in long-term care?
Steffian Bradley Architects.

Figure C-34
Otorhinolaryngology
(ENT) Ambulatory
waiting area that was
informed by the Becker
Translational Study
(see Essay 2-2).
*Weill Cornell Medical
Center (Pebble Project)
Ballinger Architecture.*

Figure C-35
One of the clinics studied by Becker and
colleagues in preparation for the Weill
Cornell project. The study revealed many
insights, one of which was the more attractive
the environment, the higher the perceived
quality of medical care and greater reported
reduction of anxiety.
*Jay Monahan Center for Gastrointestinal Health.
© Adrian Wilson, © Frederick Charles. Guenther 5.*

Figure C-36
Karmanos Cancer Center was one of the first Pebble Projects. Research reports revealed average variable costs decreased $1,000 per patient through the evidence-based design of the facility. Note the blurring of interior and exterior.
Detroit Medical Center. Beth Singer Photography, Cannon Design.

Figure C-37
Mammography suite designed to be less stressful, less clinical in its approach to design.
Martha Jefferson Hospital Outpatient Care Center. Hedrich Blessing, Steve Hall Photographer, Kahler Slater.

CHILDREN'S HOSPITALS

Figure C-38
"Exploring the Sun Coast" designed to drive down stress levels for children and families. Borrowing from another hospital project's family focus group's wish to "get to where I need to go and make me forget why I am going there" raising patient satisfaction scores.
All Children's Hospital, Renderings courtesy of Karlsberger Architect of Record/CAMA, Inc.

Figure C-39 *(left)*
A study of acoustical properties for an open waiting multiclinical space was necessary to make this environment a pleasant and healing space to occupy.
Clarian Health/Riley Hospital for Children KMD/CAMA, Inc.

Figure C-40 *(right)*
Playful spaces "Pyramid" providing a stage for interactive, memorable, stress-reducing experiences. Texas Children's Hospital.
Photography by Craig Dugan © Hedrich Blessing. Image provided by FKP Architects.

Figure C-41
Alberta Children's Hospital Exterior design becomes a landmark for clear wayfinding,
Kasian Architecture, Interior Design and Planning LTD.

Build Mock-Ups: Translational Design

As design progresses on a project there are many tools to help the interdisciplinary team make solid decisions about the evolving plan. In our computer-aided world, building information modeling (BIM) is executed by the current generation of savvy techno-artists. This three-dimensional modeling generates images that allows even the least visual to understand what a building will look like, facilitating the exchange of information about the building process and all of its systems. It is immensely important to be able to move a user to see and feel how a space ergonomically responds to the tasks that must be done effortlessly, intuitively, and free from error. It is here where the mock-up becomes invaluable.

There are three levels of mock-up one can expect to build and evaluate:

1. **Referential mock-up:** The study of one aspect of a design scheme independent of other systems. For example, parking lots are great places to map out the size and scale of a unit or other large spaces. Headwalls can be mocked-up in a spare room with foam core or with equipment brought in from a manufacturer. Details, finishes, and pieces of equipment can all be tested independent of a new building. These are important first steps in determining if the interdisciplinary team is on the right track for the desired outcome.
2. **Simulated mock-up:** The study of an entire space with all of its components in place but not mechanically operational. Often offsite due to space requirements, these mock-ups can be fully equipped where staff, patient, and family advocates can visit and respond to a number of issues that the interdisciplinary team evaluates for design approval on a project.
3. **Live mock-up:** The study of a fully operational space that includes all components of the Environment of Care in a fully functioning unit within the healthcare facility. It can include renovation of a room or a unit to test certain aspects of the design or an entire system. It is here that the entire Environment of Care is tested in the new model.

To date, there has not been research done on the effectiveness of the mock-up; design evaluations have answered many questions but more can be learned. The extensive exercise of building a mock-up has proven to be beneficial in that it has sent many a design team back to the drawing board. The investment typically avoids surprises at the opening of a project. For those who plan early there may be opportunities within a live mock-up to test results that are causing difficulty in the decision-making process. It is here where the translational design is most effective.

Keyword: Translational Design

"Drawing board to bedside." A pilot study designed to test a design hypothesis before construction of the final design begins.

Figure 4.16
Referential mock-up:
Balcony rail at Riley
Hospital for Children.
*KMD Architects/CAMA,
Inc.*

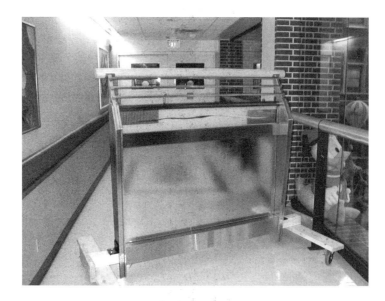

Figure 4.17
Simulated mock-up:
Dublin Methodist
Hospital (Pebble
Project) like-handed
emergency exam room.
*Photos by
Karlsberger/Jason
Meyer/Feinknopf.
Karlsberger Architects/
CAMA, Inc.*

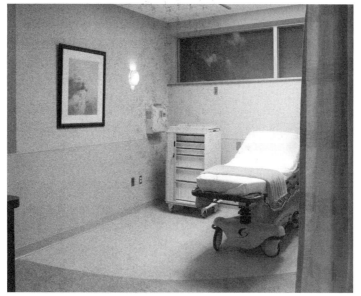

Recent notable projects have had successful mock-up experiences:

1. **Referential mock-up:** The Riley Out-Patient Center handrail design was mocked-up
   out of context but created a kick-the-tires scenario for the interdisciplinary team to

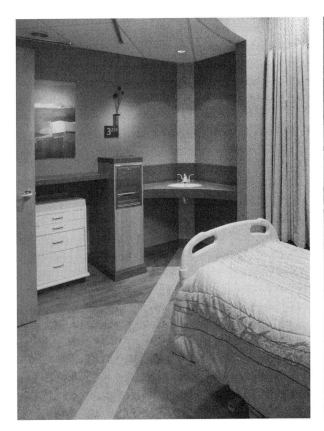
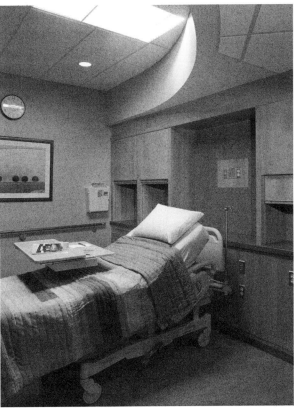

evaluate all of the necessary criteria to hypothesize a safe model for inclusion into their project's construction documents. (See Figure 4.16.)

2. **Simulated mock-up:** The Dublin Methodist Hospital, Pebble Project, built an emergency exam room, a variable acuity room, and a labor and delivery room—the latter complete with nonfunctioning bathrooms—in a warehouse space near the new construction site of its "Greenfield" hospital. Millwork, simulation of gases, plumbing fixtures, windows, furniture, equipment, fixtures, ceilings, lighting, and cubicle tracks were all installed for full evaluation. Many from within the OhioHealth system toured the mock-ups and conducted onsite reviews and simulated exercises. Changes were made to the plans before the final construction documents were completed. Many more traveled from afar to visit the mock-ups as it was an early example of a like-handed system. These mock-ups were given a fair amount of press during the project's design phases, shedding light on the importance of sharing a process with concurrent project teams. (See Figures 4.17, 4.18, and 4.19.)

Figure 4.18 and 4.19 Simulated mock-up: Dublin Methodist Hospital (Pebble Project) like-handed (a) variable acuity and (b) LDR room.
Photos by Karlsberger/ Jason Meyer/Feinknopf. Karlsberger Architects/ CAMA, Inc.

Figure 4.20
Live mock-up: Install a
lift in a patient room
and measure the differ-
ence in nurse back
injuries against this
situation.

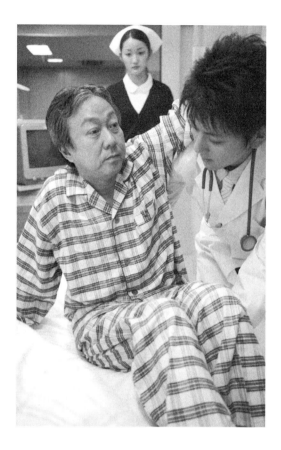

3a. **Live mock-up:** PeaceHealth's Sacred Heart Medical Center, in Eugene, Oregon, has not opened its doors at the time of this writing but has made a name for itself in the study of how to reduce nurse back injuries. In preparation for a new building program, Lola Fritz, RN, recognizing that back pain is a serious problem among nurses and nurse aides decided to address this dilemma prior to the final design phases. Taking an evidence-based approach it was easy to find supporting evidence. The American Nurses Association has documented the known benefits of a "Safe Patient Handling Program"[15] (see Chapter 6.) The PeaceHealth team installed ceiling-mounted lifts in the existing intensive care unit and neurology units. A study of reporting injuries was conducted over 60 months. Based on its analysis of the number of injuries and associated claim costs, the team at PeaceHealth found that the use of ceiling lifts virtually eliminated staff injuries from patient handling. After a cost analysis of the injuries versus equipment costs the study revealed a payback period of 2.5 years.[16] The interesting end of the story was that the public relations on this study

Figure 4.21
Live mock-up: Jay
Monahan Center for
Gastrointestinal Health.
Guenther 5 Architects.
© Adrian Wilson,
© Frederick Charles.

Figure 4.22
Live mock-up: Jay
Monahan Center for
Gastrointestinal Health.
Guenther 5 Architects.
© Adrian Wilson,
© Frederick Charles.

PATIENT SAFETY: Improve patient safety and quality of care	Design Intervention	Arch	Op	IT	EBD (Proven)	EBD (Not Proven)	INNOVATION
☆☆☆☆☆ Reduce nosocomial infection (airborne)							
☆☆☆☆ Reduce nosocomial infection (contact)							
☆☆☆ Improve quality of communication (staff to patient)							
Improve confidentiality of patient information							
☆☆ Reduce patient falls							
Improve quality of communication (patient to family)							
☆ Improve quality of communication (patient to staff)							
Improve quality of communication (staff to staff)							
Reduce medication errors							
Increase hand washing compliance by staff							

PATIENT STRESS:
Reduce stress, improve quality of life and healing for patients and families

☆☆☆☆ Patient stress (emotional duress, anxiety, depression)							
Reduce noise stress							
Improve sleep							
Reduce spatial disorientation							
Increase social support							
☆☆☆ Reduce depression							
Improve circadian rhythms							
Reduce helplessness and empower patients & families							
Provide positive distraction							
☆☆ Reduce pain (intake of pain drugs, and reported pain)							

☆☆☆☆☆ HIGH ACTION AREAS: Topics in which researchers have found many good studies linking environmental factors with the outcome or fewer strong studies that have provided convergent evidence.

☆☆☆ HIGH IMPORTANCE: Topics with relatively fewer studies. These are high importance outcome areas and additional research is needed.

☆ IMPORTANT: Topics with few studies or few studies that conclusively provide a link between environmental factors and the outcome. These are important areas that need additional research.

Figure 4.23
Evidence-based design: Checklist developed for the University Medical Center at Princeton (Pebble Project) using the Ulrich/Zimring Scorecards.
Center for Health Design/CAMA/HOK/RMJM Hillier.

brought forth a donor who has contributed to the cost of all new ceiling lifts for all rooms in the new facility. The story will continue after occupancy in August 2008. (See Figure 4.20.)

3b. **Live mock-up:** Weill Cornell Medical College/Weill Greenberg Center, in preparation for the design of their new ambulatory facility, conducted an interim study with Franklin Becker, PhD, Professor and Chair of the Department of Design and Environmental Analysis at Cornell University.[17] The study was designed to examine the ecology of the patient visit and rate several waiting rooms' physical attractiveness, waiting times, and perceived quality of care. The drivers of the design of the Weill Cornell Medical Center's waiting rooms (see Essay 2-2) were influenced by this study. (See Chapter 5, Step 4: Measure and Share Outcomes.) (See Figures 4.21 and 4.22.)

QUALITY: Improve overall healthcare quality and reduce cost	Design Intervention	Arch	Op	IT	EBD (Proven)	EBD (Not Proven)	INNOVATION
☆☆☆☆ Patient room transfers: number and costs							
Patient satisfaction with quality of care							
☆☆☆ Staff work effectiveness; patient care time per shift							
☆☆ Reduce length of patient stay							
Reduce drugs (see patient safety)							
Patient satisfaction with staff quality							
☆ Re-hospitalization or readmission rates							
STAFF STRESS: Reduce staff stress/fatigue, increase effectiveness in delivering care							
☆☆☆☆ Reduce noise stress							
☆☆☆ Improve medication processing and delivery times							
Work effectiveness; patient care time per shift							
Improve satisfaction							
☆☆ Improve workplace, job satisfaction							
Reduce fatigue							
☆ Reduce turnover							

☆☆☆☆ HIGH ACTION AREAS: Topics in which researchers have found many good studies linking environmental factors with the outcome or fewer strong studies that have provided convergent evidence.

☆☆☆ HIGH IMPORTANCE: Topics with relatively fewer studies. These are high importance outcome areas and additional research is needed.

☆ IMPORTANT: Topics with few studies or few studies that conclusively provide a link between environmental factors and the outcome. These are important areas that need additional research.

The University Medical Center at Princeton is about to build live mock-ups of patient care areas. It is their intention to measure the effectiveness of the mock-up process through the Pebble Process. This story will inform future building projects' way of appropriately mocking up live scenarios for testing. Look for insights that will be revealed throughout this process.

Share the Process

Communicating is important throughout the process. Information about the research must be shared with all on the team, but like the studies above, the sharing during the design phases can influence concurrent projects in a powerful way. In Cheryl Herbert's essay in Chapter 1, she mentions that "Each new subcontractor who joined the Dublin Methodist project went through an orientation where the vision and goals were shared, along with an expectation that they would help us accomplish them." I remember walking through the construction site and

Figure 4.24
Evidence-based design: Checklist developed for the University Medical Center at Princeton (Pebble Project) using the Ulrich/Zimring Scorecards.
Center for Health Design/CAMA/HOK/ RMJM Hillier.

being asked by the onsite manager if one operating room suite could deviate from its like-handedness because of the interference of another subcontractor's work. He was looking for an efficient way to end a mechanical run. I paused and took a moment to explain the premise behind the like-handed theory and the need to maintain consistency for our studies. With that said we agreed it was worth the question and the like-handed configuration won over ease of installation. Dublin will ultimately measure the expense of consistency to see if the efficiency and safety of an invasive procedure on a human being by a medical/surgical team was the right thing to do.

This affirms that the evidence-based process needs to be shared while it is in its early developmental phase. As more teams come on board easier ways to incorporate the evidence-based process will emerge. Although this is one of the early publications on the topic, there will be many more; some will dispute its validity, but all will be helpful in improving the process for this design methodology. The recommendation is to take it slow and document what works and what doesn't, then share. Chapter 5 reviews the options for sharing. Chapter 7 addresses the future of evidence-based design services. (See Figures 4.23 and 4.24.)

Summary

At the beginning of this chapter Ranjit Kumar suggested "that hypotheses, though important, are not essential for a study," however, they are what set a creative flow of thoughts in motion on an evidence-based project. Hypothesis, innovation, and translational design all occur within the design phases of a project, which for most teams is the most exciting. The discussions that occur here open up possibilities and excite participants with the potential for success of the evidence-based process. Although most innovation is risky, what has happened in the last eight years since the Pebble Project's inception has inspired incremental, thoughtful, deliberate forward motion in the advancement of care. Bad ideas have fallen off quickly and new ideas are emerging faster. The nine-year curve mentioned earlier is being foreshortened. (See Figure 1.24.)

The next chapter looks at the research that has occurred and should trigger ideas on how to build on the work of those teams who have passed before to see new horizons with new possibilities. Read on.

Checklist: Hypothesize Outcomes, Innovate, and Implement Translational Design

1. Hypothesize Outcomes
   - Design hypotheses state the direct relationship between a design intervention and a desired outcome used as a basis for further exploration and measurement.
   - An interdisciplinary team anticipates that the interpretation of project wisdom will:
     - Inspire a clear project vision
     - Identify the right project drivers
     - Spark the inspiration for a measurable design intervention
     - Support positive behavior in environments for the life cycle of the design
   - Evidence-based design brings:
     - Clarity from project wisdom
     - Specificity from project drivers
     - Focus from design interventions
   - Write hypotheses at the end of the schematic design phase or as early in the design process as possible so that:
     - A researcher can recommend ways to articulate a hypothesis so that it leads to a clean study
     - It can be determined if a baseline of data within the client organization exists and will support a post-occupancy study
     - A need for additional information about an existing body of knowledge can be articulated
     - Additional members can be added to the interdisciplinary team if needed, i.e., an acoustician to develop a baseline of noise for a hypothesis that will require a measurement of noise levels in the new space.
     - A determination is made to prove a known outcome or venture toward a solution that is truly innovative.
2. Design for Improvement: Dare to Innovate
   - Buros' Five Keys to Unlocking Creativity
     - Observation
     - Incubation
     - Intuition
     - Emotion
     - Stimulation
   - IDEO's 5 Steps toward the Art of Innovation
     - Understand
     - Observe
     - Visualize
     - Evaluate and refine
     - Implement
   - The Experience Economy
     - Engage customers
     - Create events
     - Customize services
     - Pick the right people
     - Change the individual
     - Create transformational experiences
     - Transform customers
   - Review Ulrich/Zimring Scorecards
     - Reduce stress, improve quality of life and healing for patients and families
     - Reduce staff stress/fatigue, increase effectiveness in delivering care
     - Improve patient safety and quality of care
     - Improve overall healthcare quality and reduce costs
3. Build Mock-Ups: Translational Design
   Translational Design: "Drawing board to bedside." A pilot study designed to test a hypothesis before construction of a final design begins.
   - Referential mock-ups: Study of one aspect of a design independent of other systems
   - Simulated mock-ups: The study of an entire space with all of its components in place but not mechanically operational
   - Live mock-ups: The study of a fully operational space within a fully functioning unit
4. Share the Process
   Just do it! Others will benefit.

Endnotes

1. Webster's Ninth New Collegiate Dictionary, Merriam-Webster Inv., Publishers, 1985, p. 594.
2. Kumar, R. *Research Methodology, A Step-by-Step Guide for Beginners,* Sage Publications, 2005; p. 79.
3. Geboy, L. Notes from Healthcare Design 07, Dallas, Texas.
4. Becker, C. (2007, December 3). "High-risk proposition." *Modern Healthcare, 37*(48), 6–7, 16.
5. Watkins, N.; Keller, A. (in press). Lost in Translation: Bridging Gaps between Design and Evidence-Based Design Research. *Health Environments Research & Design Journal.*
6. National Cancer Institute (2007). NCI-designated cancer centers: Fact sheet. Retrieved January 30, 2008 from the National Cancer Institute website: https://cissecure.nci.nih.gov/factsheet/FactsheetSearch.aspx?FSType=1.2.
7. Cram, P.; Vaughan-Sarrasin, M.S.; Wolf, B.; Katz, J.N.; Rosenthal, G.E. (2007). A comparison of total hip and knee replacement in specialty and general hospitals. *Journal of Bone and Joint Surgery, 89,* 1675–1684.
8. Eliott, J. "Someone's in the Kitchen," *Virginia Tech's Center for Real Life's Research Magazine,* Winter 2008.
9. Buros, D. *Technotrends.* Harper Collins Publishers, 1993; p. 214.
10. *Ibid,* p. 353.
11. *Ibid,* p. xvii.
12. Kelley, T. The Art of Innovation, Currency Books, 2001; 5–7.
13. IDEO, Building the Ambulatory Practice of the Future, Massachusetts General Physicians Organization, Massachusetts General Hospital, November 2005.
14. Pine, B.J.; Gilmore, J. *The Experience Economy,* Harvard Business School Press, 1999.
15. American Nurses Association, Preventing Back Injuries: Safe patient handling and movement, American Nurses Association, 2002.
16. Joseph, A.; Fritz, L. Ceiling Lifts Reduce Patient-Handling Injuries, *Healthcare Design,* March 2006.
17. Becker, F.; Douglass, S. The Ecology of the Patient Visit: Physical Attractiveness, Waiting Times and Perceived Quality of Care, *Healthcare Design,* November, 2006.

Chapter 5

Step 4: Measure and Share Outcomes

"Never measure your generosity by what
you give, but rather by what you have left."
—Bishop Fulton J. Sheen

This final step is where the measurement of the hypothesized outcomes takes place. The importance of this step is key in moving our healthcare delivery system to a new level. Although this chapter is not intended to be a research "how-to" lesson, it explains methodologies. This step also involves a call to collect economic intelligence to be able to build and share better business cases. The evidence-based interdisciplinary team takes responsibility for sharing knowledge gained as well as the process used to gather it, through presentations to fellow professionals and also through peer-review. Expert testimony and the first look at firms practicing this methodology are shared. It is here in the final component of evidence-based practice where everyone has a say in the direction of this design methodology.

To begin the work necessary within this component of evidence-based practice one must look to Len Berry's principles of "value-driven leadership" (see Chapter 3) to find the concept of generosity squarely rooted in its formula. It is what drives advancement of healing and as such inspires those responsible for the design and construction of our temples of health to hold a higher promise for the industry and hence future projects. To that end, this chapter will focus on the responsibility of an interdisciplinary team to share knowledge by venturing into at least the third level and ideally into the fourth level of evidence-based practice. This chapter will serve to inform the process, not how to conduct research.

This is the most difficult component, but also the most profound. It is here where the project's design hypotheses are proven or not. The confidence of the most secure leadership is tested by sharing not only where a project succeeded but also where it may have failed. You should know your team, project, and budgetary limitations before you commit to these two

Figure 5.1
Solomon's Seal.
Picture by Henry Domke,
www.henrydomke.com.

levels as it will take additional time and expertise to follow through completely and professionally.

It is not the intent of this chapter to tell the reader how to do research; there are others much more qualified to do so—experts with academic research backgrounds. Those qualifications are rare in the field of design but the community is growing and will continue to grow if design professionals and clients appreciating this methodology develop the demand. Those who have emerged into the specialty of healthcare evidence-based research are rigorously dedicated to growing the field. (More on the growth of the field in the final chapter.) Design-related PhD programs are organized within a few universities and their graduates are being employed within the larger firms and with healthcare product manufacturers. Firms too small to afford full-time expertise find connections within the field, at local universities or within the institutions that hire them. As the field grows the trailblazers will continue to organize within research coalitions like CHER, at The Center for Health Design, where an effort is being made to identify the gaps needed to design effectively in this method of practice. The prospect for a growing base of knowledge is great and the tools to make it all easily accessible are in development. The excitement is growing among design professionals as well as researchers because the "flashpoint" has occurred and, with the right momentum, there will be no turning back. There are two fundamental pieces of the puzzle that will follow:

1. Create a new and distinct field of study. The university programs that are building this field of study are quite excited about this prospect. The future of evidence-based design is in excellent hands—or better yet minds—that are keenly aware of the path the design professions must take.
2. Accreditation for the members of the interdisciplinary team and for evidence-based projects somewhat similar to LEED certification known as Evidence-Based Design Assessment and Certification (EDAC) (see Essay 5-4).

There are four areas to explore in this chapter that will make this last component of evidence-based design less daunting for the member of the interdisciplinary team who is not a researcher:

1. Measure Outcomes
2. Build the Business Case
3. Share with Fellow Professionals
4. Submit for Peer Review

Measure Outcomes

In order to talk about the measurement of outcomes there are several questions that need to be answered.

- Why measure?
- Who should measure and when?
- What types of studies might be conducted?

Keyword: Research

Definition:
Research is the studious inquiry or examination; especially: investigation or experimentation aimed at the discovery and interpretation of facts, revisions of accepted theories or laws in the light of new facts, or practical application of such new or revised theories or laws.[1] —Merriam Webster

Research is one of the ways to find answers to your questions. To find answers to a question, you are implying that the process:

1. Is being undertaken within a framework of a set of philosophies;
2. Uses procedures, methods, and techniques that have been tested for their validity and reliability; and
3. Is designed to be unbiased and objective.[2] —Ranjit Kumar

Practice-based environmental design research is systematic inquiry for the dual purpose of creating knowledge and solving specific design problems.[3] —Lyn Geboy, Kahler Slater

- What have we learned from previous measurement and what do we measure next?
- Where are the best practices?

Why Measure?

Without measurement trends prevail. Unless these trends are informed by evidenced-based practice, they will not meet the current expectations for creating a healing environment. Chapter 1 set up the conditions of the perfect storm. The healthcare industry is ready to make significant changes that are dependent on a supportive, safe, and effective working environment that fosters the delivery of quality care and sympathy for the human condition. Without the ability to respond confidently and rapidly with an informed base of knowledge, design professionals revert back to tried and true methods that at best turn a nine-year cycle of innovation (see Figure 1.24). That is no longer acceptable in a field that each year is making quantum leaps in technological advances let alone the resulting adjustments to care protocols. Design practices must keep pace. Inherent in the process of evidence-based design is a way to link all of the activity by sharing knowledge as fast as it is established. Those willing to measure and report immediately affect all others on the roller coaster ride, error is recorded for rapid adjustments to the course of those who keep informed.

Who Should Measure and When?

Researchers are relatively new to most design teams, sometimes making the fit awkward or unclear. The most enlightened evidence-based teams struggle to coordinate with this new team member, especially when to trigger their initiation into the process. Too many times it happens after design development, which is too late. Anjali Joseph and Amy Keller from the Research Department at The Center for Health Design prepared an outline (see Essay 5-1) showing the value of integrating the researcher at the inception of a project. This outline should serve to clarify the role of the researcher and allay any hesitations about the process.

Essay 5-1
The Role of the Researcher in the Design Process
Anjali Joseph, PhD, and Amy Keller

Healthcare organizations and architecture/interior design firms are becoming increasingly sophisticated in using different types of credible information to support design decision-making in their building projects. Assessing the effectiveness of design decisions on clinical and financial outcomes is a benefit for both the architecture/interior design firm and the healthcare organization. Researchers are a critical part of the evolving multidisciplinary design team in healthcare building projects. Researchers may be employed with the architecture/interior design firm, with the healthcare client or may be an independent consultant or university researcher. The researcher has the ability to bring a lot to the different stages of the design process. The extent of involvement of the researcher at different stages may vary depending on which organization the researcher represents (architecture/interior design firm, healthcare organization, independent) and how far the team wants to go in terms of conducting new research (e.g., information gathering, information sharing, conducting research). The full potential of an evidence-based design process is realized by going through the full cycle—of using the evidence, creating the hypotheses, and then measuring the effectiveness of design innovation. Here are some ways that a researcher can contribute during the different stages of an evidence-based design process:

During the **visioning phase** the researcher might:
- Help articulate project goals in terms of projected impacts on desired outcomes.
- Identify key sources of information on the impact of environment on project goals and desired outcomes. This might involve doing literature reviews, surveys with staff or patients, and focus groups.
- Educate the team about how the physical environment and other factors (technology, culture) together impact outcomes in healthcare in order to spur innovative thinking and new ideas.
- Develop an information repository—organizing and categorizing available information and information sources and defining key terms so that this information is readily available to different individuals on the design team.

During **master planning** stages the researcher might:
- Work with hospital staff and administrators in evaluating current practices to develop a baseline.
- Help connect project goals and objectives to desired clinical and financial outcomes through well-articulated research hypotheses. This is a critical aspect of an evidence-based design process.
- Help identify evidence-based design interventions (through literature reviews, focus groups, etc.) that will help in achieving the desired improvement targets (i.e., reduction in infection rates, increase in efficiency, etc.).
- Assess scope and potential for research.
- Formulate preliminary research budget.
- Identify potential sources of grant funding for research (both internal and external).

During **functional programming and schematic design stages**, a researcher might:
- Help to translate existing evidence to design recommendations (e.g., by annotating drawings, by reviewing preliminary design solutions).

- Document evaluation of proposed budget alongside baseline of current hospital costs to project ROI (return on investment).
- Conduct workshops with team members to drill down on research topics that
  - Identify metrics of interest.
  - Define detailed research plan for selected topics.
- Collaborate with hospital administrators to obtain funding from internal sources or submit grant proposal to external sources.
- Submit research plans for review by Institutional Review Board (IRB) (many hospitals have their own) to make sure that there is adequate protection for human subjects who may participate in the research.
- Conduct onsite measurements—to measure outcomes of interest *before* design intervention is constructed.

During **design development stage**, a researcher might:
- Help the design team identify relevant evidence to support specific design decisions or conduct quick turnaround studies to guide decision-making (e.g., a study to assess which type of carpet is most effective from the perspective of rollability).
- Document evaluation of budget alongside baseline of current hospital costs to project ROI.
- Conduct interviews, focus groups, and research archival notes to document design process used.
- Many of the steps from the functional programming phase might also occur during this phase (depending on the timing of the project).

During the **construction phase**, a researcher might:
- Develop detailed research plans.
- Conduct IRB.
- Identify metrics of interest.
- Collect "before" data in existing facility.
- Continue documenting costs and design decisions during construction phase.

During **post-occupancy**, a researcher might:
- Collect data (outcomes research, post-occupancy evaluation, surveys, time-motion studies, plan analyses).
- Analyze data.
- Make recommendations and evaluate lessons learned.
- Publish and present research in peer-reviewed journals and magazines.

What Types of Studies Might Be Conducted?

"Studies can either be initiated with a focus on outcomes or a focus on design. A design-focused research project, such as one initiated by an architect, may ask how a particular design feature or set of features affects one or more outcomes. An outcome-focused research project (e.g., one focusing on increasing patient safety) might ask how a particular outcome was impacted by the manipulation of different types of environmental factors."[5]

—Joseph, The Center for Health Design, Hamilton, Texas A&M

"At a philosophical level some researchers, myself included, are concerned with issues of epistemology as they relate to research."[6]

—Geboy, Kahler Slater

For the interdisciplinary team to better understand an approach to research in accessible terms, a very good primer for the nonresearcher is *Research Methodology, a Step-by-Step Guide for Beginners* by Ranjit Kumar. Kumar defines research as a process for collecting, analyzing, and interpreting information to answer questions. In order to qualify as research, he states, the process must have certain characteristics: It must, as far as possible, be controlled, rigorous, systematic, valid and verifiable, empirical, and critical.

Specifically he defines:

- Controlled: in exploring causality in relation to two variables, a study is set up in a way that minimizes the effects of other factors affecting the relationship.
- Rigorous: procedures followed to find answers to questions that are relevant, appropriate, and justified.
- Systematic: procedures adopted to undertake an investigation that follows a certain logical sequence.
- Valid and verifiable: the basis of the findings is correct and can be verified by you and others.

Keyword: Institutional Review Board (IRB)

Under FDA regulations, an IRB is an appropriately constituted group that has been formally designated to review and monitor biomedical research involving human subjects. In accordance with FDA regulations, an IRB has the authority to approve, require modifications in (to secure approval), or disapprove research. This group review serves an important role in the protection of the rights and welfare of human research subjects.

The purpose of IRB review is to assure, both in advance and by periodic review, that appropriate steps are taken to protect the rights and welfare of humans participating as subjects in the research. To accomplish this purpose, IRBs use a group process to review research protocols and related materials (e.g., informed consent documents and investigator brochures) to ensure protection of the rights and welfare of human subjects of research.[4]

- Empirical: based upon hard evidence gathered from information collected from real-life experiences or observations.
- Critical: the process of investigation must be foolproof and free from any drawbacks.

For Kumar, in order for a process to be called research, it is imperative that it has the above characteristics.[8]

In the Pebble handbook and in an article for *Building Research and Information*, Anjali Joseph, PhD, and Kirk Hamilton documented the coordinated efforts of the research process undertaken by the Pebble Projects.[9] Listed below are the study types with an explanation using the methodology of the evidence-based process discussed in this book:

- Documentation studies: The documentation of internal intelligence to create a baseline or the documentation of the process used for an evidence-based design approach to a specific project.
- Original data collection: During the development of an innovative design intervention the need may arise to collect "new knowledge to answer specific research questions…collecting new and original data."
- Randomized controlled experiments: "Such studies usually manipulate or vary the independent variable (e.g., lighting levels) to test the effect on dependent variables (e.g., medication dispensing error)."
- Natural experiments: "Perfect experimentation conditions (where all other potential causes have been eliminated or controlled for) are difficult to produce in real-life situations.
- Before/after studies: Mock-ups allow for this kind of study where a design intervention is measured before it is finalized and again after it is installed permanently.

Keyword: Epistemology

Research is only one way of "knowing." The branch of philosophy that deals with this subject is called "epistemology." Epistemologists generally recognize at least four different sources of knowledge:[7]

1. Intuitive knowledge—takes forms such as belief, faith, intuition, etc. It is based on feelings rather than hard, cold "facts." It is used when coming up with an initial idea for research.
2. Authoritative knowledge—based on information received from people, books, etc. Its strength depends on the strength of the sources. It is used when reviewing the professional literature.
3. Logical knowledge—arrived at by reasoning from "point A" (which is generally accepted) to "point B" (the new knowledge). It is used when reasoning from findings to conclusions.
4. Empirical knowledge—based on demonstrable, objective facts (which are determined through observation and/or experimentation). It is used when engaging in procedures that lead to these findings.

- Prospective studies: "The characteristics of subjects are assessed and then examined again after they have been exposed to some kind of event or condition."
- Retrospective studies: "Past behaviors or events are examined for relationships."
- Simulation studies: Mock-ups can allow for a simulation study where "by carefully designing the study, measuring and documenting the environmental intervention and the observed outcomes."
- Just-in-time studies: When participatory decisions are made regarding choices, "these types of participatory situations can also be the subject of a research study."
- Ethnographic studies: "…provide in-depth qualitative information about a setting or design issue. These studies are useful in identifying how things actually work within a setting and what corrective measures may be instituted to remedy conflicts."

What Have We Learned from Previous Measurement and What Do We Measure Next?

The Ulrich/Zimring analysis of documented research has concisely summed up what is known from research projects that have followed the rigor outlined above. The Pebble Project currently has 50 institutions following a matrix that looks at a variety of issues (clinical; safety; economic; patient-, family-, staff-based; and sustainability) across a variety of populations (single patient, patient groups, all patients, community, staff, organizational culture, and family) while allowing each project to introspectively examine a strategic objective that is driving their own building project, e.g., PeaceHealth and their motivation to eliminate nurse back injuries. Following these studies is easy due to The Center for Health Design's well-oiled marketing machine that keeps these projects and the intelligence gained from them in popular, professional, and peer-reviewed journals. There are always additional studies going on independent of the more visible opportunities. There are also many more healthcare facilities measuring design-related outcomes everyday. Many architectural firms are also measuring topics specific to their interests. Universities with design-related interests are measuring topics as the opportunities present themselves. With the Pebble Project the flurry of interest in evidence-based design has redirected many health-related manufacturers to step up their rigor and study similar topics as they relate to the development of product that answers the current need. The excitement of keeping pace with all of this activity is what has caused this "flashpoint." There are many more areas to be studied—too many to mention them all. I offer the following four for discussion here.

1. Natural Design Features
   Roger Ulrich's landmark studies on views of nature from a patient's bed[10] and views of artwork with long views of nature[11] have proven to be the motivating force about making such a strong connection to nature in healthcare facilities. (See Figure 5.2.)

Figure 5.2
University Medical Center of the Rockies, sustainable project exterior garden with natural walking path and waterfall.
Joel Eden photography, Heery.

The U.S. Green Building Council (USGBC)'s Leadership in Energy and Environmental Design (LEED) program has caused the development of the Green Guide for Health Care dealing with the unique set of circumstances within the operations of a healthcare facility that would accommodate a green or sustainable building system. (See Figure 5.3.)

In their recent book on sustainable healthcare, Robin Guenther and Gail Vittori state that it truly is an interdisciplinary issue to move toward a sustainable health facility: "What is clear is that the work does not reside just within the walls of the healthcare facility—success requires coordination at the community, regional, and global levels, and among manufacturers and educators as much as policy makers."[12] (See Figure 5.4.)

E.O. Wilson and others have "fostered satisfying contact between people and nature in the built environment—known as positive environmental impact, or 'biophilic' design. Biophilic design includes two basic dimensions: organic (or naturalistic) design and vernacular (or place-based) design. Organic design (see Figure 5.5) involves the use of shapes and forms in building and landscape; vernacular design (see Figure 5.6) refers to buildings and landscapes that foster an attachment to place by connecting culture, history, and ecology within a geographic context."[13] Janine Benyus has opened the eyes of a generation of designers with the attention she has drawn to Biomimicry, or the

Figure 5.3
Discovery Health Center
is the first ambulatory
care center to achieve
LEED-certified status.
Perkins + Will.

design of the built environment and the products it is comprised of being inspired by nature.

2. Long-Term Care/Cooperative Care/Home Care

In Essay 5-3, Maggie Calkins admits little has been studied about the impact the built environment has had on the elderly. There are, however, many references to studies that build a case for evidence-based innovation in this area of specialty. The focus has been on long-term care and the varieties of assisted living, but more rehabilitative centers will be developed as less invasive procedures occur, and more cooperative care centers are needed for recuperative time. (See Figure 5.7.) That is not to say that our homes cannot be more universal. Cynthia Leibrock has been a life-long advocate of universal principles in the standard home, providing individuals more independence and less disruption in their sense of normalcy. (See Figures 5.8 and 5.9.) Many multigenerational households are evolving and require a very different paradigm to the standard approach to home building solutions that involve impediments like stairs. And in the event of chronic illness where home care is an option—what evidence exists to support that genre of health and well-being?

Can a design team turn to the evidence available from acute and long-term care and apply it to a residential application? (See Figure 5.10.) As stated in ASID's new release

Figure 5.4
Dublin, Ohio community zoning requirements complimented the design of the automotive parking lot at Dublin Methodist Hospital (Pebble Project) becoming a "Park Walk" using evidence-based design. *MSI—Landscape Architects.*

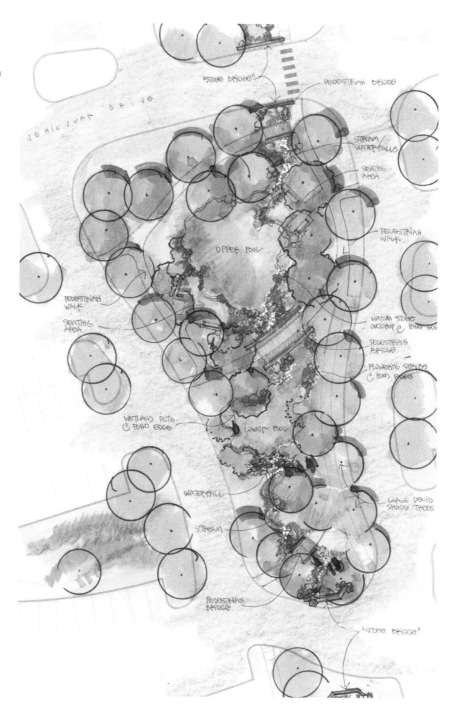

Figure 5.5
"The Biophilic Organic Design Dimension" as seen in the interior design of the Credit Valley Hospital's lobby.
Farrow Partnership Architects, Inc., Peter Sellar, KLIK Photography.

Figure 5.6
"The Biophilic Vernacular Design Dimension" as seen in the exterior of the Southcentral Foundation: Anchorage Native Primary Care Center.
Courtesy NBBJ
© Assassi Productions.

Figure 5.7
Cooperative care patient/guest room as offered by the American Cancer Society in their NYC "Hope Lodge." Respite care for patients receiving cancer treatment at area health facilities.
SLCE/CAMA, Inc.

Figure 5.8
Universal design for a residential bathroom as part of an exhibit done by Cynthia Leibrock with the Kohler Design Center.
Courtesy of Kohler Co.

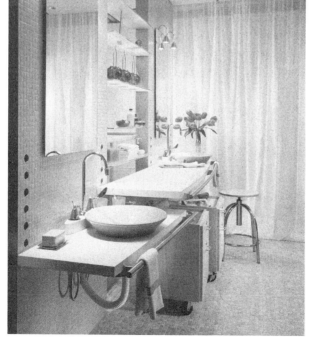

on Healing Homes, "when asked where they [Baby Boomers] want to live as they age, 90 percent state they want to live in their own homes…To complicate matters, the design of many boomers' homes will make their goal of staying at home while they age very difficult."[14]

3. Technological Advances

Emerging technologies are like a crystal ball a view of the possibilities that come with the delivery of more accurate diagnoses, less invasive surgeries, more effective communications, and possibly, more personalized interiors. Our evidence-based knowledge will help channel the development of new technology for the best impact. For example visualize an iHome station, with personalized healing sounds and imagery. A space that, by virtue of an electronic connection—wireless or not—becomes customizable to personal preferences. Those preferences could include music and views of the natural environments that resonate most with the user.

4. Materials Management

Nothing is more unnerving than to walk onto a nursing unit and see clutter. Is it a necessary evil or a nonfunctioning materials management system? This dilemma clearly adds to the inefficiencies the nursing profession is desperately trying to cure. We have explored in previous chapters the on-stage/off-stage model (see Essay 4-2), or the

Figure 5.9
Universal design for a residential bathroom as part of an exhibit done by Cynthia Leibrock with the Kohler Design Center.
Courtesy of Kohler Co.

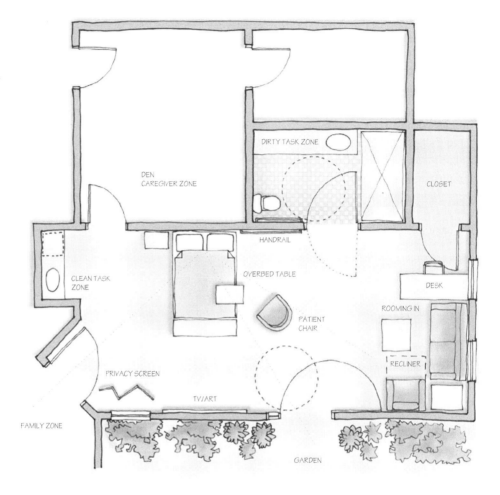

Figure 5.10
Evidence-based design principles of an acute care patient room applied to a residential bedroom when an infirmed member of a family is cared for at home.
CAMA study.

resurgence of the Friesen model of "Nurse Servers." (See Figure 5.11.) These are not new issues and the struggle to solve them is delayed only by finding solid pieces of evidence to drive the appropriate business decision. See the next section of this chapter.

Best Practices

Through the course of writing this book several firms were contacted to share how they embraced the emerging practice model of evidence-based design. Their struggled to formulate answers inspired a questionnaire about participation at each level of practice (see Chapter

Figure 5.11
"Nurse servers" as de-
picted at St. Mary's
Medical Center North.
Photo courtesy of HDR by
© Peter Vanderwarker.

An excerpt from The Hospital: A Social and Architectural History
by John D. Thompson and Grace Goldin

In an attempt to rebuild St. Anthony's at Cheam, Surrey, the sister administrator toured Britain, Germany, Sweden, Italy and Ireland and then flew to America to consult Mr. Friesen in Washington. She returned with a "revolutionary plan" for a 300-bed hospital of all single rooms, complete with nurse servers, central supply system, and a closed-circuit television network for patient-nurse communication. In a published statement the hope was expressed that this hospital, then scheduled for completion in 1971, would permit almost 100 percent bed occupancy and that automation would effect a 30 percent savings in domestic and other ancillary labor, while enabling nurses to give 100 percent patient care.[15]

---

7). Four firms responded with a great deal of detail—Anshen + Allen offered a comprehensive review of their culture. The next chapter is dedicated to a closer look at their efforts and subsequent cultural transformation around an evidence-based practice model.

HKS, Ellerbe Becket, and Kahler Slater shared the following insights.

Evidence-Based Design Practice and Research at HKS Architects

Debajyoti Pati, PhD

1. Why does HKS embrace evidence-based design? As a leader in healthcare design, it is HKS's responsibility to define and shape this new paradigm of healthcare design practice and to set the bar for commitment within the architectural community.

- Our objectives in engaging in research are summarized as follows:
  - Improve patient outcomes (LOS, patient recuperation)
  - Increase productivity/operating efficiencies (workflow, resource access, direct care time)
  - Reduce operating or capital cost (staffing, materials)
  - Increase user satisfaction (patient, physician, staff)
  - Assist risk management (patient safety/reduce errors)
- HKS adopted the evidence-based design (EBD) paradigm to further enhance its ability to design safe and therapeutic environments for patients and caregivers in healthcare settings.
- Evidence from empirical research, where available, helps structure our discussions with clients and arrive at consensus at all phases of the design cycle.

2. How does HKS integrate EBD into studio culture?
- Three tools help in integrating EBD into studio culture:
  1. A design quality checklist that aggregates the collective regulatory requirements, best practice recommendations, and research evidence in the domains of patient safety, infection control, staff well-being, and patient satisfaction, among others, constituting the current key issues in healthcare settings. These tools are used by designers daily and serve as a measure of quality delivery in formal design progress reviews.
  2. The HKS Info Byte Series is an online dissemination/education about recent research findings that are relevant to healthcare design. These announcements are not project-specific and are aimed at elevating the consciousness of evidence to support our work and assist our teams by increasing their awareness of a knowledge they may not have discovered on their own.
  3. HKS delivers bi-monthly Brown Bag presentations to our entire network of regional offices engaged in healthcare design. This service is a strong vehicle for focusing on evidence that can make our planning and design stronger and more effective.
- We are also working on an EBD Balanced Scorecard developed by our HKS Research team to better integrate practice evidence with myriad other issues that must be addressed in the design and construction process.

3. How does HKS integrate EBD into the design process?

In addition to the cultural influences already described, HKS has hired a number of individuals who have years of experience as clinicians or administrators in healthcare. This team of nurses, physicians, technicians, therapists, pharmacists, and administrators comprise our Clinical Advisory Group, a team of professionals who work within the design process. They also serve as the investigative team HKS utilizes in its research and Functional Performance Evaluations (a kind of post-occupancy evaluation tailored to assess performance of our completed healthcare projects). This group uses their experience and knowledge to champion the gathering of evidence from research.

This team has a formal structure for how they infuse into the design process, from initial meeting to begin a project with our clients, through programming and planning, schematic design, and design development phases of our projects.

4. What are the EBD strengths/benefits for a project outcome?
- Ability to predict outcomes
- Informed decision-making
- Structured designer-client-consultant dialogue

5. What are its weaknesses?
- Perception of additional time requirement for project delivery
- Perception of slowing down of the programming and design processes
- Perception of increase in initial capital expenditure

6. Project Overviews
HKS has adopted two distinct lines of approach: EBD knowledge application and EBD knowledge generation.

The first approach is research conducted within a specific project to support specific design decisions. The second type of project constitutes applied research studies not attached to any specific healthcare project that are aimed at generating knowledge to support design decision-making across projects. Abstracts of two examples of each are included. The specific examples are:
1. EBD Knowledge Application
- Emory Neuro ICU unit (an example of Action Research)
- Houston Medical Center inpatient unit design (an example of simulation research)
2. EBD Knowledge Generation
- Inpatient Unit Flexibility Study (multiple site)
- Nature View–Acute Stress/Alertness Study (two hospitals)

1. EBD Knowledge Application Example
A) Emory University Hospital Neuro ICU Project
EBD Project Type: Decision support through action research.
Academic Collaborator: Dr. Craig Zimring, Professor, College of Architecture, Georgia Institute of Technology
Background: A temporary Neuro ICU expansion project to cater to an increasing census was undertaken as an experimental project to inform a subsequent large-scale expansion of the Emory University Hospital.
Project Objectives:
To collate and apply existing knowledge on best practice Neuro ICU designs. To design the ICU environment to facilitate family-centered care. To extract and make use of the rich informal knowledge of the then-current users of the Neuro ICU through a collaborative design process that uses existing evidence and best practice benchmarks as the informational backdrop for informed decision-making.
Design:
A detailed study of 10 award-winning ICU designs was conducted to extract best practice benchmark data. Structured observation protocols of existing Neuro ICU to identify key performance parameters. A series of design charrettes with the end users in a highly collaborative environment.
Setting: Emory Neuro ICU, Atlanta, GA
Project Period: 2005–2006
Design Innovations:
- More spacious patient rooms. Family space inside the patient room designed to optimize family involvement in patient care
- Family amenities: chair-cum-beds, sink, table, TV, Wi-Fi network
- Large windows for natural light
- Public areas with appropriate amenities: kitchen, lounge, wide corridors

What Proved Positive:
- Anecdotal evidence suggests high patient satisfaction. Further data collection in progress.

What Proved Negative:
- Large floor plate
- Longer walking distances for staff
- More difficulty in finding assistance

B) A MedModel decision-support study to assess the relative impact of nurse servers over central medication rooms on nursing efficiency

EBD Project Type: Decision support through simulation research.

Academic Collaborators:
Clarissa Lima, Graduate Student, College of Architecture, Georgia Institute of Technology
Godfried Augenbroe, Professor, College of Architecture, Georgia Institute of Technology

Background:
Excessive nurse walking on inpatient units has attracted attention, with some studies showing 3 to 5 miles of walking during typical shifts. Such excessive walking potentially interacts with operational stressors to create fatigue and hence impacts efficiency and patient safety. Moreover, undue walking takes valuable time away from direct patient care. One reason for walking involves getting medications for patients.

Study Objectives:
To assess through a MedModel simulation study the relative impact of nurse servers in patient rooms over central medication rooms on nurse walking distance and time with patients.

Design:
MedModel simulation runs on a floor plan with nurse servers and an identical floor plan with central medication room. Study focused solely on walking related to gathering medication and supplies.

Setting:
Houston Medical Center

Participants and Data type:
Walking distance, time spent

Data Collection:
The year 2006

Data Analysis:
Comparison of predicted walking distances and time spent

Findings:
For tasks related to medications alone, the nurse server alternative reduced walking by 576 feet during a typical 12-hour shift, thereby increasing time at bedside by 30 minutes. Based on study results, Houston Medical Center decided to adopt the nurse server design alternative for their new bed tower.

2. EBD Knowledge Generation Examples
A) Inpatient Unit Flexibility: Defining the design characteristics of a successful adaptable unit.

Project Status: Complete

Academic Collaborator:
Carolyn L. Cason, PhD, Professor, School of Nursing, University of Texas at Arlington

Background:
Flexibility in healthcare design is typically addressed with an architectural bias. The problem lies in the absence of knowledge on what flexibility means to stakeholders of inpatient units.

Study Objectives:
To understand what flexibility means to stakeholders of inpatient units. To identify physical design elements that influence stakeholders' flexibility. To identify design elements that promote or hinder stakeholders' flexibility.

Design:
Qualitative, exploratory study of inpatient units in six hospitals across the United States. The selected (purposive sampling) units demonstrated variability in size, age, shape, circulation configuration, nursing model, nurse-to-patient ratio, and presence of universal rooms.

Setting:
Parker Adventist Hospital, Parker, CO; Clarian West Medical Center, Avon, IN; Laredo Medical Center, Laredo, TX; McKay-Dee Hospital Center, Ogden, UT; Bon Secours St. Francis Hospital, Charleston, SC; and St. Rose Dominican Hospital–Siena, Henderson, NV.

Participants and Data Type:
Semi-structured interview with 50 participants from nursing, respiratory therapy, materials management, environmental services, pharmacy, and dietary services at the six hospitals. Systematic walk-through of inpatient units.

Data Collection:
September to November, 2006

Data Analysis:
Content analysis of interview transcripts

Findings:
In total, nine operational flexibility issues are affected by physical design. Of the nine issues, seven pertain to flexibility to adapt, and one each to flexibility to convert and expand. Flexibility to adapt issues include: 1) peer line-of-sight, 2) patient visibility, 3) multiple division/zoning options, 4) proximity of support, 5) resilience to move/relocate/interchange units, 6) ease of movement between units and departments, and 7) multiple administrative control and service expansion options. Flexibility to convert and expand is related to convertibility and expandability of support core spaces.

Funding Support:
AIA 2006 research grant
Herman Miller grant

Dissemination:
Conferences:
AIA National Convention, San Antonio, 2007
EDRA International Convention, Sacramento, 2007
Healthcare Design Conference, Dallas, 2007
Industry Journals:
Health Facilities Management

Healthcare Design
Peer-Reviewed:
Environment and Behavior (in press)
B) Relationships between Exterior Views and Nurse Stress: An Exploratory Examination

Project Status: Completed

Academic Collaborators:
Paul Barach, MD, MPH, Professor, Anesthesia and Patient Safety, Center for Patient Safety, Utrecht University Medical Center, Netherlands

Advisors:
Gary Evans, PhD, Professor, College of Human Ecology, Cornell University, USA
Craig Zimring, PhD, Professor, College of Architecture, Georgia Institute of Technology, USA

Background:
High stress and fatigue in nursing jobs are typically addressed through operational interventions. The physical environment, however, has been shown to modulate stress in building occupants. This study extended earlier studies focused on the positive impact of view on patients, to look at possible influences on caregivers.

Study Objectives:
To explore the association between duration of exposure to external view and view content on both chronic and acute stress and alertness of nurses.

Design:
Prospective, survey-based study. Statistical control measures.

Setting:
Two hospitals under the Children's Healthcare of Atlanta.

Participants and Data Type:
Thirty-two nurses from 19 different units at the two hospitals. Chronic stress, acute stress, and alertness data before and after 12-hour shifts. Duration of exposure to external view and view content (nature versus non-nature). Environmental stressors (lighting,

noise, thermal, ergonomics), organizational stressors, work load, age, and experience.

Data Collection:
November, 2006

Data Analysis:
Paired sample comparison, multivariate regression, joint partial F-test, multivariate regression with interaction terms.

Findings:
View duration has significant influence on both acute stress and alertness. It is only second in magnitude to organizational stress on its impact on alertness. Similarly, it is only second in magnitude to environmental stress on its impact on acute stress. For nurses whose alertness level remained the same or increased and acute stress level remained the same or

decreased between the beginning and end of the shift, a considerable proportion were exposed to view (and nature view). For nurses whose alertness level decreased and acute stress level increased between the beginning and end of the shift, a considerable proportion were exposed to no view or only non-nature view.

Dissemination:
Conferences:
EDRA International Convention, Sacramento, 2007
Healthcare Design Conference, Dallas, 2007
ASHE-PDC Conference, Orlando, 2008
Peer-Reviewed:
Health Environments Research & Design Journal (accepted for publication)

Evidence-Based Design Practice and Research at Ellerbe Becket

Terri Zborowsky, RN, BID, MSc, PhD Director of Healthcare Education & Research

1. Why does Ellerbe Becket embrace EBD?

Building upon Ellerbe Becket's nearly 100-year legacy as innovators in the design of healthcare facilities, we feel compelled to be at the forefront of this initiative as well. As one of only a handful of firms in the country with a formalized healthcare education and research program, Ellerbe Becket has set forth a research agenda that promotes:

- The use of design research internally among all our staff,
- Initiatives to help our clients make more informed design decisions, and
- Programs that will promote research within our larger design community.

Our approach to the dissemination of this information is to be open and share among our colleagues…with the overarching goal of elevating the

bar within the field of healthcare design.

For years social science researchers have explored ways to validate design decisions or design hypotheses. The recent attention paid to the role of research in helping to define "best practices" in healthcare design as it relates to improving patient and staff outcomes may prove to be the best way to integrate research and practice. This has implications not only for practice but also in the academic realm: how design is taught and what curricula are important. This movement, should it endure, could transform our world of healthcare design.

2. How does Ellerbe Becket integrate EBD into studio culture?

"Well, quite frankly, with pizza and lots of humor." In reality there is a great deal of truth to this: People learn better in an atmosphere of trust, respect and with their stomachs full. Our research efforts are accompanied by a learning program that infuses EBD into many different aspects of our studio culture. Design charettes are conducted starting with research-based criteria, and our projects include relevant research to help inform design decisions. In fact, our entire healthcare practice embraces EBD as relevant information to be integrated into our projects. Our clients demand it and our practioners embrace it.

Some examples of our practice-based research efforts:

Ellerbe Becket has undertaken a number of initiatives to make practice-based research an integral part of the firm's culture. Among them:

In-House Healthcare Research Database: Accessible to all employees, this database contains over 200 peer-reviewed research articles and health-care-related websites, and provides "one-stop research shopping" for employees.

Funded Research: Practice-driven research questions that Ellerbe Becket funds/co-funds to move forward the healthcare design discipline. The goal is to promote the role of practice-based research; to explore the role of research in understanding the world of healthcare design; and experiment with research methods most appropriate to the complex social science world of healthcare. This is the firm's way of using its assets to promote research and development in our field.

Healthcare Connection: Monthly firmwide meetings, held via Webex, used to share healthcare project information, current research in a particular topic area, or updates on healthcare conferences attended by employees. All employees of the firm are invited to participate. On occasion, clients are invited to participate as well.

Speaker Series: Employees share their integration of research within the firm and experiences with

using research in projects at conferences throughout the world. We are also co-sponsors (with the University of Minnesota Center for Spirituality and Healing) of a speaker series on Optimal Healing Environments, which brings leading thinkers in healthcare research to the Twin Cities for public lectures.

Research Used in Projects: Client-driven requests to integrate research into the design decision-making process.

Mock-Ups: Study of the effect of full-scale mock-ups on facility users, both functionally and aesthetically. A variety of methods can be used to study the questions at hand.

3. How does Ellerbe Becket integrate EBD into the design process?

Beyond the above-noted initiatives, we are embarking on an intense process of post-occupancy evaluation (POE) this year. This is where we can make the most significant strides on many levels. First, POEs will help us collect useful research information for our design teams. In essence, this research is the "missing link" to complete the cycle of design for our teams, helping to inform design decision-making on all subsequent projects. We believe this is critical to help our design teams effectively work within their own process. In this way, research is internalized and impacts each design team member's process intimately—this is a powerful way to use research to impact practice. By engaging in a formal research study, practitioners also become more familiar with research and research methods, enhancing their competency and comfort level with research. It's a win-win for everyone.

4. What are the EBD strengths for a project outcome?

I believe for the client, an important strength of EBD is in informing design-making. For example, it can help a client make stronger cases for a return on investment to their board of directors, on criteria such as single-handed patient rooms or decentralized nursing units. For designers, in working with our clients, it is important to finally be able to validate our collective design decisions with "evidence." Being able to link our design decisions to patient and staff outcomes is empowering. We suspected it was true, but now that we can *see* it is true, and we can work toward changing the field of healthcare design…we can improve the environment that our clients work in and by doing so, impact their quality of life by impacting their quality of work and by improving the quality of life of patients, families, visitors, and staff.

5. What are the weaknesses?

One downside to EBD is that research takes a commitment of time and money unlike any other movement in healthcare design that we have seen to date. The question is this: Will our field of design, which is relatively new to the world of academia, be willing and able to embrace the world of research? The answer to this question will become clear as we see academic programs' willingness to integrate research into curriculum development. EBD will only succeed if we begin to integrate research into our educational systems of design; research will only be fully embraced by practice if practitioners understand the nuances of research.

6. Give a project overview—Project Description

We recently designed a significant expansion to a large urban hospital that was trying to reconcile how to design for three different types of patients—Critical Care, Telemetry, Medical/Surgical—in a new bed tower. Using the research of Ann Hendrich on Acuity Adaptable rooms and John Reiling's documentation on the patient safe room in West Bend, WI, it was determined that a same-handed patient room would be the prevailing template used throughout the patient tower. After much evaluation, this decision was modified slightly after the patient room template was set, in that the hospital elected to move forward with mirrored patient rooms—retaining the building

infrastructure that will allow the facility to accept same-handed patient rooms in the future. Half of the patient rooms will be dedicated to med/surg, the other half to critical care. Remarkably, the client decided to build fewer patient rooms to accommodate this model, a true case of using research to inform design decision-making. Their belief in the Acuity Adaptable room as a good ROI provided the impetus to move forward with this design approach.

Research Agenda—Create a patient-safe experience, minimize patient transfers, minimize staff travel.

7. What proved positive?

Having research that could springboard the dialogue needed to develop a design that satisfied all types of patient acuity.

8. What proved negative?

While the research available was great to provoke dialogue, they are case studies (one a research case study, the other anecdotal documentation). No research exists to date to validate these decisions.

9. What were the design innovations?

The above case study described resulted in a prototype that will be ready for a complex research study once the building is complete. We are able to identify the data needed to conduct a thorough pre- and post-research study. This research study will be able to help inform us all on the importance of the relationship between the head of the bed to the toilet to patient safety in both a medical/surgical unit as well as a critical unit. This project will be an important study of room layout as it relates to patient safety.

10. How has the EBD approach influenced a future project of a similar nature?

Many of our patient tower projects now start off using the templates reviewed for the above project. The research underlying our case study has set off a flurry of discussions in our office about how to integrate research into the design as well as the design decision-making process.

Evidence-Based Design Practice and Research at Kahler Slater

Lyn Geboy, PhD

I believe evidence-based design can be effectively synthesized for design professionals as having three main activities that can be listed in order of difficulty: finding, applying, and doing. As settings have increased in complexity, research-related activities and individuals who excel at finding design-related research have grown in importance in the minds of conscientious design professionals. The fact that there are design research professionals now on staff in design firms or successfully consulting is true confirmation of the increased recognition of the need for research knowledge in the design field.

Applying research is for me where the action is right now. Ensuring context in terms of a project or plans for research findings is usually a win-win situation. Finding efficient, effective ways to ensure that designers have the information they need, when they need it, and in a form that they can immediately understand is what we spend most of our time on. The best designers I work with want to know that they are making design decisions that reflect their best abilities, decisions that are supported by research evidence whenever possible.

Doing research is trickier. Gutman and Wohlwill, writing decades ago, noted a fundamental difference in the problems of researchers and practitioners: researchers' problems are questions that seek answers in research data—often non-contextual—and practitioners' problems are questions that demand concrete, contextual, and immediate environmental solutions. From my desk, I don't see this difference has changed much. The pursuit of "methodological rigor" has compelled many researchers to limit their attention to non-contextual measuring of discrete environmental stimuli and partitive analysis in the effort to attain "definitive" cause-and-effect relationships. Practitioners, on the other hand, are still responsible for solving complex problems in context, under the ever-increasing pressures of intractable budgets, exigent deadlines, and rising client expectations. Because I see the role of the researcher-practitioner as providing designers with information they can use to make their designs more effective for users, I see researchers-practitioners as working in support of designers, and our research—and research methodologies—must be oriented toward resolving practical needs.

What types of research are suited to research in practice? I believe design firms should be involved in any and all types of research, as long as the research method fits the question at hand. Quantitative, qualitative, and mixed methods are all suitable. Regardless of method, however, whatever research is done in firms should accomplish two objectives: build designers' general knowledge base and solve immediately pressing problems.

Like the Evidence-based Design Wheel, I developed a conceptual model that organizes the research knowledge base into 12 environmental factors that contribute to the healing environment. (See Figure 5.-12.) It's been very useful in making the critical mass of research information more accessible to designers and clients. Making research understandable is the first step in getting designers to apply it in their own practice.

We regularly send out emails with article links and research summaries, and encourage designers to share items of interest with others in our multiple offices as well. We lead participatory sessions that we call "Topic Charrettes," where we summarize research and health-related topics, then discuss design implications.

Figure 5.12
Kahler Slater's "Evidence-Based Design Wheel"—a tool for their design staff.
© 2007 Kahler Slater, Inc.

THE EVIDENCE BASED DESIGN WHEEL:
Environmental Factors that Affect Outcomes

So what are the challenges and opportunities in practice-based research today? First, I think that there is still work to do to get designers on board with the idea that research is a help, not a hindrance, to creative design. Second, in our experience, clients are valuing what EBD is bringing to the table, but the realities related to budget and time don't always allow for them to pursue research to the degree that they might like. Third, I anticipate there will be lots of fits and starts in building a shared body of knowledge among organizations—for profit and not-for-profit—that compete for market share.

In terms of opportunities, there are many. The demand for research-informed design is continuing to grow, particularly in healthcare settings, where addressing complexity requires new and better information produced through research. And finally, the current boom in designing and constructing healthcare facilities will provide us with all the field settings we can handle—a boon for researchers like us!

The Outpatient Care Center for Martha Jefferson Hospital
Charlottesville, Virginia

The Outpatient Care Center for Martha Jefferson Hospital (MJH) (opened: 2005) displays evidence-based design features, including human scale, flexible furniture groupings, generous use of windows and inspirational view of and direct access to nature. (See Figure 5.13.) The human scale of the café at

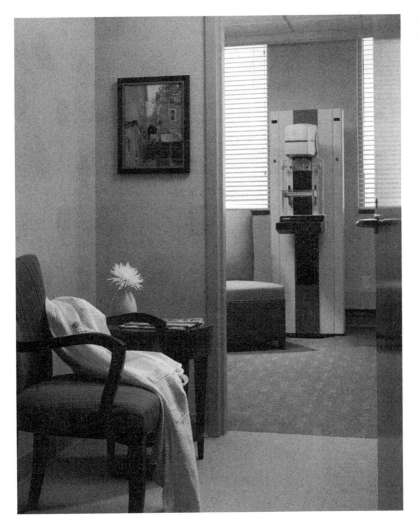

Figure 5.13
Martha Jefferson Hospital's mammography unit.
Hedrich Blessing, Steve Hall photographer.

MJH makes for a warm and welcoming space. Tables for two or four people support social interaction at an intimate level. Abundant windows let daylight into space, allow guests a close look at landscaping details, and afford views of the magnificent Blue Ridge Mountains in the distance.

The library at Martha Jefferson Hospital affords on-site access to resources, increasing patients' sense of control and responsible engagement with their healthcare issues. (See Figure 5.14.) A central evidence-based objective, sense of control, is associated with stress. Loss of control results in stress, which in turn, negatively affects outcomes. Provisions for control in the healthcare setting such as this library improve a patient's ability to deal with stress, experience less stress, and support better health.

Figure 5.14
Martha Jefferson
Hospital's library.
*Hedrich Blessing, Steve Hall
photographer.*

Build the Business Case

The process of justifying the expenditure of multi-millions and in some cases over a billion dollars on the construction and outfitting of a healthcare facility misses vital information if it does not consider evidence-based data that calculates the return on investment (ROI). There is little evidence that links that kind of spending to the ROI, but it is growing. The current methodology for budgeting these complex building types helps establish a great chasm between a guaranteed maximum price (GMP) and the return on investment of an efficient operating system. Inherent in the evidence-based process are mechanics that help close that gap. Linking first costs with operational savings will equip a new generation of facilities with a business model featuring better efficiency for employees in these vast systems as well as enhanced safety for patients and staff alike.

In 2004, the magic that occurs when a smart group of big thinkers gets together happened around this very topic. Data was coming in from the first four Pebble Projects and someone asked the question if The Pebble effort was recording the costs savings from the improved

Figure 5.15
HDR's St. Alphonsus Regional Medical Center (Pebble Project), one of the first four Pebbles to report data from studies after Bronson Methodist, Clarian-Health, and Karmanos Cancer Center. It was from these four projects that the Fable Hospital was invented.
Photo © VanceFox.com.

outcomes from these design interventions. (See Figure 5.15.) It wasn't long before six Center for Health Design board members jumped in to meet the challenge. The legendary "Fable Hospital"[16] was invented, utilizing all of the proven design features and showing a payback almost within its first year of operation, which when compounded presented a very attractive financial model for a new building. Blair Sadler elaborates in Essay 5-2.

Evidence-based value engineering was discussed in Chapter 1 as a way to align rising construction costs with operational savings. Construction managers are keenly aware that this opportunity exists, but enough data has not been generated to address all of the issues needed to make the case strong enough to follow through. In the not too distant future, we stand to gain a better base of knowledge due to the contribution of the 50 Pebble Projects on board with The Center for Health Design. Their shared economic analyses will help the program decide where it is best to spend the dollars that create the best return on the investment. This will ease the pressure on teams during the cost reduction process where cuts should focus on where evidence proves less return on investment rather than on a perception of savings. Like-handed rooms were thought to be expensive because of the inefficiency of the plumbing layouts. Turner Construction did an analysis of all of their like-handed projects and projected an average cost of $3,500 over the cost of a mirrored room. It is too early to tell if the savings associated with this

Essay 5-2
Why Evidence-Based Design Makes Good Business Sense

Blair L. Sadler, J.D. Past President + CEO Rady Children's Hospital,
San Diego and Senior Fellow, Institute for Healthcare Improvement

With all the evidence now available to show that connection between the physical environment and improved safety/quality for patients, families, and staff, why haven't all hospitals insisted on including evidence-based design in their projects? Some have. For those who have not, the barriers are often perceived to be economic.

This is understandable due to the rapidly escalating costs of construction and, until recently, we did not have the evidence upon which to base solid financial operating impact assessments.

Based on published evidence and actual experience of pioneering health-care organizations, in 2004 a multidisciplinary team analyzed the data and designed a hypothetical Fable hospital. It was called a Fable hospital because it had not then been built but it could at any time (and a few, like Dublin, would qualify). In Fable, the hospital's leaders decided to incorporate all the appropriate, evidence-based design innovations (Frontiers of Health Care Management, Berry et al).

After detailed analysis, they estimated that including these would require a relatively modest one-time capital cost of $12 million (or 5 percent of the $240 million base cost). When they analyzed the operating cost savings resulting from reducing infections; eliminating unnecessary intra-hospital patient transfers; minimizing patient falls; lowering drug costs; lessening employee turnover rates; as well as improving market share and philanthropy, they were amazed. The additional $12 million capital cost would be more than offset by the end of the second year. With effective management and monitoring, the financial operating benefits would continue year after year, making the additional innovations a sound long-term investment. In short, there was a compelling business case for building better, safer hospitals.

Since 2004, construction costs have skyrocketed but the business case has become even stronger. Significant new research has been published that provides additional support for evidence-based design features and a comprehensive review of the literature has been completed (Ulrich and Zimring submitted to *HERD Journal* April, 2008). For example, single-patient rooms are now a basic requirement of most hospitals being built today.

Studies show that installing ceiling lifts can significantly reduce the costs of workforce injuries resulting from lifting patients (Joseph and Fritz, 2006). The costs of treating patients with hospital-acquired infections or who have suffered injuries from falls has escalated.

The acuity-adaptable room remains one of the most powerful innovations to improved care by reducing unnecessary intra-hospital transfers, having a threefold benefit of reduced errors and falls, significantly increased patient satisfaction, and reduction in non-productive staff time. Dublin has implemented these rooms throughout the entire hospital. (Edwards, 2007; Ulrich and Zhu, 2007).

Noise-reduction innovations: Acoustical ceiling tiles are very economical as is providing positive, anxiety-reducing distractions through appropriate art and music.

On the revenue side of the equation, dramatic new changes are occurring as well. A fundamentally new concept has emerged in the reimbursement of hospitals and physicians. It is called value-based purchasing or pay for performance (P4P) and it will have a profound impact on the business case for quality improvement, including the environment in which people work and care is received. The Center for Medicare Medicaid Services (CMS) has announced that there will be NO reimbursement for certain hospital-acquired infections and patients' injuries (including falls).

Also significant is the increasing transparency about reporting patient experiences in hospitals. The Hospitals are Quality Information from the Consumer perspective (HCAHPS) was developed to: (1) produce comparable data on patients' perspectives of care, through public reporting; (2) create incentives for hospitals to improve care; and (3) increase public accountability through increased transparency of care. Of the survey's 27 items, 18 address critical aspects of the hospital experience including cleanliness and quietness of the hospital environment and the overall rating of the hospital. (Sadler et al., submitted to *HERD Journal*, April, 2008).

Conclusion

Since the landmark Fable Hospital article in 2004, the business case for implementing proven evidence-based design intervention has become even stronger. The costs of unnecessary patient harm are larger, public and employer expectations and demands far higher, the importance to customer satisfaction greater, and the reimbursement implications of the pay for performance revolution are profound. As part of their management and fiduciary responsibilities, hospital leaders must include cost-effective, evidence-based design interventions in all appropriate programs or suffer the economic consequences in an increasingly competitive and transparent environment.

type room, especially as it contributes to efficiency and safety justify the construction costs, but the projects are in place to measure. St. Joe's in Wisconsin and Dublin Methodist have it on their research agenda. Decisions that are informed by outcomes and not by scale will inform the new wave of smart construction. Imagine selling the concept of a new building based on the return on investment or, better yet, on the safety improvement or efficiency improvement over its cost per unit. We need a paradigm shift toward this way of project decision-making. Watch for future reporting to see if the financial model will work.

Share With Fellow Professionals

Chances are if you are reading this book then you are likely to attend or speak at your professional conferences or read or write for your professional journals. It is about sharing current practices that gets us to participate actively or passively. The need in an evidence-based practice to share is great since the speed of innovation is dependent on the last published or toured concept. The next big idea needs to germinate from the current big idea. It happened with Ann Hendrich's studies at Clarian, and Frank Becker's studies at Weill Cornell, and Lola Fritz's study at PeaceHealth, and Sue Olson's studies at Bronson. It will occur with Dublin and St. Alphonsus as data is reported in. All will grow and change their design methodologies from the lessons learned at these living labs.

I would like to thank all the contributing essayists for the time they put into sharing their wisdom on the very important topic of evidence-based design. Their insight hopefully brought some of your questions about the process into clearer focus. It sparked for me different perspectives and showed that it was our collective "group brain" that got us to this place in time. There are many opportunities to share your projects and if they are evidence-based then the story is even more important to tell. From the germination of a strategic initiative, to the investigative stages. For mapping of wisdom gained, to the "aha" moment and the big idea. And finally, from inspired trial studies translating into improved outcomes, fostering research projects, and sharing with professionals ideally via peer-review.

There are sizeable gaps in the research making it clear we need an agenda to move forward. Maggie Calkins, a pioneer in the field of long-term care, shares her insights on the road that lies ahead for further studies in this subspecialty.

Essay 5-3
What We Know: Evidence-Based Design in Long-Term Care Settings

Margaret Calkins, PhD
President IDEAS, Kirtland, OH

Much of the environment-behavior research in long-term care settings has focused on individuals with dementia, who comprise up to 85 percent of nursing home residents and 50 percent of individuals in assisted living (ALFA, 1999; Maslow and Ory, 2001; Teresi, Holmes, and Ory, 2000).[17,18,19] This focus on the needs of individuals with dementia has spurred a dramatic and fundamental change in the overall approach to the provision of care and the design of these shared residential settings.

The earliest research in nursing homes focused on the negative consequences of what Goffman called the "total institution" (Goffman, 1961)[20], specifically, lack of control and lack of privacy. Research on privacy found that appropriate interpersonal socialization increased when individuals were afforded greater privacy (Lawton, 1977; Sommer and Ross, 1958).[21,22] A number of other studies have clearly demonstrated that higher satisfaction (resident and family) and better clinical outcomes (in terms of fewer nosocomial infections and hospitalizations) are associated with private bedrooms (Kane, Baker, Salmon, and Leazie, 1998; Mosher-Ashley and Barrett, 1997; Terakawa, 2004; R. Ulrich and C. Zimring, 2004; R.S. Ulrich, 2004).[23,24,25,26,27]

Another area of research that was initiated with individuals with dementia but has spread to the whole long-term care continuum relates to the number of residents who are grouped together. Traditionally called units, but more recently referred to as households or neighborhoods[28] (see Calkins, 2003, for a typology of these terms), these groups were traditionally determined by staffing ratios. Typically, one nurse can serve 60 residents on a nighttime shift, thus 60 beds was a very common unit size. Research, however, has shown that these larger units (30 to 70 residents) are associated with higher anxiety/aggression, faster cognitive decline, and greater emotional disturbances, while smaller units (9 to 19 residents) are associated with less anxiety and depression, less psychoactive drug use, greater social interaction and friendship formation, more resident-staff interaction, and more positive activity and less negative activity[29] (Day and Calkins, 2002).

Building design impacts an individual's ability to be oriented to certain locations. Several studies have demonstrated that meaningful, personalized memorabilia at the bedroom entrance can improve the ability for residents to identify their own bedroom (Namazi, 1990; Nolan, Mathews, Truesdell-Todd, and VanDorp, 2002; Zeisel, Hyde, and Levkoff, 1994)[30,31,32] and potentially reduce unwanted intrusions into others' rooms. One study found an eightfold increase in toilet usage (37 versus 285) when the toilet was directly visible versus being behind a curtain (Namazi, Rosner, and Rechlin, 1991).[33] Other studies focused on factors including signage and landmarks/reference points find that lack of visual differentiation and poor signage lead to both disorientation and anxiety (cited in Joseph, 2006).[34] (See Figure 5.16.)

Lighting and exposure to sunlight have also been evaluated as being related to several different resident outcomes. A number of studies have shown that exposure to bright light—either sunlight by spending some time outside or bright light therapy—can improve sleep hygiene (Campbell, Dawson, and Anderson, 1993; Kim, Song, and Yoo,

2003; Koyama, Matsubara, and Nakano, 1999; Satlin, Volicer, Ross, Herz, and Campbell, 1992).[35,36,37,38] Low light levels are associated with increased agitation and disruptive behaviors (Sloane et al., 1998)[39], while high light levels have been shown to reduce agitation and depression (LaGarce, 2004; Lovell, Ancoli-Israel and Gevirtz, 1995; Sumaya, Rienzi, and Moss, 2001).[40] (See Figure 5.17.)

There are several gaps in the research. Most fall-related research is so multimodal that it is virtually impossible to determine the effect size of environmental interventions, such as handrails or flooring surface. Much of the environmental sleep research fails to take into account whether the person is in a private room or a shared room, which has clear implications for sleep hygiene. While the evidence on the value of private rooms over traditional (side-by-side) shared bedrooms is strong, few studies have examined the impact of enhanced shared rooms on psychosocial, clinical, or operational factors.

An agenda is clearly articulated for those who practice in this specialty. Find the forward-thinking interdisciplinary team members to spur further thinking on these and other topics so that this industry is ready for the fussiest of consumers—the Baby Boomers.

Submit for Peer Review

Submitting for a peer-review journal requires a certain style of writing. Work with a researcher to document processes, methodologies, and findings. Read the journals you are interested in publishing in and get a sense of the type of studies that apply to a project's agenda. A new, peer-reviewed journal relevant to this area of practice has been released called *Health Environments Research and Design Journal,* or *HERD.* Its inaugural issue was unveiled at the Healthcare Design 07 Conference. It is an interdisciplinary, peer-reviewed journal whose mission is to enhance the knowledge and practice of evidence-based healthcare design by disseminating research findings, discussing issues and trends, and translating research into practice. It publishes the most relevant healthcare design–related studies that meet academic rigor. *HERD* will feature research papers, opinion papers, theory papers, metanalysis/metasynthesis book reviews, case studies, independent post-occupancy evaluations, letters to the editors, and responses to letters and papers. All are welcome to submit a manuscript to *HERD*; submissions will be accepted online through HERD's online journal office at http://herd.edmgr.com.[41] (See Figure 5.18.) Other journals in design include the *International Journal of Design* (see Figure 5.19), the *Journal of Interior Design, Journal of Architecture and Planning Research, Landscape Journal,* and others. A good source to keep pace with many of these publications is through the Environmental Design Research Association

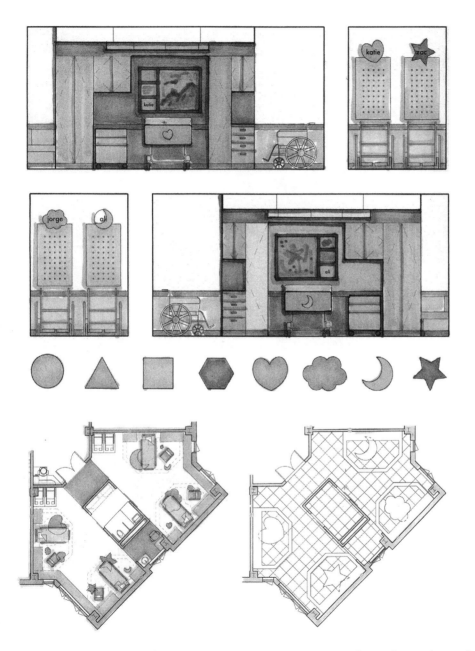

Figure 5.16
Elizabeth Seton Pediatric Center's personalized bed's located in a household configuration in a Neighborhood for this pediatric long-term care facility.
Perkins Eastman/CAMA, Inc.

(EDRA)'s publication *Research Design Connections*. It is important to know the emphasis of each of these publications to know where the proper fit is for your documented project research and then submit accordingly.

Figure 5.17
At Linden Ponds, daylight is captured through skylights in this long-term care facility's library.
Steffian Bradley Architects.

Essay 5-4
Research and Competitive Advantage
By D. Kirk Hamilton, FAIA, FACHA

Leaders of every design firm should be asking themselves how they can become proficient at evidence-based design, and how to do so quickly, because it has the prospect of becoming a powerful differentiator in the design marketplace. In the last few years, for just one example, there have been a number of major healthcare systems that have begun to ask for credentials in evidence-based design. Clients are increasingly savvy about the results associated with project designs. They want to know what the firm and its members have done in the way of designing with evidence, and are especially interested in learning what results the firm can claim.

Develop committed experts: Each firm that intends to practice in an evidence-based model will need a qualified staff who are familiar with the process of designing with evidence and who have a reasonable understanding of research. This means they should understand something about the different types of research, be capable of finding it, and making an evaluation of its quality. They will need to be able to use critical thinking to interpret the implications of research for the unique circumstances of each individual project.

Use a consistent process: The firm should be able to describe its design process to a prospective client, an engineer, or consultant collaborator. Of course a key feature of the process will be the way in which the firm assures that research informs major design decisions for every client. The process should have enough formal documentation to guide a design team, and to indicate when the team is intentionally varying from it. The design process should be universal for the firm; not reserved for clients who request an evidence-based design.

Predict and document the intended outcomes: A key to credibility in the marketplace will be the firm's ability to document how evidence-based design concepts have produced results. There should be a fully documented chain of logic that runs from research findings, through interpretation of their implication for the project, to a design concept that is related to a hypothesis about the result that can be expected when it is built. Results that have been predicted are far more credible than random observations made after the project has been completed.

Measure the results: When the designer has predicted an outcome, it is incumbent upon them to devise a means of verifying whether their prediction has come to pass. Measurement of project outcomes is absolutely required in any evidence-based process. Firms will make no progress with evidence-based design and clients who request it until they have begun to rigorously collect credible information about their projects. An important step is to recognize what data will be required and make arrangements to collect it both before and after the project. The client will have a number of types of data they would like to see. The firm will have others.

Most design practitioners will need to learn to avoid the tendency to believe they have "proved" something with their findings. In the complex worlds of human behavior in the context of the physical environment with all of its confounding variables, it is sufficient to say the hypothesis was supported.

Share the findings: Once data has been collected and there are findings to report, the evidence-based practitioner should be prepared to share them with the field. Good or bad, findings that result from an appropriate study method are of use to the entire field. Firms that fail to openly share their findings will be less credible to prospective clients than those who do. Firms that only share their positive results will find skeptics among their listeners. Firms that openly share all, indicating what they have learned from every set of positive and negative findings, are most likely to be perceived as believable, honest, and authentic.

Avoid unsupportable claims: Some practitioners may be tempted to inflate their credentials or exaggerate their results in order to benefit from the marketplace advantage.

Figure 5.18
The cover of the new
Health Environments Re-
search and Design Jour-
nal or HERD Journal,
Vendome Group, LLC.

FALL 2007 VOL. 1, NO. 1   WWW.HERDJOURNAL.COM

HERD

Health Environments Research & Design Journal

Welcome

Letters to the Editors

Editor's Column

Research Methods for Evidence-Based Healthcare Design

Opinion

Design of the Physical Environment for Changing Healthcare Needs

Evidence-Based Design: Strong Support and Healthy Skepticism

Innovation, Architecture, and Quantum Reality: Synthesis in a New Age for Healthcare

The Healthcare Design Decade

Leading Change: The Academy of Architecture for Health Foundation Grants

The Time Has Come

Reflections on Healing Environments and Evidence-Based Design

Editor's Column

Bridging Design & Research

Articles

Medical Complications of Intra-Hospital Patient Transports: Implications for Architectural Design and Research

Centralized and Decentralized Nurse Station Design: An Examination of Caregiver Communication, Work Activities, and Technology

Nursing Unit Design and Communication Patterns: What Is "Real" Work?

ISSN 000X-0234

VENDOME GROUP   THE CENTER FOR HEALTH DESIGN

IJDesign

ISSN 1991-3761

■ International
Journal of
Design

No. 1 / Vol. 1

April. 2007

Figure 5.19
The cover of the International Journal of Design.
IJDesign.

Inability to live up to such claims could have disastrous implications for the firm, and to some degree all of the design professions.

Collect the stories: In order to make the marketing case to prospective clients, the firm will need to collect findings from many or most projects, along with the stories of the ways in which these results were achieved. Compiling data will be helpful, but capturing the emotions from stories will help convince the listeners of the firm's commitment and passion for this fascinating process.

I will confidently predict that firms which have a credible track record in evidence-based design, along with qualified staff and properly documented findings associated with their past projects, will have a significant advantage in the marketplace. I believe this advantage will be sustained into the future. This is not a fad. I am equally convinced that firms which cannot demonstrate competence in the evidence-based process and who have not provided public access to positive findings will unfortunately suffer in the marketplace. For me, the choice is clear.

Summary

There is much to understand and incorporate into practice. If you are just beginning an evidence-based practice, take each of the suggestions in each of the four steps of Chapters 2 through 5 and find your comfort zone to adjust your conventional practice. Some projects will be easier than others. Once you wholly own the methodology, evidence-based design becomes infinitely easier to embrace. You will find that the client seeking an evidence-based approach will find you and your team as the playing field is currently small, but in time it will grow and become much more competitive. Use the resources mentioned here and find your unique set of "connectors" to guide you. You will soon be on your way.

Checklist: Measure and Share Outcomes

1. Measure Outcomes
- Place a researcher on a project's interdisciplinary team—asap.
- Be rigorous in research methodologies.
- Add to the existing body of knowledge but innovate as well.
- Become a student of other firms' research methodologies.

2. Build the Business Case
- Collect a baseline of costs for issues under consideration for research.
- Monitor changes throughout the duration of the project.
- Record changes in first year of occupancy and again as time goes by.

- Report and contribute to the larger body of the business case.

3. Share with Fellow Professionals
- Identify and then fill in the gaps of research documentation.
- Speak at conferences in and outside of your profession.
- Submit writings to professional journals.
- Document process of all EBD projects.

4. Submit for Peer Review
- Write up research findings.
- Identify appropriate journals.
- Learn from process.

Endnotes

1. *Webster's Ninth New Collegiate Dictionary*, Merriam-Webster Inv., Publishers, 1985, p. 1002.
2. Kumar, R. *Research Methodology, A Step-by-Step Guide for Beginners,* Sage Publications, 2005; p. 6.
3. Geboy, L. Notes from Healthcare Design 07, Dallas Texas.
4. U.S. Food and Drug Administration, www.fda.gov/oc/ohrt/irbs/faqs.html.
5. Joseph, A.; Hamilton, K. "The Pebble Projects: Coordinated Evidence-Based Case Studies," *Building Research & Information*, 36:22, pp. 129–145.
6. Geboy.
7. Henrichsen, L.; Smith, M.; Baker, D. "Taming the Research Beast," Brigham Young University, Linguistics and English department, 1997.
8. Kumar, p. 7.
9. Joseph, A.; Hamilton, K. pp. 133–136.
10. Ulrich, R. "View through a Window May Influence Recovery from Surgery," *Science*, 1984, pp. 420–421.
11. Ulrich, R.; Lunden, O. "Effects of Nature and Abstract Pictures on Patients Recovering from Open Heart Surgery," Paper presented at the International Congress of Behavioral Medicine, Uppsula, Sweden, 1990.
12. Guenther, R.; Vittori, G. *Sustainable Healthcare,* John Wiley & Sons, 2008, p. 386.
13. Kellert, S. *Building for Life, Designing and Understanding the Human-Nature Connection,* Island Press, 2005, p. 5.
14. Coleman, T. "Creating a Healing Home for Older Adults and Persons with Disabilities," ASID, Healing Homes, 2008, p. 48.

15. Thompson, John; Goldin, G. *The Hospital: A Social and Architectural History*, Yale University Press, 1975, p. 225.

16. Berry, L.; Parker, D.; Coile, R.; Hamilton, K.; O'Neill, D.; Sadler, B. Can Better Buildings Improve Care and Increase your Financial Returns?, ACHE/HAP, 2004.

17. ALFA (1999). Guide to Research Information for the Long-Term Care Industries: Assisted Living Communities and Nursing Homes. Fairfax, VA: Assisted Living Federation of America.

18. Maslow, K.; Ory, M. (2001). Review of a Decade of Dementia Special Care Unit Research: Lessons Learned and Future Directions. *Alzheimer's Care Quarterly, 2*(3), pp. 10–16.

19. Teresi, J.; Holmes, D.; Ory, M. (2000). The Therapeutic Design of Environments for People with Dementia: Further Reflections and Recent Findings from the National Institute on Aging Collaborative Studies of Dementia Special Care Units. *The Gerontologist, 40*(4), p. 417.

20. Goffman, E. (1961). Asylums: Essays on the Social Situation of Mental Patients and Other Inmates. Garden City, NY: Anchor Books.

21. Lawton, M.P. (1977). The impact of the environment on aging and behavior. In J. Birren & K.W. Schaie (Eds.), *Handbook of the Psychology of Aging* (Vol. 1, pp. 276–303). New York: Van Nostrand, Reinhold.

22. Sommer, R.; Ross, H. (1958). Social interaction on a geriatric ward. *International Journal of Social Psychology, 4*, pp. 128–133.

23. Kane, R.; Baker, M.; Salmon, J.; Leazie, W. (1998). Consumer perspectives on private versus shared accommodations in assisted living. Washington, DC: AARP.

24. Mosher-Ashley, P.M.; Barrett, P.W. (1997). *A Life Worth Living: Practical strategies for reducing depression in older adults.* Baltimore, MD: Health Professions Press.

25. Terakawa, Y. (2004, June 2–4). *The relationship between environment and behavior at the institutional setting for the elderly.* Paper presented at the Environmental Design Research Association 35th Annual Conference, Albuquerque, NM.

26. Ulrich, R.; Zimring, C. (2004). The Role of the Physical Environment in the Hospital of the 21st Century: A Once in a Lifetime Opportunity: The Center for Health Design.

27. Ulrich, R.S. (2004). Evidence-based environmental design for improving medical outcomes.

28. Calkins, M. (2003). On getting our terms straight. *DESIGN, 53*(March), pp. 17–20.

29. Day, K.; Calkins, M.P. (2002). Design and Dementia. In R.B.A. Churchman (Ed.), *Handbook of Environmental Psychology.* New York: John Wiley & Sons.

30. Namazi, K.H. (1990). Effect of personalized cues at bedrooms on wayfinding among institutionalized elders with Alzheimer's disease. Paper presented at the American Psychological Association, Boston, MA.

31. Nolan, B.; Mathews, R.; Truesdell-Todd, G.; VanDorp, A. (2002). Evaluation of the Effect of Orientation Cues on Wayfinding in Persons with Dementia. *Alzheimer's Care Quarterly, 3*(1), pp. 46–49.

32. Zeisel, J.; Hyde, J.; Levkoff, S. (1994). Best practices: An environment-behavior model for Alzheimer special care units. *The American Journal of Alzheimer's Care and Related Disorders & Research, 9*(2), pp. 4–21.

33. Namazi, K.H.; Rosner, T.T.; Rechlin, L.R. (1991). Long-term memory cuing to reduce visuo-spatial disorientation in Alzheimer's disease patients is a special care unit. *The American Journal of Alzheimer's Care and Related Disorders & Research, 6*(6), pp. 10–15.

34. Joseph, A. (2006). *Health promotion by design in long-term care settings.* Concord, CA: The Center for Health Design.

35. Campbell, S.S.; Dawson, D.; Anderson, M.W. (1993). Alleviation of Sleep Maintenance Insomnia with Timed Exposure to Bright Light. *Journal of the American Geriatric Society, 41*(8), pp. 829–836.

36. Kim, S.; Song, H.H.; Yoo, S.J. (2003). The effect of bright light on sleep and behavior in dementia: An analytic review. *Geriatric Nursing, 24*(4), pp. 239–243.

37. Koyama, E.; Matsubara, H.; Nakano, T. (1999). Bright Light Treatment for Sleep-Wake Disturbances in Aged Individuals with Dementia. *Psychiatry Clin Neurosci, 53*(2), pp. 227–229.

38. Satlin, A.; Volicer, L.; Ross, V.; Herz, L.; Campbell, S. (1992). Bright Light Treatment of Behavioral and Sleep Disturbances in Patients with Alzheimer's Disease. *American Journal of Psychiatry, 149*(8), pp. 1028–1032.

39. Sloane, P.; Mitchell, M.; Preisser, J.; Phillips, C.; Commander, C.; Burker, E. (1998). Environmental Correlates of Resident Agitation in Alzheimer's Disease Special Care Units. *Journal of the American Geriatric Society, 42*, pp. 862–869.

40. LaGarce, M. (2004). Daylight interventions and Alzheimer's behaviors—a twelve-month study.

Part III
Dublin Methodist
Hospital (Pebble Project).
Courtesy of OhioHealth/
Dublin Methodist Hospital,
George C. Anderson
Photography, Karlsberger
Architects/CAMA, Inc.

PART III
NEXUS

"To do easily what is difficult for
others is the mark of talent."
—Henri Frederic Amiel.

Chapter 6
Evidence-Based Design in Practice

"By experience we find out a short way by a long wandering."
—Roger Ascham

This chapter, like in the one before, allows the reader to take a good look into the operations of a firm that has fully embraced the evidence-based process. It is through the generosity of firms like Anshen + Allen that this process will grow and become commonplace. Their methodology should serve as an inspiration for others.

A Look Into an Evidence-Based Practice That Recognizes the Need for Research That Improves Clinical Outcomes

I have left this chapter to two legends, Derek Parker, FAIA and Bill Rostenberg, FAIA, of Anshen + Allen Architects, San Francisco, because of their conviction about championing the practice of evidence-based design thoughtfully, methodically, and wisely. They offer on the following pages brilliant insight and a masterful road map toward organizing knowledge within the design firm. Derek will be the first to say that evidence-based design is in its infancy and as such, needs time to develop. He rightfully points out the fear of most that evidence-based design is at a marketing level but not embraced by those who are responsible for the design of our healthcare facilities. This momentum needs to be built cautiously and protect itself against proprietary interest, and engage practice only when it is ready. It is Derek's conviction that we take a conservative approach and not run too quickly to market. Both Derek and Bill offer a serious look at the issues plaguing healthcare and how a slow, steady pace of redefining the design process helps to develop improved clinical outcomes.

Figure 6-1
Gaudy Sanguin shells.
*Picture by Henry Domke,
www.henrydomke.com.*

Essay 6-1
Why Has Anshen + Allen Embraced Evidence-Based Design?

*Derek Parker, FAIA, Director, Anshen + Allen Architects,
Director Emeritus, The Center for Health Design*

Anshen + Allen holds deep convictions about the importance of health to the foundation of a society's sense of well-being and liberty. Each new project is looked at as an opportunity to advance the state of design of a healthcare project that would in turn further the goals of the healthcare organization in helping their community to thrive. We also believe that architecture, as expressed in the built environment, is a legitimate therapeutic modality. However, we lacked, until recently, evidence to support our intuition.

We Believe, with John Dewey, That "Health Is the First Liberty."
People can use that liberty to become educated.
Healthy, educated children are the foundation of a
community and, one might say, of a civilization.

Our co-founding and support of The Center for Health Design was driven by the need for research to support our beliefs. The research of the Pebble Projects, the Pebbles who are also Anshen + Allen clients, together with the firm's own work has produced a rich and challenging body of knowledge which only now is being incorporated into real projects in design.

We have developed an evidence-based design matrix, with complete references, which organizes the research findings into an easy-to-use guide for the project designers. Spreading what we know throughout the firm is a formidable task. Our commitment of resources, the identifying of principals with assigned responsibility for research, is beginning to make the difference and we are seeing some headway. Research and evidence-based design principles are one of the benchmarks used during internal design quality reviews, which a project must pass before proceeding to the next phase. Our clients have responded well to the evidence-based design initiative and the design teams are pleased with the additional dimension and professionalism that the research has added to the practice.

This is, though, early days; we have much to learn, but we have started and there is no turning back.

Essay 6-2
Cultivating a Culture of Inquisitiveness:
Integrating Evidence-Based Design Knowledge
Into a Design Practice at Anshen + Allen

Bill Rostenberg, FAIA, Principal and Director of Research Anshen + Allen Architects

Anshen + Allen is dedicated to creating architecture that enables our clients to excel. Our strategic plan describes our commitment to discovering and sharing new ideas essential to our clients in order for them to advance their leadership as providers of healthcare and us as innovative designers. To this end we have developed an organizational structure—comprised not of studios nor of departments—but in a matrix fashion with project teams along one axis and practice areas (such as planning, design, technical quality, and research) along the other, where each practice area supports all project teams as a unique firm-wide resource providing vital expertise within a multitude of disciplines. (See Figure 6.2.)

Project teams evolve around design projects and practice areas function as specialized knowledge bases informing the project teams so as to improve design-related outcomes. It is precisely this relationship between design decisions and their impact on outcomes (clinical, financial, sustainable, social, etc.) that is at the heart of evidence-based design. Through our matrix structure we have created a perpetual feedback loop where practice

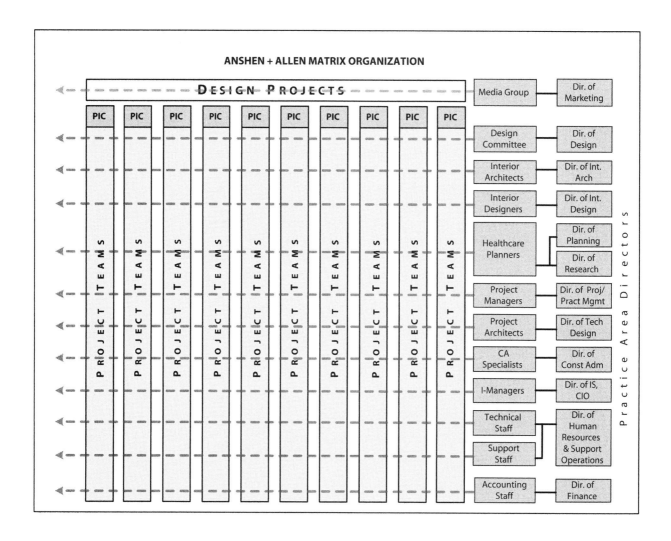

Figure 6.2
Anshen + Allen
Organizational Matrix.
The matrix organiza-
tional model encour-
ages research knowl-
edge to be shared
firm-wide.
© 2008 Anshen + Allen.

areas leverage the capacity of each project team and project teams in turn inform the practice areas with new knowledge that can immediately be applied to the next project. With this structure in place each practice area supports project teams across our contin-uum of offices and enables us to conduct research as one integrated firm.

In order to improve the ratio of resources we invest (people, time, and dollars) rela-tive to our knowledge gained, Anshen + Allen supports three distinct types of research and knowledge cultivation. Our first approach, internal knowledge dissemination, shares the extensive expertise already possessed by our diverse staff to expand the skills and understanding of others within the firm. Our second approach, acquisition of external knowledge, examines what we can learn from others—our clients, our peers, and from other professions—to further expand our internal knowledge. Our third approach, focused research, is used selectively to study issues at the forefront of architecture, healthcare, and medicine. In this way, evidence gained can be integrated into design solutions which in turn will improve the impact that our buildings' performance will have on specific outcomes for patients, staff, and administrators. Each type of research supported at Anshen + Allen is described as follows:

INTERNAL KNOWLEDGE DISSEMINATION:
How do we organize and disseminate what we already know?

Our staff is our greatest asset. Therefore, we choose to invest in continuous knowledge development utilizing a variety of tools, techniques, and discussion formats:

- **Planning Review Committee:** an ad hoc committee focusing on healthcare planning and design. This group is made up of two components; a core committee meets semi-monthly to review project status and knowledge development opportunities, and an extended group meets bimonthly to discuss and review healthcare topics of common interest in an open forum. Knowledge sharing and dissemination is also continuously encouraged through electronic distribution member lists for "open forum" communication.
- **Sustainability Committee:** a committee dedicated to setting high standards and leading our staff in eco-effective design and best practices of sustainability. This group meets monthly to review project status, share newly acquired knowledge, review industry best practices, and to mentor others in preparing for and taking the LEED® certification exam. A subcomponent of the Sustainability Committee—The Green Team—meets regularly to foster new sustainable practices within the environments of our multiple offices. Knowledge sharing and dissemination is also continuously encouraged through electronic distribution member lists for open forum communication. Many of our sustainability leaders are known for their activism on local, regional, and national initiatives.
- **Virtual Building Committee:** a technical committee fostering our commitment as pioneers in virtual building and building information modeling. This committee is comprised of leaders in the AIA/TAP (Technology in Architectural Practice) Knowledge Community and are liaisons to BIM industry leaders. The group meets periodically to review best practices in information modeling, supports our project teams in transitioning to intelligence-rich design tools (a commitment we have made for all projects), and seeks opportunities for BIM to support our "impact of design on

outcomes" research. In addition, the Virtual Building Committee holds regularly scheduled meetings examining specific challenges of building information modeling.

- *First Thursday Healthcare Dialogues:* ongoing firm-wide monthly knowledge sharing forum in which Anshen + Allen staff are encouraged to pursue healthcare topics of their own personal interest and report back to the office, at large, with the knowledge they have gained through self-directed, but firm-supported, exploration. Often outside guests with expertise related to our topics of interest are invited to supplement these dialogues.

- *Informal "Deep Dives":* oftentimes multiple project teams are serendipitously facing similar design challenges in order to achieve best practice outcomes, such as determining optimal dimensions for acuity-adaptable patient rooms or examining alternative configurations for surgical and interventional procedure rooms driven by the latest emerging technologies. To maximize the sharing of knowledge across multiple project teams—who might otherwise miss the opportunity to learn what their colleagues are discovering because each team is managing its project's deadlines and milestones—we periodically conduct multiproject, deep dive studies to objectively review the design topic at hand and the different ways it relates to the specific design challenges of each project. Deep dives are typically brief immersive single-topic studies which are conducted "virtually" across multiple office locations.

- *Healthcare 101 Series:* internal series of presentations and dialogue that focus on interactive learning sessions examining the basics of healthcare planning and design. 101 Series presentations are often supplemented by more advanced "deep dives," as described above.

- *The Fable Hospital, Evidence-Based Design Matrix and Flight-Ready Checklist:* In 2004, the landmark article, "The Business Case for Better Buildings," appeared in Frontiers of Health Services Management magazine[1] and subsequently in the November, 2004 issue of Healthcare Financial Management.[2] The purpose of this peer-reviewed article was to describe an ideal "fable" hospital incorporating all the best-practice evidence-based design features known at that time and to build a business case comparing the potential savings of each feature against its respective first costs. In essence, the fable hospital concept formalized the first quantitative argument suggesting that "better" buildings could improve not only clinical outcomes, but financial outcomes as well. Co-author of the article, Derek Parker, Director of Anshen + Allen and co-founder of The Center for Health Design, has led our firm in an ongoing pilgrimage to extract the essence of the Fable Hospital into the core values of our design culture. To this end, since the time the article was first published, we have developed:

1. EVIDENCE-BASED DESIGN MATRIX: A comprehensive evidence-based design matrix expanding the fable hospital concept with individual best practice design elements along one axis and descriptive categories along the other. For example, a descriptive category such as "target populations" identifies whether each design element affects nurses, physicians, administrators, patients, families, etc.; "physical location" identifies whether each design element has its greatest impact in nursing units, diagnostic and treatment areas, etc.; "outcome hypothesis" identifies whether the assumed outcome is most closely related to safety, stress, finances, etc.; and various descriptive categories, such as "Documented Design Guidelines," "Documented Outcomes," "Regulations and Standards," "References," "Date of Publication," "Author," and "Comments" direct the reader to additional relevant data describing the potential value of each design element.

2. EVIDENCE-BASED DESIGN DATABASE: This is an interactive database extracted from the above matrix. Users can select a design feature (ceiling lifts, hand-washing sinks, etc.), targeted user group (RNs, MDs, etc.), healthcare facility location (nursing unit, operating room, etc.), clinical outcome (reduced patient falls, reduced medication errors, etc.), and access published articles, regulatory guidelines, and even anecdotal descriptions of each best-practice design feature through a series of interconnected pivot tables.

3. FLIGHT-READY CHECKLIST: This is a draft "flight-ready checklist" (see Figure 6.3) to help isolate and emphasize the most important design features we can provide to improve clinical outcomes in the buildings we design. Based on the application of aeronautic-style "flight-ready" checklists that surgical teams use in the operating room to assure they are appropriately prepared to commence a surgical case, this design checklist further refines the best-practice design categories described in the above matrix and database to focus the design team to integrate research and design. It enables the team to identify during a project's inception the greatest opportunities for applying best-practice design knowledge and prioritize which research topics might be best informed through the design process.

- *Succinct Communications Tools/Flashcards:* Recognizing that even the best-intentioned scholars are often too busy to read volumes of text and that design professionals are typically visual learners who relate well to graphic iconography, a variety of initiatives are underway to capture relevant knowledge and disseminate it in a ready reference graphic format for easy access and understanding. For example, Anshen + Allen is currently in the process of creating a set of "flashcards" (see Figure 6.4) designed to succinctly convey industry best practices in healthcare design, "evidence-based design," The Center for Health Design's Pebble Projects, research benchmarks, Anshen + Allen

Flight Ready Checklist of Best Practices

Phase:	ANSHEN+ALLEN
Project Name:	Project Number:

Does project provide the following? If not, do not proceed to next design phase w/out a clear strategy.

→ PATIENT/STAFF EXPERIENCE	PM sign off	→ PATIENT/STAFF SAFETY	PM sign off
☐ Clear wayfinding		☐ Visibility of patients	
☐ Daylight @ interior		☐ Dbl door access (toilet)	
☐ Patient privacy		☐ Dbl door access (treatment)	
☐ Artwork strategy		☐ Grab bar: bed to toilet	
☐ Operable windows		☐ Ceiling lifts (patient rms)	
☐ On stage / off stage		☐ Ceiling lifts (treatment)	
☐ Noise reduction		☐ Non toxic materials	
☐ Short travel distances		☐ ACR MRI safety	
☐ External views		☐ Interview Radiation Physicist	
☐ Patient choices		☐ Interview Chief Safety Officer	
☐ Convenient parking		☐ Align design w/ safety policies	
☐ Staff Respite			

→ REDUCED MEDICAL ERRORS	PM sign off	→ REDUCED INFECTION RATE	PM sign off
☐ Low distraction pharmacy		☐ All private patient rms	
☐ Low distraction meds rooms		☐ Convenient sinks and gel	
☐ Convenient consult spaces		☐ Robust air and ventilation	
☐ Lighting design strategy		☐ HEPA filtration strategy	
☐ Communications syst. strategy		☐ Interview Infect. Control staff	
		☐ Materials selection strategy	

→ OPERATIONAL EFFICIENCY	PM sign off	→ LIFE CYCLE FLEXIBILITY	PM sign off
☐ Separate flow (pts, staff, mtrls)		☐ External expansion strategy	
☐ Separate flow (IP/OP)		☐ Internal conversion strategy	
☐ Separate flow of (adult/child)		☐ Excess capacity of bldg systems	
☐ Nursing unit configuration strategy		☐ Adequate flr to flr height	
☐ Remote support strategy		☐ Column bay spacing strategy	
☐ Vertical transport analysis		☐ Modular prog/planning	
☐ Adequate parking by type		☐ Bldg systs zoning: horiz	
☐ Supply inventory strategy		☐ Bldg systs zoning: vert	

→ FINANCIAL PERFORMANCE	PM sign off	→ BEST PRACTICE CONCEPTS	PM sign off
☐ Energy performance modeling		☐ Acuity adaptable rms	
☐ Best practice dgsf & bgsf multipliers		☐ Acuity convertible rms	
☐ Best practice dept program allocations		☐ Handed patient rms	
☐ Best practice flr to flr heights		☐ Integrated Interventional	
☐ 1st cost/life cycle strategy		☐ e ICU	
☐ Philanthropy strategy		☐ Other:	

RESEARCH PRIORITIES FOR INVESTIGATING THE IMPACT OF DESIGN ON OUTCOMES:

1
2
3
4

projects, and Anshen + Allen design principles. Future refinements of flashcards will be keyword searchable and each flashcard category can be expanded to drill down to greater levels of detail while remaining brief and succinct.

PeaceHealth Sacred Heart Medical Center at RiverBend
Springfield, Oregon

PeaceHealth installed ceiling lifts in patient rooms in two units of its existing facility. Administrators report that the annual cost of patient handling injuries in those two units is approximately 99% less than before. Applying this data "house wide," they estimate that the $1.64 million cost that they will spend making all 306 patient rooms in their new facility lift ready will be paid back in approximately 1.88 years. [1]

1. The Center for Health Design, Pebble project data

Figure 6.4
Flashcard describing use of patient lifts. Flashcards, developed for a wide variety of topics, provide instant orientation on a subject, and navigate the reader to additional informational resources.
© 2008 Anshen + Allen.

- *Enhanced Collaborative User Process:* Interaction between the design team and our clients' facility end users is one of the most important activities necessary for aligning design concepts with operational models. At the same time, the interactive user process can be very time consuming for both the design team and our clients. Therefore, we have invested significant resources into developing an enhanced and collaborative user process that prepares the entire team during pre-design to be effectively and efficiently organized in order to design the project.

Each of our clients has a different culture and process for healthcare delivery. Each enters the design process with different needs and different levels of expertise and prior experience in designing a new facility. Our *Enhanced Collaborative User Process* provides a road map and critical path for decision-making and offers various models of interaction between our design team and our clients. For example, some clients prefer larger user groups where everyone has an opportunity to participate in the design of the area(s) they will be working in. Others prefer smaller groups where only a few individuals represent the interests of larger constituents. Regardless of which approach is used, the enhanced collaborative user process informs the team of the sequence of decisions that need to be made throughout each phase of design.

ACQUISITION OF EXTERNAL KNOWLEDGE:
How do we obtain and disseminate knowledge from others?

Information organization and integration requires a variety of techniques to ensure that all participants are reviewing valid and relevant information. In order to ensure credibility of the information being sought for informing design, there needs to be a level of discretion brought to the process of searching for and applying evidence.

Anshen + Allen has developed an educational hub to collect and distribute information in a variety of formats to staff. This hub is known as the *Information Resource Center (IRC)* and is managed by two full-time professionally trained librarians. The librarians are responsible for collections maintenance, reference/research, and knowledge dissemination. The following tools are utilized to distribute the vast amounts of knowledge contained within the IRC hub:

- Newsletter emails
- Intranet content management
- Creation of "tacit knowledge" repositories
- Educational seminars
- Training and orientation sessions
- Coordination of the IRC with ongoing continuing education activities
- Daily distillation and distribution of current events and relevant news in abbreviated formats
- Dedicated reference support to project teams

Our clients are often our best source of state-of-the-art knowledge. We are fortunate to work with some of the brightest and most innovative pioneers shaping the future of healthcare. Whenever possible we endeavor to collaborate with our clients in such a way that the design process itself yields new knowledge that is mutually beneficial to both the design team and the facility owner and occupants.

Early in the design process we identify opportunities to study the impact of specific design decisions upon clinical and operational outcomes. Because many of our clients are research-focused organizations we often are able to identify design studies that can benefit the interests of both our clients and ourselves. For example, one of our Pebble Projects, PeaceHealth's Sacred Heart Medical Center at RiverBend in Springfield, Oregon, examined the benefits of ceiling lifts in patient units to reduce staff injuries. First, research was conducted tracking the number of injuries associated with patient handling and the costs of claims over a five-year period. This provided the foundation for design research studying both the functional and financial impact of installing ceiling lifts in patient rooms. After a prototype nursing unit was designed, a cost benefit analysis was performed comparing rooms with lifts against those without lifts. The results were so positively conclusive, that the benefit of ceiling lifts in patient units has now become industry-wide accepted knowledge, and illustrates the tangible value of how Pebble Project–related research can benefit the professions of both architecture and healthcare.

Another Pebble Project, Palomar Pomerado Health, took a broad approach to evidence-based design. Champion teams were formed to serve as a "think tank" in order to identify, evaluate, and challenge innovative design concepts across four domains: financial strength, customer service, quality, and workforce and workplace development.[3] The champion teams then formed topic-specific subteams to examine six areas of design innovation:[4]

1. Acuity adaptability subteam: studied the advantages and disadvantages of acuity-adaptable patient rooms and decentralized nursing stations.
2. Interventional platform subteam: evaluated strategies for developing universal procedures rooms and concepts for integrating surgery, interventional radiology, and interventional cardiology into one multispecialty department in order to improve life-cycle flexibility and cross-departmental collaboration. (This concept is described in more detail later in this chapter.)
3. Sustainability subteam: evaluated sustainable facility design strategies and their impact on cost and operations.
4. Healing environments subteam: evaluated methods and techniques such as art, lighting, views to nature and positive distractions in order to promote patient well-being.
5. Technology subteam: recommended strategies for providing optimal infrastructure and information technology systems. The work of this group evolved into developing an improved process for selecting and approving new medical technology.
6. Diverse, nontraditional alternatives (DNA) subteam: promoted innovative, nontraditional solutions to traditional challenges that could be resolved in new creative ways.

A third Pebble Project, Laguna Honda Hospital and Rehabilitation Center, addressed challenges of both sustainability and evidence-based design. Listed as one of the "Top 10 Green Hospitals in the U.S." the project also studied the effectiveness of pharmacy system automation on reducing medical errors and of wireless patient bed and chair exit alarms on reducing fall rates. (See Figure 6.5.)

Figure 6.5
Pebble Project: Laguna
Honda Hospital and
Rehabilitation Center.
  The Laguna Honda
Hospital and Rehabilita-
tion Center (LHHRC) re-
placement project in-
cludes 150,000
square feet of historic
renovations and
700,000 square feet
of new construction to
provide a complete
continuum of long-term
health services (includ-
ing acute general med-
ical facilities, acute
general rehabilitation,
and skilled nursing facilities). As a Pebble Pro-
ject, the LHHRC practi-
tioners are conducting
two research initiatives.
The first initiative will
determine the impact of
pharmacy automation
and medication pass
systems improvements
in reducing medication
errors and increasing
safer medication prac-
tices by staff. The sec-
ond initiative will test
the effectiveness of
wireless bed and chair
exit alarms in a long-
term care facility with
the assumption that
wireless systems (as op-
posed to standard
alarm systems) will have
no bearing on the num-
ber of incidents of pa-
tient falls.
© 2008 Anshen + Allen.

Anshen + Allen attracts individuals with a variety of specialized interests, expertise, and the desire to participate in numerous professional organizations. Many of our senior staff have leadership roles in both architectural and medical societies. Thus we are able to improve our internal knowledge base by simultaneously contributing to the collective knowledge of our own profession as well as those of our clients. These relationships are also beneficial in raising the educational benchmark of our firm. By fostering and cultivating these relationships we are able to create formal and informal liaison networks with a variety of organizations such as:

- Center for Health Design (CHD)
- AIA/Academy of Architecture for Health (AIA/AAH)
- AIA/Technology in Architectural Practice (AIA/TAP)
- American College of Healthcare Architects (ACHA)
- American Hospital Association (AHA)
- American Society for Healthcare Engineering (ASHE)
- US Green Building Council (USGBC)
- National Association of Children's Hospitals and Related Institutions (NACHRI)
- Association of Perioperative Registered Nurses (AORN)
- Radiological Society of North America (RSNA)
- Environmental Design Research Association (EDRA)
- Society for Imaging Informatics in Medicine (SIIM)

Anshen + Allen encourages its leaders to foster relationships with academic institutions in diverse roles such as consulting, teaching, and advisory positions. Maintaining ties with academic institutions through intern development programs also provides opportunities for recruiting research-minded graduates into our organization. Relationships with academic institutions conducting research can prove beneficial when the time comes to develop and perform rigorous research projects, which we believe are best conducted by partnering with external researchers who lend an objective perspective to each topic of inquiry. Academic institutions that Anshen + Allen has partnered with in teaching or research roles include:

- Clemson University
- Texas A&M University
- Harvard University
- University of California, Berkeley
- Cornell University
- California College of the Arts
- University of Hawaii
- University of Cincinnati

FOCUSED RESEARCH: How do we perform rigorous research to add to the collective pool of evidence/knowledge?

Topics and issues frequently arise on projects that necessitate a broader or dedicated scope of consideration and review. When these situations arise, the director of research and the research coordinator selectively organize "research initiative" teams composed of multidisciplinary members, who collaboratively work together to craft an implementation plan to best capture knowledge, contribute credible evidence, and translate findings so they can be better integrated into project-specific design solutions.

Project research initiatives often consist of (1) reading and analyzing articles written by others, (2) developing white papers and/or publishing articles written by our own staff, (3) designing solutions integrated into ongoing project work, and (4) soliciting review and commentary by our clients' end users and the medical and architectural professions at large.

Examples of ongoing focused research initiatives at Anshen + Allen include:

- *John M. Patterson, AIA Traveling Fellowship:* Every year since 1998 we have conducted an in-house research grant competition, where any staff member can submit a proposal for a focused traveling research study. This annual award, established in memory of John Patterson, an esteemed Anshen + Allen colleague, enables a staff member to conduct a study endeavor for a limited period of time where he or she can be free of daily project responsibilities and travel to a location unique to the research project's scope. Proposals are reviewed based on the value to the firm of the knowledge gained, the social and educational value of the topic, and the research quality of the proposal itself. Anshen + Allen provides the winning staff member with paid time off and specified traveling expenses for the proposed research topic. The recipient is required to present the topic and a description of his or her travel experience to the entire office. Awards have been given to a broad variety of topics, such as providing Third World countries with solar-powered electricity and studying sustainability practices in other continents.

- *Eco-Effective Design (EED) and Evidence-Based Design (EBD)—Removing Barriers to Integration:* A research project co-funded by Anshen + Allen, the American Institute of Architects–College of Fellows and the Boston Society of Architects designed to review similarities and disparities between incorporating EBD principles with those of EED. Our thesis is that while both eco-effective design and evidence-based design are topics of considerable recent popularity, few projects solve the challenges of each endeavor simultaneously. In fact, we assume that many design solutions addressing the issues of sustainability may unintentionally create additional challenges to solving evidence-based design requirements, and vice versa. The goal of this study is to analyze best practices of both EED and EBD and to develop guidelines where solutions within one arena can provide positive contributions to the other.

- *Green Patient Room (GPR):* Traveling exhibition developed in conjunction with International Facility Management Association (IFMA) Healthcare Council, Corporate Realty, Design & Construction and Skanska to illustrate how sustainable design practices can improve patient care by increasing efficiency and reducing the anxiety of medical staff, patients, and families. (See Figures 6.6 and 6.7.) The room also serves as an educational tool for healthcare administrators, showing how they can adopt green practices now. In a recent national exhibit, leaders in healthcare were invited to review, critique, and comment on the green patient room. In an informal "pre-occupancy evaluation" their comments were recorded and summarized so they could be applied to future design iterations of this concept.

- *Reading Room Prototype:* An ongoing multidisciplinary dialogue, with mini design charrettes, involving designers, human factors specialists, radiologists, workplace furniture manufacturers, and industrial work process analysts. This group meets periodically in search of new solutions for creating reading room environments where radiologists can interpret soft copy data in a more efficient and effective manner than the traditional reading room environment typically yields.

- *Virtual Building Design Pilot:* Ongoing research collaboration project with Lawrence

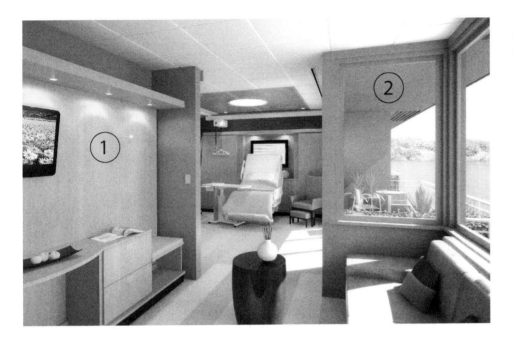

Figure 6.6
Green patient room family area: 1. Family zone: Hospitals moving toward hospitality models need to consider amenities for the patient's visitors, as well as adequate space for them to be a part of the healing process. 2. Terrace zone: Providing outdoor spaces has moved from an amenity to a necessity, given the proven benefits for both the patient and the facility in terms of energy savings and passive survivability.
© 2008 Anshen + Allen.

Berkeley National Laboratories researching different alternatives for utilizing Building Information Modeling techniques to analyze energy efficiency hypotheses.

• *Medergy:* An innovative medical waste–processing concept that simultaneously solves aspects of two key challenges in health facility design: safer and more economical processes for disposing of medical waste and more environmentally effective processes of powering healthcare facilities, by converting waste to energy. Since Medergy's inception, Anshen + Allen has been involved in this San Francisco-based corporation that offers a service to use its licensed small-scale bio-refinery "clean tech" noncombustion technology to convert healthcare institutions' hazardous and conventional waste materials into valuable hydrogen and other "green" eco-products.

Compared to traditional landfill methods of waste disposal, Medergy waste removal is less expensive because waste-generating institutions do not need to transport their waste to a fill site (many of which are being closed, and are thus in short supply). It is also less damaging to the environment because there is no combustion or measurable greenhouse gas emissions. Thus, Medergy can reduce a healthcare institution's emissions fees and often can qualify for carbon credits, renewable energy credits, and other local, state, and federal incentives. (See Figure 6.8.)

Figure 6.7
Green patient room
patient area: 3.
Restroom/building sys-
tems: The patient rest-
room has been scruti-
nized for safety and
resource efficiency.
Water conservation
provides almost equal
energy conservation
throughout the facility;
nylon surfaces (for grab
rails) are known to har-
bor fewer bacteria than
brushed stainless steel;
and recycled content
materials for counter-
tops, floor tiles, and
other finishes contribute
to resource efficiency.
4. Staff zone: All case-
work in the room is
modular, meaning it
can be reconfigured or
relocated as operations
and technology
evolves, with minimal
downtime and drasti-
cally reduced waste.
5. Patient zone: Giving
the patient control of
their environment has
many positive benefits,
both in health out-
comes as well as satis-
faction. In this sce-
nario, the observation
window (privacy), light-
ing (multiple levels and
types), and the TV
(entertainment, educa-
tion, art, concierge,
etc.) are all controllable
by the patient.
© 2008 Anshen + Allen.

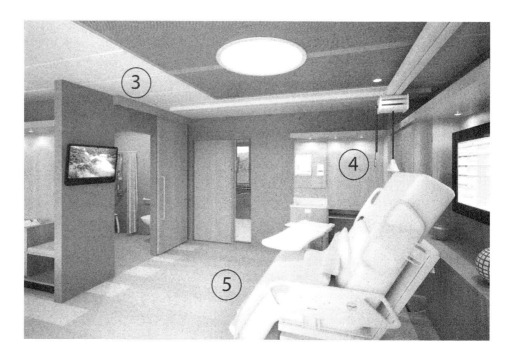

- *Integrated Interventional Platform:* An innovative design concept that responds to the growing convergence of surgery and interventional radiology and cardiology, provides long-term facility flexibility, and promotes multidisciplinary collaboration among diverse providers of procedural medicine. Anshen + Allen has researched, promoted, presented, and published this concept widely and has incorporated numerous varia-tions of the integrated interventional platform into the design of current projects. (A detailed description of this initiative follows.)

3. THE INTEGRATED INTERVENTIONAL PLATFORM

OVERVIEW

Nowhere within the healthcare environment are issues of advanced medical technology, facility design, politics, turf, tradition, culture, cost, and future flexibility combined within a more complex arena than when developing a concept known as the integrated interventional platform (IIP). This concept departs from the traditional "departmental" separation of surgery, interventional radiology, and interventional cardiology, which in the past have typically been located, configured, and operated independently from one another. In contrast, it seeks to create a singular, more unified physical and operational

Figure 6.8
Medergy provides a
safe and economical
process for disposing
of medical waste while
also converting that
waste into useable
energy.
© 2008 Anshen + Allen.

entity that reflects the growing convergence of the three services and enables healthcare facilities to more easily evolve and adapt to future changes in healthcare delivery and accompanying medical technology. (See Figures 6.9 and 6.10.)

Drivers of the integrated interventional platform include:

1. Much of surgery is becoming less invasive. Minimally invasive techniques now dominate surgical procedures and have altered the nature and equipment utilized for many activities taking place within the operating room.
2. Surgery is becoming increasingly reliant on advanced image guidance and thus is benefited by new forms of medical imaging equipment within the operating room.
3. Much of interventional radiology and interventional cardiology (also referred to as cardiac catheterization) is becoming more interventional and thus, more surgical like in nature.

4. Interventional radiology and interventional cardiology include both diagnostic and interventional procedures. As much of the diagnostic workload shifts to noninvasive modalities, such as computed tomography angiography (CTA), magnetic resonance angiography (MRA), nuclear medicine (NM), and ultrasound (US), those procedures that continue to be performed within interventional procedural suites are the more invasive, or surgical-like, procedures. Therefore, interventional suites require surgical-like environments (including greater air-handling capacities, greater space requirements, restricted access and egress, adjacent pre-operative and post-operative services), and can benefit from co-location within the surgical suite.
5. Pre-operative and post-operative space and staff are often in short supply. Increased flexibility and efficiency can be achieved by co-locating these spaces for all three services and cross-training staff.

Our hypothesis is that in spite of this recent convergence, many architects and planners still design surgical suites based on one traditional model and interventional suites based on a different traditional model. We believe a new singular integrated design "partí" should be considered; one that recognizes both the commonalities and the differences in surgery, interventional radiology, and interventional cardiology, and enables further convergence to be accommodated in the future without requiring extensive and costly facility renovation.

Anshen + Allen has pioneered the development of the integrated interventional platform through the design of many of our recent advanced medical centers. Our goal is to establish a new benchmark for the design of procedural medical environments by (1) analyzing traditional models of surgery and interventional medicine and their associated design solutions, (2) tracking current—and predicting future—changes in medical practice, (3) identifying how traditional design solutions may no longer respond to current practices, (4) developing new design models that respond to current and anticipated practice changes, and (5) integrating these solutions into the design of new buildings through extreme collaboration among our design team, the surgical and interventional end users of the facilities we design, and national leaders influencing the future of medical care and the development of advanced medical equipment.

In a manner paralleling that of translational medical research (which translates basic medical research into clinical practice), iterative design of the integrated interventional platform provides us with an ideal opportunity to translate theoretical evidence-based design concepts into tangible and testable architectural design partís. The following describes our assumptions regarding the potential benefits and frequent challenges as well as our typical approach to designing the integrated interventional platform.

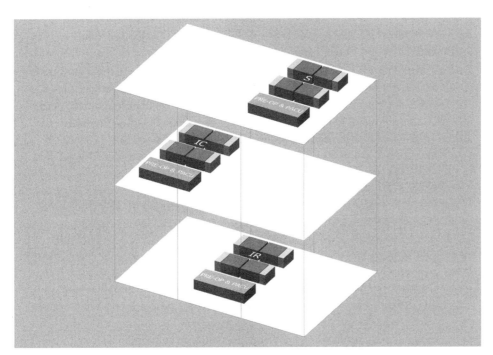

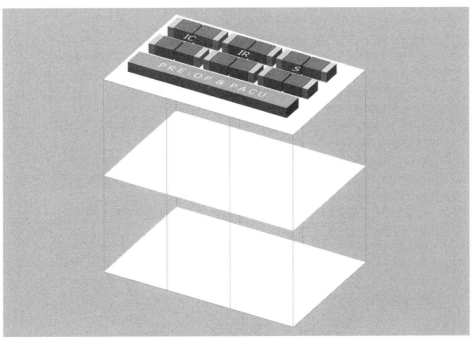

Figures 6.9 and 6.10 Traditional separation of surgery, interventional radiology, and interventional cardiology. The integrated interventional platform anticipates the growing convergence of surgical and interventional services within a collaborative, multispecialty environment. © 2008 Anshen + Allen.

ASSUMED BENEFITS AND POTENTIAL CLINICAL OUTCOMES OF THE INTEGRATED INTERVENTIONAL PLATFORM

Surgery, interventional radiology, and interventional cardiology are often the most costly healthcare services to operate and staff, yet also are usually the greatest revenue producers. They require expensive and often unpredictable facility modifications as both technology and medical practice change. Potential benefits of incorporating these services into one integrated interventional platform include:

- Reduced duplication of pre-op/recovery space
- Reduced duplication of pre-op/recovery staff
- Reduced duplication of procedure room spaces that might have low utilization from only one service line
- Improved efficiency of building systems design due to co-location of multiple users of robust building systems, such as those requiring surgical-quality air-handling, increased structural capacities, minimum vibration tolerance, etc. Specific zones of excess infrastructure capacities can be identified to provide additional future flexibility without requiring the entire floor—or multiple floors—to be designed beyond a typical capacity.
- Reduced rates of infection when interventional radiology and cardiology services are located within a controlled and restricted "surgical red-line" instead of within non-controlled "street clothes" accessible zones.
- Increased facility flexibility to accommodate evolving changes in operating room design, such as adjacent control rooms and electronics equipment closets (similar to those typically employed in catheterization labs and interventional radiology suites), by:
  - Utilizing modular procedure room pods or clusters with strategically placed "soft space" that can be converted into control rooms and/or electronics closets
  - "Loose-fit" programming that provides adequate soft-space available for future conversion into the above functions
- Ability to accommodate new types of personnel, such as surgical imaging technologists and surgical IT specialists; enabling them to support surgical procedures (within the control room) without entering the "sterile" procedure room itself.
- Increased facility flexibility to accommodate growing needs of image-guided surgery, such as hybrid OR/MRI suites by:
  - Utilizing modular procedure room configurations where multiple rooms can accommodate a variety of equipment types and configurations and/or be combined into "super procedure rooms" that integrate functions that have traditionally been separated, such as interventional MRI (I-MRI) and surgery

- Locating "fixed" vertical building elements (such as stairs, elevators, shafts, etc.) toward the edges of the building footprint in order to maximize the length and width of zones that can be easily modified
  - Increasing vertical floor-to-floor height and/or coordinating building systems to yield greater usable floor height in order to accommodate special equipment requiring excessive vertical clearances
- Increased potential for multidisciplinary collaboration due to co-location and sharing of support spaces among traditionally separated clinical services.
- Increased potential for integrated and more efficient materials management systems due to co-location of various key equipment and supply users.

CHALLENGES IN DESIGNING THE INTEGRATED INTERVENTIONAL PLATFORM

While design challenges to be overcome are complex, it is the political and cultural challenges that are often the most demanding. Success of the integrated interventional suite requires alignment of both operational goals and architectural solutions.

- Individual departmental desires must be balanced by nondepartmental champions who will advocate for the benefit of the entire medical enterprise. This requires a clear executive-level vision that values multispecialty collaboration over inter-departmental competition, the latter often being tied to financial rewards for patient referrals and revenue generation.
- Tradition and culture are difficult to change. Historically and presently, competition for space, equipment, and revenue among surgery, radiology, and cardiology remains strong and complex.
- There is a cost for providing flexibility; typically either a moderate premium added to the initial construction cost of a facility or a significant renovation and disruption cost incurred to modify a facility that has no excess capacity beyond its initial anticipated utilization. Medical technology and clinical practice tend to change more rapidly than the lengthy time required to design and construct a medical facility easily permits. Furthermore, change will take place long after a facility is opened. It is easier and less expensive for a facility with excess capacity to evolve as technology evolves than to renovate and add infrastructure to one with no surplus capacity. Thus, strategic decisions need to be made regarding how much excess capacity to build into the facility initially and where to place it, while recognizing that all the excess capacity may never be fully utilized.

ONE APPROACH TO DESIGNING THE INTEGRATED INTERVENTIONAL PLATFORM

While the design of the integrated interventional platform cannot easily be summarized into a simple formula, the following steps describe how to determine if this concept is appropriate for a given project, and how to facilitate a collaborative process to align a healthcare organization's operational philosophy, culture, and vision with the physical design solution.

1. Facilitate discussion among executive leaders, physicians, nurses, and clinical managers to determine both an organization's interest and resistance to this concept because the integrated interventional platform likely differs from their present physical and operational model. Representatives should include—but not be limited to—surgeons, interventionalists, anesthesiologists, and ancillary staff. Both individual departmental and multidisciplinary cross-departmental discussions should take place. These discussions need to occur throughout both programming and design phases. A well-crafted design that does not align with an institution's vision and goals will not yield a successful project. Thus it is important that there be an internal champion to hold and maintain a vision for this concept. This does not suggest that there will be unified opinions on the subject.

2. During concept design and block planning, develop a floor plate large enough and of a configuration that can accommodate surgery, interventional procedures, and pre-operative and post-operative services (including their necessary support spaces) with adequate space for growth and expansion.

3. Integrate building systems in much the way one would design a research laboratory—by bringing fixed vertical elements to the building's perimeter, thus creating a flexible internal planning zone. (See Figure 6.11.) One challenge of designing a large flexible floor plate is to also penetrate the area with multiple sources of natural daylight.

4. Develop a universal room configuration that can accommodate a variety of surgical and interventional procedures and equipment. This room becomes an incremental building block that will be used to form modular activity clusters.

5. Within the floor plate array these modular clusters, where each cluster or pod contains roughly four to six universal procedure rooms. (See Figure 6.12.)

6. Although each cluster is identical, or at least similar, they may not all function in the same manner. For example, pods of rooms used as operating rooms might be oriented around a central clean core. Because surgical procedures utilize a significant amount of reprocessed instruments it is often desirable to separate the flow of clean goods from that of soiled materials, although even this concept has been

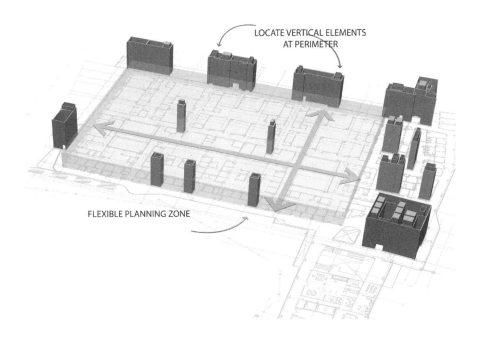

LOCATE VERTICAL ELEMENTS
AT PERIMETER

FLEXIBLE PLANNING ZONE

Figure 6.11
Flexible floor plate.
Flexibility of the inte-
grated interventional
platform is achieved
in large part by the
strategic placement of
fixed building system
elements.
*© 2008 Anshen + Allen
Architects for Palomar
Pomerado Health.*

debated. Because interventional procedures utilize a significant amount of dispos-
able supplies, such as catheters and guide wires, these rooms are often oriented
around a central staff core which tends to separate the flow of staff from patients
rather than separating clean goods from soiled. (See Figure 6.13.)

7. Designing an integrated interventional platform can be compared to an urban
   planning study where neighborhoods are created to segregate different populations
   via separate traffic routes. For example, it may be desirable to separate the flow of
   surgical patients, interventional radiology patients, and interventional cardiology
   patients. (See Figure 6.14.) Thus within one environment there are multiple
   degrees of separation: clean from soiled; staff from patients; and separation
   between surgical patients, radiology patients, and cardiology patients.

8. It is desirable that both pre-operative and post-operative areas are proximate to
   each of the procedural areas while at the same time the spaces can flex between
   surgery, radiology, and cardiology. Similarly, it is desirable for pre-operative areas—
   which will be heavily used in the morning—to be able to flex as level-two recovery
   spaces—which will be heavily used in the afternoon.

9. One of the greatest challenges in designing the integrated interventional platform
   is to achieve consensus from surgery, interventional radiology, and interventional

Figure 6.12
Modular clusters of universal procedure rooms. Universal procedure rooms can be arrayed in modular clusters. Variations in workflow and operations can be accommodated by orienting these clusters in different directions.
© 2008 Anshen + Allen Architects for Palomar Pomerado Health.

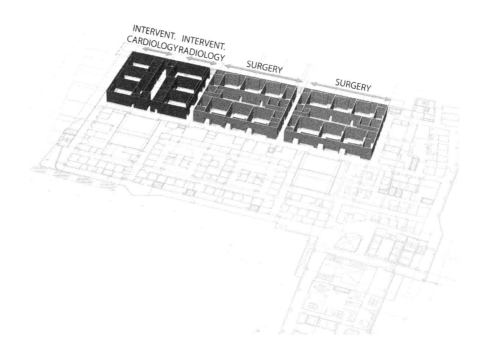

Figure 6.13
Modular procedure pods utilizing different workflow processes. Variations in cluster orientation enable the separation of dissimilar types of workflow.
© 2008 Anshen + Allen Architects for Palomar Pomerado Health.

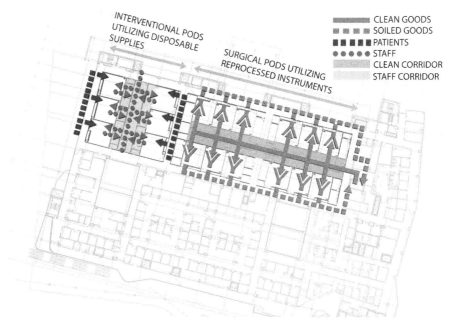

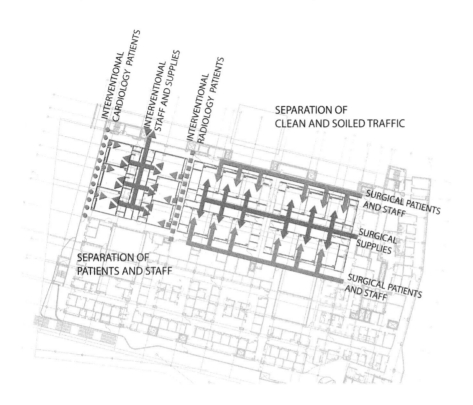

INTERVENTIONAL CARDIOLOGY PATIENTS

INTERVENTIONAL STAFF AND SUPPLIES

INTERVENTIONAL RADIOLOGY PATIENTS

SEPARATION OF
CLEAN AND SOILED TRAFFIC

SURGICAL PATIENTS AND STAFF

SURGICAL SUPPLIES

SEPARATION OF
PATIENTS AND STAFF

SURGICAL PATIENTS AND STAFF

Figure 6.14
Workflow neighborhoods within the integrated interventional platform. Separation of workflow creates segregated clinical neighborhoods. For example, the flow of patients can be separate from staff; the flow of supplies can be separate from people; or surgical patients can be separate from interventional patients.
© 2008 Anshen + Allen Architects for Palomar Pomerado Health.

cardiology that each of their pods should be placed behind the restricted surgical red-line. While surgical staff would agree that access to the operating rooms should be restricted by the red-line, interventional radiology and interventional cardiology staffs may be less likely to agree with this. By separating the flow of surgical, radiology, and cardiology patients as described in item 7 above, it is possible to create a "virtual red-line," where the boundaries of the red-line can change simply by changing a decision, rather than through extensive renovation. In this way the red-line can envelope only the operating rooms (see Figure 6.15); the ORs and the interventional radiology rooms (see Figure 6.16); or the ORs, the IRs, and the interventional cardiology rooms (see Figure 6.17).

Figure 6.15
"Virtual" red line:
Surgery only. Diverse
opinions among sur-
geons, interventional
radiologists, and inter-
ventional cardiologists
regarding whether their
procedure rooms
should be inside versus
outside of a controlled
"red line," make it chal-
lenging for a single
design solution to solve
this diverse set of protocols. A "virtual red
line" enables the
design to accommo-
date changing proto-
cols while minimizing
the need to physically
modify the environ-
ment.
© 2008 Anshen + Allen.

Figure 6.16
"Virtual" red line:
Surgery and interven-
tional radiology.
© 2008 Anshen + Allen.

Figure 6.17
"Virtual" red line:
Surgery, interventional
radiology and interven-
tional cardiology.
© 2008 Anshen + Allen.

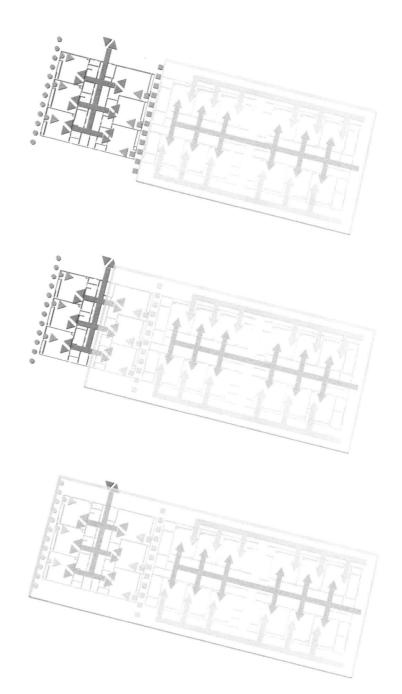

Endnotes

1. Berry, K.; Parker, D.; Coile, R.; Hamilton, D.K.; O'Neill, D.; Sadler, B. "The Business Case for Better Buildings," *Frontiers of Health Services Management*, 21:1 Fall 2004 pp.3–26, Chicago, IL.

2. Berry, K.; Parker, D.; Coile, R.; Hamilton, D.K.; O'Neill, D.; Sadler, B. "The Business Case for Better Buildings," Healthcare Facilities Management Association, November 2004, Westchester, IL.

3. The Center for Health Design and Palomar Pomerado Health; Innovation Through Participation: Improving Healthcare Facility Designs for Palomar Pomerado Health; September 2006.

4. *Ibid.*

Chapter 7
Growth Opportunities for the Design Professional

> "The empires of the future are
> the empires of the mind."
> —Winston Churchill

The close of this book is about the next frontiers, the future of the practice and the educational system that will fuel its advance. It reaches to the nonprofits that will hold the discussions about practice reform and leadership. The evidence-based certification process is discussed and the future of this methodology for designing our healthcare facilities is forecasted.

Dial back to the late 1970s when fewer were focused on the design of healthcare facilities. The market of resources was slim and the attitude about occupants focused primarily on the needs of the physician. It was almost impossible to be as sensitive to the needs of patients as we are today. While the traditional spaces for birthing were being challenged, the real excitement was around equipment innovations that offered new insights on diagnostics and treatment. Much has happened since the 1970s that allows us to design more sensitively for patients and staff. It is now acceptable to measure the stress of those who occupy these buildings, or the environmental cause of a medical error, or the efficiency of a caregiver. More importantly, members of an interdisciplinary team are empowered to launch informed innovation on the shoulders of tried and true design applications. It is therefore time for an evidence-based approach to healthcare design to come into its own. In this closing chapter the future thinking that is fueling this push to the next plateau will be explored. We are in the infancy of truly understanding the power of place as it relates to healing the human body—we still have much to learn. Let's look at the influence that will create a more informed future.

When I speak to a group of people, I use an icebreaker that has changed the way I think about the development of the interiors for healthcare facilities. The consistent results have

Figure 7.1
Foxtail.
Picture by Henry Domke,
www.henrydomke.com.

made me realize that it doesn't matter where you hail from, when you are stressed it is a basic need that your senses prefer to be completely and favorably engaged by elements within a natural environment. Try the exercise below and see for yourself.

Typically, 95 percent of those polled answer outdoors, either on a beach or in the mountains. The other 5 percent were indoors, comforted by a familiar room that has access to a view of nature. When asked to be more descriptive about the environment, the detail is described in the variability of each element's color and texture and how those qualities subtly engage all senses. One neurology patient described the engaging view out his window as "eight shades of green." So why can't the design of our interior healing environments do just that—engage our senses. If you are reading this indoors, then look around you and note what

Exercise: Full Sensory Engagement

Take a deep breath and relax. Remember the last most stressful moment in your life—if you could have been transported anywhere in the world to a place that offered serenity and calmness, where would you have gone? Visualize that environment and focus on the elements that support your sense of well-being. Now answer the question: Were you indoors or outdoors? (See Figures 7.2 and 7.3.)

Figure 7.2
Indoors?

Figure 7.3
Outdoors?

you see, feel, smell, hear. More than likely, you see solid-color walls, with one even light source, smell someone else's lunch cooking in the microwave, and hear the whir of machines. We have the capability to design into our environments more soothing solutions that demonstrate connection to nature. Why aren't we doing so? Are we utilizing the engineering profession correctly to create whole healing environments? Will we in the future because it will be proven as the healthy thing to do?

Next Frontiers

In a search for facilities in which the design came close to achieving a true connection to nature, the one that resonated most with my less-than-scientific study is the Credit Valley Hospital in Mississauga, Ontario. The facility opened its new Carlo Fidani Peel Regional Cancer Centre and Ambulatory Care Centre in the spring of 2005. Having used evidence-based design, the Farrow Partnership Architects, Inc., was awarded a grant to measure the effects of space and design on staff and patient satisfaction. Specifically, emphasis was placed on the creation of efficient circulation and workflow patterns, access to natural light, and direct views to landscaped courtyards and therapeutic gardens. The main lobby was programmed as the "village gathering place" where wood was selected to be used for its inherent emotive qualities, and its ability to evoke feelings, meanings, and sentiments by connecting our inner and social selves. (See Figure 7.4.) The design project hypothesized to:

- Eliminate resource waste (staff)
- Increase direct patient care time
- Create an exceptional patient care experience,
- Provide balance with the characteristics of a healing environment
- Support models for future delivery of care while solving patient flow problems.

The design and operational strategies to achieve these goals were:

- To reduce the number of steps necessary for nurses to obtain supplies and prepare for the clinic
- Rework the care delivery model and provide more space for interdisciplinary collaboration and decision-making
- Increase the number of private/confidential spaces for clients
- Increase the proximity of key structures to staff to reduce client wait times and transfers
- Increase treatment space to accommodate higher volume and minimize delays for placement of patients and waiting times in holding areas
- Eliminate equipment duplication and unsafe clutter in the treatment areas and hallways
- Maximize technology for efficiency
- Provide for teaching and education of patients and caregivers to encourage prevention and self-care.

Figure 7.4
A "village gathering" space using materials that "emote qualities that connect with social and inner selves, evoking feelings, meanings, and sentiments."
The Credit Valley Hospital, Farrow Partnership Architects, Inc., Peter Sellar, KLIK Photography.

Results from the studies indicate a positive direction in the levels of satisfaction, efficiency, and effectiveness as well as a positive change in the overall distribution of time. Satisfaction with physical comfort, information, communication, education, and respect for patient preferences all increased in the new site.

- Direct patient treatment time increased by over 62 hours per week or 6 hours per RN (4 percent).
- Administration decreased by 7 hours or 42 minutes per RN (6.5 percent).
- Clinic preparation time decreased by 4 hours or 24 per RN.
- "On-foot" travel time increased for RNs post-occupancy from 29 hours at baseline to 59 hours at time 1. Clearly the additional space has meant more travel time.

Patient Satisfaction Results

- 8 percent increase in patient satisfaction with physical comfort
- 3 percent increase in patient satisfaction with access to care

The research team was led by Karen Parent, a professor in the department of physical medicine and rehabilitation at Queen's University. In an interview before the study was conducted, Professor Parent notes "there is growing research worldwide into rigorous evidence-based process. If this study confirms the superiority of the process, it could find its way into greater use by developers of all types of commercial buildings. In fact, I would argue that it would be negligent not to do so."[1]

This project and its interdisciplinary team have embraced the evidence-based approach. From the photography it looks as though it has created a remarkable facility, but more importantly, from the data reported it has created a safe, efficient, and satisfying environment in which to heal. How many firms out there are working on projects such as Credit Valley and yet fall below the radar screen? It continues to be worthwhile to ask the question that seeks out the most innovative projects and to learn from their frontiers.

Percentage of Firms Practicing Evidence-Based Design

For the last three years *Interior Design Magazine* has reported the top "Forty Healthcare Giants," where design firms report top billings in healthcare interiors. This annual business survey of Healthcare Interior Design Giants ranks the largest firms by healthcare design fees for a 12-month period from July to June. Healthcare design fees include fees attributed to:

1. All healthcare interiors work
2. All aspects of a firm's healthcare design practice, from strategic planning/programming to design/project management.
3. Fees paid to a firm for work performed by employees and independent contractors who are "full-time staff" equivalent.

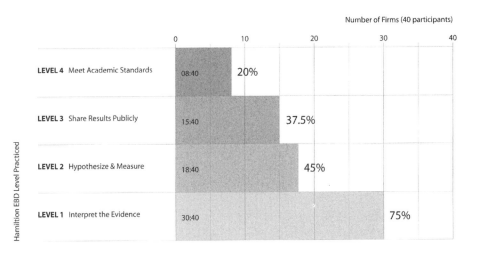

Number of Firms (40 participants)

Figure 7.5
Top healthcare firm survey on the acceptance of an evidence-based approach to practice for the design of healthcare facilities.
Cama/Leung with Interior Design *Magazine.*

Of the **40** firms surveyed, **37** engage in evidence-based design.

Wing Leung, Interior Design Magazine's research director, was gracious enough to partner with me in surveying all of the firms who have made the list over the last three years to see where they fared with respect to engaging in an evidence-based practice. Fifty firms were polled, forty responded, giving us an 80 percent response rate. Of the forty, 92.5 percent said they engage in evidence-based design. Seventy-five percent practice at Level 1 (see the checklist in Chapter 1), or they use peer-review journals as a way to inform design concepts; 45 percent practice at Level 2, or they hypothesize an expected outcome and measure the results; 37.5 percent practice at Level 3, or share the knowledge through articles written in professional journals or lectures at professional conferences; and 20 percent practice at Level 4, or submit found conclusions to a peer-review journal. (See Figure 7.5.)

Half of the respondents made comments about the desire to follow an evidence-based practice, citing that there is still not enough data to draw from or clients are not yet ready to engage in follow-up measurement. They also expressed concern about the marketing of this design methodology before the necessary rigor is put in place on each project to produce the appropriate database of knowledge.

The survey results are much more encouraging than I found in my initial quest for participating projects at the start of this book. There is much more to do, but design professions are poised to build a body of knowledge, use it in the formulation of design hypotheses, and test their design concepts born out of the intellectual analysis of data that gives birth to innovative concepts. As many of us undo old methodologies the question arises: How do we prepare a next generation of design professionals to take a more rigorous approach to their design interventions?

Future of Design Education and Practice

The National Institutes of Health (NIH) has instituted a road map for the direction of medical research.[2] The University of Connecticut in a collaborative effort to align with the NIH's
road map is now offering a clinical translational master's degree, designed as a bridge between
research and practice, reflecting an NIH priority to speed, streamline, and improve the delivery of research findings to patient care and encourage innovation. The new master's degree
expects to attract physicians, medical and dental students, and graduate or post-doctoral students in psychology, nursing, pharmacy, bioengineering, and other fields. The degree is not
terminal but can be completed as part of an MD, DDS, or PhD program, or as post-doctoral training.[3] The University of Connecticut no longer offers degrees in Interior Design
and never offered a degree in Architecture, but this program seems primed for graduates from
a design program who can offer a perspective on the built environment that serves to heal.
(See Figure 7.6.)

The University of Connecticut program is intriguing in that it recognizes research as integral not separate from advanced degrees in medicine and related medical fields. Does the
study of healthcare design follow a common path for improving a health outcome? It is worth
the challenge to see how pioneers of this program might feel about a graduate design student
entering into the discussion. A few years ago, Denise Guerin, PhD from the University of

Minnesota, visited my office to observe our practice and to share her thoughts about an integrated design educational offering the University of Minnesota was exploring. Though shifts in thinking about healthcare seem to take years this shift in academia is very encouraging and promises to accelerate the future of design education and practice. It is due to her forward thinking that I asked her to express her thoughts on evidence-based practice and how the base of education may change as a result.

Essay 7-1
Embracing an Evidence-Based Design Approach in Education and Practice

Denise A. Guerin, PhD, FIDEC, ASID, IIDA, College of Design, University of Minnesota

We often hear from interior designers, architects, landscape architects, and engineers that they are using an evidence-based design approach in their design problem solving. (See Figure 7.7.) Using evidence to inform their design decisions reflects a change in their design process that is significant; it is the future of all built environment design practice. In the past, design practitioners acquired information from a variety of sources including manufacturers' data, representatives' knowledge, practitioner periodicals, and professional organization studies. A problem that can occur with practitioners' use of these information sources is that there can be product bias, inappropriate data-collection methods used, or incomplete analysis.[4]

Design researchers try to avoid these problems by following prescribed data-collection and analysis methods, basing their inquiry on theory, and reporting the results objectively in scholarly journals. Yet, this research is often inaccessible to design practitioners, written in a language that is unfriendly to designers, and the findings are seldom translated into design criteria, which would allow their application in a design problem. In 2002, InformeDesign® (www.informedesign.umn.edu) was launched, and a solution to this problem was now only a click away. An evidence-based design approach was supported because practitioners now had easy access to research findings that were transformed into evidence-based design criteria—and it was free.

The major feature of InformeDesign is the searchable database of design and human behavior research. To date, there are over 2,000 Research Summaries, a 2- to 3-page bulleted summary of research articles that are published in referred journals. About 300 Research Summaries are added annually. InformeDesign has had a steady increase in usage over the last five years; an average of 65,000 Research Summaries are downloaded monthly; and users come from around the world (users from China are often second to the United States. In 2008, the search engine was optimized, registration became mandatory,

Figure 7.7
Art sculpture designed
to enhance a view of
a brick wall from a
patient room.
*MSI—Landscape
Architects.*

and usage soared. Research Summaries can be searched via keyword and are used by designers in programming, schematic design, and design development to inform them of recent research findings. Other research-based features include:

- *Implications,* a monthly newsletter focusing on specialized topics
- *Improve,* the continuing and professional education curriculum, fee-based
- *Inquiry,* a research brief summarizing all InformeDesign research on a single topic, fee-based

InformeDesign has pioneered the market transformation to evidence-based design.

Educators have been preparing for this transformation for several years. Design faculty members have introduced the use of evidence as a means to inform design choices into courses, and some are transforming their curriculum. The most important effect this has on interior design practice is formally putting human behavior and human needs at the center of design problem solving.

Many undergraduate interior design programs have begun integrating an evidence-based design approach into design process activities via programming, schematic design, and design development. For example, at the University of Minnesota, in the first semester of the freshman interior design studio, students are introduced to InformeDesign®, taught the difference between evidence and information, and asked to create user need criteria for a specific design problem that is supported by evidence found on InformeDesign…after that, no student addresses a program without knowing what evidence exists to support user needs or design decisions. This is the first of many sequenced activities experienced by students that teach them the complexity of programming spaces in ways that protect people and support their needs. Additionally, students explore how evidence helps them make informed decisions as they create schematics and continue through design development.

A key issue faculty address is to expose students to understanding the difference between information that students find on the Internet, in books, or provided by manufacturers and evidence that has been validated in a systematic, research process. It is appropriate to use both, but it is also necessary to understand the difference and when each type of data can be used to produce the best solution. By teaching an evidence-based design approach, educators are trying to close the gap between research and practice, to see practice as a contributing partner to research about the field, and to have a level of discussion and reflection that moves practice from a vocational skill model to a skill/knowledge model where choices and directions reflect theory and researchable findings.[5]

This is not to imply that evidence-based design requires designers to rely only on evidence for design decisions, but to develop a balance among evidence, information, their own practice experience, and their critical and creative problem solving. This is the future of design practice—and education is preparing new designers who are learning how to acquire this balance.

The University of Minnesota does not stand alone on this design methodology. Poking around online as I explored this subject I found the following course offering at Parsons, the New School for Design in the Department of Design and Management:

Parsons: Design Research Methods

Description: An introduction to qualitative research methods that are commonly used in design projects, this course covers the gathering, analysis, and application of research as it informs different stages of the design process. Techniques covered will include participant observation, in context interviews, self-documentation, participatory design, and interactive test-ing. Texts and materials will be drawn from several fields in the social and behavioral sciences, including anthropology, and sociology. This course will include individual and group research assignments and applications of findings to real-world design problems. (Required)[6]

Credit Hours: 3

In *Implications,* a newsletter by InformeDesign, an article "Closing the Research-Design Gap,"[7] written by Franklin Becker, PhD, notes the gap that exists within some portions of the related design fields regarding this newly formalized approach to design. He states: "There is widespread confusion, skepticism, and resistance to the value of what has become known as evidence-based design." He continues and notes the Cornell College of Architecture, rated number one in the country, has one social scientist and no required course focused on "environmental behavior…Interior Design, as a profession, has been a much stronger advocate of incorporating the social sciences into the design curriculum. CIDA (Council for Interior Design Accreditation), for example, mandates that accredited programs include defined course work related to human-environment relations, including but going beyond human factors/ergonomics. But interior designers fight their own battles with the architecture profession to avoid marginalization and achieve the recognition and acceptance. The gap continues within the design community." He goes on to say the exceptions in the communities are lead by individuals and firms who have worked to close the gap. Becker refers to the drive the client imposes that initiates the shift and that is exactly what has happened in healthcare. In the last few years the invitations to come to the table earlier in a project have been more plentiful than ever before. Is it because of knowledge of this practice model or knowledge from my professional capabilities? I think the former. It has shifted the practice of studios within firms but not entire firms, so the gap remains but it will not remain for long if we keep up our end of the evidence-based equation and measure and share our findings. It is that very action that has tipped the healthcare industry's reception to this methodology—hopefully it will find its way to other bastions that are holding out.

As more and more of our design programs prepare students for an evidence-based approach, will the profession be ready to offer positions in the field? We see that clients have accepted the methodology and ask for it in their "requests for proposals." What are the professional organizations doing to keep practitioners poised for this shift in design delivery?

Essay 7-2
ASID, Design Research and the Future of Interior Design

Michael Berens, MS, PhD, Director of Research and Knowledge Resources
American Society of Interior Designers

In 1931, with the nation caught in the grip of the Great Depression, a group of furniture manufacturers and interior decorators met in Grand Rapids, Michigan, to discuss the formation of an association that would be mutually beneficial to their respective business interests. That meeting gave birth to the American Institute of Interior Decorators, of which the American Society of Interior Designers is a direct descendent. Times have changed greatly since then, but, regrettably, perceptions have not. The words "designer" and "decorator" are still used interchangeably in most circles, including the media who cover the industry and, by now, should know better. Likewise, the practice of interior decoration and interior design are usually regarded as being more or less similar, despite the fact that they have been evolving away from each other for some time.

Interior design is still celebrated largely for its aesthetic achievements, but in practice it has increasingly become more about the application of a diverse body of technical and behavioral knowledge. The pervasive adoption of sustainable design is the most notable example of this trend, but it is also apparent in the expectation that today's designers have the education and know-how to create environments that positively impact productivity and collaboration in the workplace, customer satisfaction in hospitality environments, safety and recovery in healthcare settings, learning and socialization in educational facilities, and safety in government and other public buildings.

The obvious question is why the perception of interior design has not kept up with the practice. There are many reasons for this, not the least of which is that the areas in which interior design has become more technical are those that are most difficult to demonstrate to nonpractitioners. One can take a photograph that illustrates the designer's aesthetic choices, but behavioral effects or the absence of environmental factors that might negatively affect occupants, such as pollutants or fire hazards, are not so easy to capture.

Outcomes must be measured and documented. If interior design professionals practice in an evidence-based way and demonstrate improved outcomes then, when that evidence is amassed with some consistency, interior design will emerge in a new light.

The leaders of ASID realized the importance of design research and evidence-based design decades ago. In the early 1990s, the Society developed the first of a series of white papers grounded in research. (See Figure 7.8.) Each year ASID presents two awards recognizing outstanding design research, one to a design educator or professional and one to a graduate student in design. We take great pride in being the Founding Sponsor of

Healing Homes
Design to Promote
Recovery and Well Being

InformeDesign, the online database of Research Summaries on design and human behavior, and a major supporter of the effort to codify the interior design body of knowledge.
ASID exists to encourage and promote the profession of interior design, and recognizes
that demonstrating how design affects quality of life and impacts the health, safety, and
welfare of occupants is integral to that mission. Recently, we expanded the ASID
Foundation to create an endowment that will fund research and educational efforts for
years to come.

Further research and evidence-based design will help to clarify what interior design is
and what interior designers do. In the not-too-distant future, interior designers will look
back and wonder how there ever could be any confusion about the purview of their profession. And we who occupy and use the spaces they create will benefit from their understanding of how we co-exist with our man-made environments.

AIA has many efforts in place that embrace evidence-based design. Its Academy of Architecture for Health has joined forces with The Center for Health Design to share the same conference venue that is steeped in evidence-based practice. Its new healthcare awards programs will showcase healthcare design–oriented research while the Boston Society of Architects awards grants for research. These are just the few programs of which I am aware.

The professional societies are on board with the shift toward accountability that is occurring. I must admit my bias, the real reason for the shift in design methodology is the result of The Center for Health Design, an organization that creates a common denominator around the specialty we serve, and true to the practice of evidence-based design is interdisciplinary in its structure and governance. Due to its multidisciplinary approach The Center for Health Design has the nimbleness to help move this design methodology forward without concern for disenfranchising any constituencies.. It has reached across the table to the universities, professional associations, healthcare providers, regulators, manufacturers, and private enterprise to build an infrastructure that will house and disseminate knowledge. Its network will identify gaps and initiate the research that is missing. It will advocate for the best possible health experience for all who enter the system. The Center was founded as a non-profit research, education, and advocacy organization whose mission is to transform healthcare settings into healing environments that improve outcomes through the creative use of evidence-based design.

It is with this mindset that qualified individuals have responsibly taken on the practice of this methodology, leading the way to a discussion about certification.

Professional Certification

As the profession prepares for a more accountable method of practice, how will we know who is adequately trained and informed? This begins the discussion about certification. A few years ago, Kirk Hamilton, FAIA, and Alberto Salvatore, AIA, hosted a discussion at Health Design 05 to see who would be interested in a formalized certification program and the room filled. Was it fear of being left behind in a topic that was gaining momentum within our design sector? From that very busy day, a smaller group of dedicated professionals emerged and have been working with the staff of The Center for Health Design to formulate and create a certification program.

Essay 7-3
The Evidence-Based Design Assessment and Certification Program
Alberto Salvatore, AIA, Salvatore Associates

The development of evidence-based design (EBD) is consistent with a much larger shift to a new global understanding of the relationship between things. This new global understanding is based on

1. responsibility
2. accountability
3. transparency

It impacts individuals by drawing them to EBD, as it impacts the largest, most complex organizations by changing their culture.

The culture within these organizations is shifting from a machine age culture that has a product focus and is based on linear, independent activities to a culture focused on ideas, based on interdisciplinary, simultaneous activities. This shift in culture redefines the evaluation criteria for successful organizations from a single bottom line (economic, regardless of the consequences) to multiple bottom lines (economic, social, and environmental simultaneously evaluating the effects of one bottom line on the other):

1. as a process through which facility projects are undertaken;
2. taking responsibility for one's actions;
3. being accountable for the consequences, outcomes of those actions; and
4. documenting the process and the outcome so anyone who is interested can review those activities.

EBD practitioners understand that this shift in organizational culture also directly applies to the organization's understanding of the overall Environment of Care (EOC) within which EBD is practiced. EOC has been traditionally understood to be comprised of six independent components (concepts, people, systems, layout/operations, **physical environment**, and implementation) that are manipulated and separately evaluated by individuals without considering the consequences of changes in one component on the others. Our new understanding informs us that ideally, these components must be simultaneously developed and evaluated by interdisciplinary teams to achieve the greatest return on investment.

This dramatic shift in understanding can affect which project delivery system is chosen to implement an organization's project. It is possible to use a traditional linear, segmented project delivery system with EBD, but the results of EBD interventions in this system are, at best, incremental. In an effort to maximize an organization's return on investment in each of their bottom lines, the Interdisciplinary Design Team (IDT) approach to project delivery is the ideal implementation process for EBD.

Given this shift in understanding, what tools or indicators can organizations use to assemble the appropriate teams to develop their projects? How can an organization that understands the value of the EBD process know that the professionals that they work with have the base knowledge that they need? How do they know that these team members understand the process involved in order to maximize their investments? The Evidence-Based Design Assessment and Certification Program (EDAC) was developed to do just that. The EDAC program was developed by The Center for Health Design (CHD) with funding from the Robert Wood Johnson Foundation. Over a three-year period, working with a national group of volunteers and a psychometric firm specializing in the development of examinations, EDAC has defined EBD, provided the base knowledge required to become an EBD practitioner, and outlined the ideal process for its implementation.

Individuals who feel that they may benefit from a better understanding of how to maximize the investments in their facilities through the use of EBD are eligible to take the seminars and use the study guides to improve their understanding of this process. Further, if any individuals feel that they would benefit from taking an examination that will verify their understanding of this knowledge, EDAC will offer an examination for that purpose.

Organizations may then use this assessment and certification program as one of the many means of evaluating the increased likelihood of success working with professionals who have completed this exam or attended seminars on the subject. In addition to the assessment of individuals, a Project Certification Program is also being developed by the CHD. This project certification program will work to validate the process and the outcome.

The publication of this information will lead to a better understanding of how to efficiently design facilities to increase the quality of care for everyone who is exposed to the healthcare delivery system (i.e., patients, family, visitors, clinical and support staff, physicians, and other care providers). This new global understanding of the relationship between things will identify EBD as the most responsible, accountable, and transparent way to invest in the development of any facility.

Two organizations that have emerged work toward professional accreditation of architects and interior designers who practice in healthcare. They are the American College of Healthcare Architects, or ACHA, and the American Academy of Healthcare Interior Designers, or AAHID, respectively. EDAC will test for a different set of research-based design skills independent of traditional professional design knowledge.

What Comes After What Comes Next

This is just the beginning, and by the time this book is published much will have developed pushing us and the way we practice to yet another plateau. I asked Debra Levin, President and CEO of The Center for Health Design, to paint a picture of the future of evidence-based design through the eyes of the Center.

Essay 7-4
The Future of Evidence-Based Design
Debra J. Levin, President and CEO, The Center for Health Design

To map out the potential future for evidence-based design, we need to take a moment to reflect on how significantly our field has evolved in a short period of time. Our understanding of the relationship between the built physical environment in healthcare settings and outcomes connected to those environments has come a long way in just the last decade.

"First, healthcare design was a subspecialty, then it moved into being an industry, and now as an industry we are marching together into being a field of study."

As design professionals, many of us may have grown up being aware of the space around us in a way that was unique from our peers. Most likely we always intuitively knew that the physical space around us had to have an impact on how people behaved. I can remember in college reading anything I could get my hands on about color theory, psychoneuroimmunology, and environmental psychology. These disparate pieces of information informed the way I thought about design, physical environments, human behavior, and even being human. Nowhere do these impacts become both more apparent and more important than in healthcare settings—a place where people are often at their most vulnerable and frightened.

In recent years there has been a growing desire for empirical evidence that validates our intuitions about the impact the physical environment can have on outcomes. The Center for Health Design has been at the forefront of leading that charge. Supporting others to make design decisions influenced by research—aptly named evidence-based design—is the basis of the Center's work. Initially we helped build a multidisciplinary community of professionals to start the conversation through educational conferences and seminars. Later we helped to focus this community through advocacy work that pushed for changes in the codes and standards that regulate the design of healthcare buildings—work that is ongo-

ing. Today, we continually dedicate resources to making relevant research more easily accessible and helping to translate the findings into accessible, useful information relevant to building design.

When we look at the latest generation of healthcare facilities there is a great deal to be proud of. As a whole, healthcare facilities are moving toward being safer, greener, and more efficient and have a level of design quality and sophistication not seen in healthcare a decade or two ago.

Such state-of-the-art healthcare facilities are not yet commonplace. Despite all of the great progress we are making in the industry, many are still being built every year without taking into account what the research tells us about outcomes. Furthermore, they are designed without knowledge of new products available to market that can significantly reduce the impact of that facility on the community. To continue to move from an industry to a field, we need to commit to measuring the outcomes of these buildings and to making those findings readily available. (See Figure 7.9.)

We have already started to create an educational road map for students just starting down the pathway of design as well as for professionals returning for continuing education. Many universities are starting to offer degrees that take a multidisciplinary approach to their curriculum, bringing together schools of architecture, health, medicine, nursing, and engineering under one umbrella degree which focuses on the unique need of healthcare institutions. As an industry we need to support these efforts and help to encourage even more institutions of higher learning to look at these programs as models for their own curricula.

The Center has committed to developing a set of measurement tools and metrics over the next few years to create a more standardized approach to how we measure outcomes in healthcare facilities. We need to agree upon and create an industrywide dashboard of metrics that all across the field will use to monitor progress. We must be able to measure if we are in fact creating better outcomes from year to year. Are hospitals safer across the board because of these new designs and products? Are we as an industry consuming fewer resources and producing less waste? Have we reduced the spread of nosocomial infections? Are more families involved in patient care?

The Center for Health Design is devoted to continuing to lead this charge. We are focusing our energy and resources on funding research through our Research Coalition and making the findings available through our website, in our *Healthcare Design* magazine and *HERD Journal*. Our Pebble Project research initiative is growing globally and publishing the findings. We bring together industry thought leaders and provide high-level education throughout the year with our conferences and webinars. And we keep advocating for change to building codes and standards through the volunteer work of our Environmental Standards Council.

Most of all, we remember that the body of evidence is just a road map to make sound decisions about design and resources. In the end, it is the perfect marriage of both art and science that makes a truly memorable building, one that celebrates the spirit of the soul, one you know values you as an individual. And it is exactly these types of buildings that we should aspire to build because nowhere can design truly elevate those in need more than in healthcare settings.

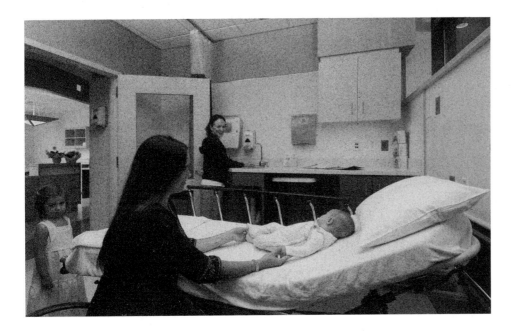

Figure 7.10
Generations that are counting on us! Children's Hospital at Yale–New Haven Emergency Department.
© 2008 C.J. Allen. Salvatore Associates, CAMA, Inc.

Summary

This is the beginning of a new era. Much will be written about this topic as time goes on, about the evolution of a process but more importantly about the body of knowledge we will amass. It is my hope that evidence-based design will inform next generations of construction, building, new habitats for the human body, mind, and spirit that will promote a sense of well-being and foster the kind of support needed to perform at our best. It will take time and as time goes on we will find better ways to access this knowledge and synthesize it into better solutions. The "flashpoint" has sparked a change—be a part of how we shape our future as designers who create interior environments that improve outcomes! (See Figure 7.10.)

As I complete this endeavor I realize I am just scratching the surface of this emerging discipline. I will continue to develop a more complete understanding of the full potential of an evidence-based practice, but I discover that in my own liberal arts approach to this research there are obstacles and challenges. I hope to maintain a zest for this practice with an eye on transforming the field. As pioneers in this interdisciplinary approach to implementing this methodology I realize we need to philosophically align the mechanics of this practice with how we ask questions and find answers. The ongoing challenge for our academic and professional colleagues is to be aware of the release of new insights, to continue to incorporate new concepts in future work and to embrace the notion of sharing results of research for the greater good of healthcare design.

Checklist: Evidence-Based Design

1. Identify desired level of evidence-based practice
2. Determine which component of evidence-based service will be offered/requested
3. Select value-driven leadership
4. Identify who will serve on the interdisciplinary team
5. Conduct internal investigations
6. Search literature and tour facilities with best practices
7. Document front process
8. Define desired outcomes and necessary project drivers
9. Map vision
10. Establish a research agenda
11. Begin design process
12. Hypothesize outcomes
13. Dare to innovate
14. Build mock-ups
15. Continue to document process
16. Build and occupy
17. Measure outcomes
18. Build the business case
19. Share with fellow professionals
20. Submit for peer review
21. Celebrate!

Endnotes

1. Taylor, G. The Globe and Mail, January 25, 2005, 89.
2. National Institutes of Health, http://nihroadmap.nih.gov.
3. Weiss, C. Grad student first to complete master's in clinical, translational research, University of Connecticut Advance, 2008; 26:1.
4. Guerin, D., Dohr, J., Bukowski, K. (2004). Research 101: An introduction to research, Parts I, II, and III. Available at: http://www.informedesign.umn.edu.
5. *Ibid.*
6. www.parsons.edu/departments/courses.
7. Becker, F. "Closing the Research-Design Gap," *Implications*, 5:10.

INDEX